BOMBER CREW

BOMBER CREW

Taking On the Reich

JOHN SWEETMAN

LITTLE, BROWN

A *Little, Brown* Book

First published in Great Britain by Little, Brown in 2004

Copyright © 2004 John Sweetman

A CIP catalogue record for this book
is available from the British Library.

ISBN 0 316 72771 7

Typeset in Baskerville by M Rules
Printed and bound in Great Britain
by Clays Ltd, St Ives plc

Little, Brown
An imprint of
Time Warner Book Group UK
Brettenham House
Lancaster Place
London WC2E 7EN
www.twbg.co.uk

CONTENTS

ACKNOWLEDGEMENTS

Apart from those listed in the Sources, Appendix A, I am indebted to a wide range of individuals and institutions. Sqn Ldr T. C. Iveson DFC (Chairman, Bomber Command Association), Robert Owen (Official Historian, 617 Squadron), Dr Neil Young (Imperial War Museum) and Peter Elliott (RAF Museum Hendon) have been especially helpful, and I am extremely grateful to them.

The staff of the following libraries and archives have supplied me with material and patiently answered a multitude of questions:

British Library
Department of Aviation Records, RAF Museum Hendon
Imperial War Museum: Department of Documents,
    Department of Photographs, Sound Archive
Ministry of Defence, Air Historical Branch
National Archives, Kew
Royal Military Academy Sandhurst

I readily acknowledge permission to use the information that they have produced and I particularly thank the Controller of Her Majesty's Stationery Office for permission to reproduce photographs and to quote from records under Crown copyright, the Trustees of the Imperial War Museum and of

Acknowledgements

the RAF Museum Hendon for allowing reproduction of photographs and to quote from documents held at those locations.

I am grateful, too, to the Woking branch of the Aircrew Association for allowing me to draw upon the recollections of its members contained in the publication *Upside Down Nothing on the Clock*.

Seven Men

'Like a commando raid'

Shortly after 1 a.m., in bright moonlight and utterly alone, the four-engine bomber skimmed the North Sea as it approached German-occupied Europe. While the two gunners tested their weapons, the navigator manipulated his various aids, the wireless operator listened for broadcast information and the bomb aimer checked the load, the pilot and flight engineer kept the machine on course at its designated speed. Ahead searchlights weaved menacingly and pockets of flak threatened the night sky. They eased through unscathed and crossed the Netherlands unchallenged. Over the Rhine, the peaceful scene suddenly changed. A spiteful wall of flak confronted them. The pilot circled warily while, as the wireless operator recalled, 'some debate took place about the best method of approach and the considered opinion was "head down, keep low and go through"'. So the pilot hugged the ground and flew beneath the adjoining trees along a forest fire-break to safety, a 'very, very nasty' experience. Skirting the Ruhr, the Lancaster approached its special target to the south. Amid 'wooded, valley-marked country with little or no features on the map' and swirling mist adding to his difficulties, the navigator strove to locate the right spot. Even then he was unsure, but the others remembered the briefing photographs and confirmed his choice. Dipping low, the pilot attacked and, as he climbed away, a gigantic explosion took place behind. With the sky already lightening, there was no time to linger. Dreading the appearance of fighters, the aircraft brushed the hedges to survive unchallenged until the coast. There it faced a barrage of shells from the Frisian Islands, some bouncing off the water and over the fuselage. Turning hastily to starboard, the pilot by-passed the danger area to 'sneak out' further north. Six and a quarter hours after takeoff, AJ-0 landed at RAF Scampton, Lincolnshire. The bomber had lost one engine, the windscreen was obscured by a thick coating of oil, causing the pilot to peer out of the quarterlight as he came in downwind to bump uncomfortably ('it seemed like twenty-four times') over the grass. The crew, though, were unharmed. In total isolation, they had found and bombed their target as ordered.

During the morning of Sunday 9 June 1940, at RAF Driffield in Yorkshire, home of 102 (Bomber) Squadron, Pilot Officer Geoffrey Leonard Cheshire learnt he would be flying his first operation that evening in a twin-engine Whitley captained by a New Zealander, Pilot Officer F. H. 'Lofty' Long. Long closely questioned his new second pilot about his training experience and detailed knowledge of the Whitley: how to fly it, operate its guns (the second pilot became front gunner, when not at the controls), navigate and drop bombs. The pilot stressed that all crew members must be utterly reliable in their own jobs and able to fulfil the duties of any other in an emergency.

After this grilling, Long and Cheshire went out to the dispersal point to meet the navigator, wireless operator and rear gunner, who made up the five-man crew. Long led them through the escape drills and checked that the ground crew had prepared Q-Queenie for the forthcoming operation. Each crew member then carried out the series of pre-flight checks, precisely as he would immediately prior to takeoff. After these were completed, Long took the Whitley up for an air test, and only when he was thoroughly satisfied did he land. It had been an exhausting experience for Cheshire. Long, though, had sharply reminded him how interdependent were the members of a bomber crew, whose own lives quite literally depended on the vigilance and efficiency of each other.

That evening, Cheshire looked down on a peaceful summer scene as the Whitley climbed towards the coast and its target in northern France. He could see people walking and cycling below, occasionally stopping to wave, and wondered whether any of them thought of the bomber as more than 'a mechanical entity', which actually contained 'five ordinary humans'.

Before long, RAF bombers were flying further afield – into the heartland of Germany. On 9 December 1940, the *Daily Telegraph*'s banner headlines read 'RAF Leave Düsseldorf "Mass Of Fires"'; on 18 April 1941 'Berlin Is Chequered With Fires'; and, two months later, on 10 June, 'Biggest Bombs On Mannheim'. In the next three years, raids would become heavier, as one hundred, two hundred and even a thousand bombers at a time struck German targets. The aircraft would fly greater distances, have four engines instead of one or two, be equipped with more sophisticated aids to increase navigational and bombing accuracy. Crews would expand to seven, eight or even ten, instead of three to five as in the opening months of the war. So the postscript to each published report of an operation – ten, fifteen, thirty 'of our aircraft are missing' – meant the loss of far more men than the bald statistic of non-returning aircraft. On 31 March 1944, officially ninety-five bombers (more than 650 men) failed to come back from a disastrous attack on Nuremberg.

T. E. Lawrence once remarked that a death in action produced a 'ripple of sorrow' like a pebble cast into a pond. When a bomber was lost, the family, friends, former work colleagues in civilian life and even casual social acquaintances of each crew member were deeply affected. Agonising weeks, frequently stretching into months, would pass before their fate was confirmed. Some would have become prisoners of war, thus prolonging the anguish of relatives anxious for their welfare and survival. Of others, no news would ever be received; and they would eventually be listed 'missing believed dead'.

Analysing the strength of Bomber Command at the beginning of 1943, Sir Arthur Harris would reflect that nearly 40 per cent of its pilots were from overseas; principally the air forces of Australia, Canada, South Africa and New Zealand. There was a sprinkling from other dominions, of Americans serving in the RAF, Royal Canadian Air Force (RCAF) or wearing the uniform of the United States Army Air Force (USAAF), as well as men from the occupied countries of Europe and neutral Ireland. This diversity of background was not confined to the pilot's seat, as illustrated by the Englishman living in New York who joined the RCAF as a navigator before flying operationally. Including personnel living in the United Kingdom, RAF Bomber Command was, therefore, a truly cosmopolitan force.

Being part of a bomber crew, whose efficiency and very survival depended on each individual member, as 'Lofty' Long so firmly underlined to Leonard Cheshire, was the common denominator for those flying. Seventeen airmen would win the Victoria Cross 'in recognition of most conspicuous bravery' for their actions in European skies, several directly related to saving fellow crew members. Many other pilots, unrecognised with awards, would also sacrifice themselves to preserve the lives of their crew.

Each bomber crew, like that of AJ-O returning from the Dambusters Raid, comprised men from different air forces and nationalities and became central to the very existence of its members. Flight Sergeant Peter Brown, a 10 Squadron Halifax bomb aimer, thought every operation 'like a commando raid against the whole might of the German defences'. A 617 Squadron Lancaster rear gunner from Canada, Flying Officer Dave Rodger, agreed: 'Every time we went out, it was seven men against the Reich.'

CHAPTER 1

Countdown to Conflict

'The bomber will always get through'

Formation of the Royal Air Force (RAF) on 1 April 1918 acknowledged the arrival of a third dimension to war – the air, in addition to land and sea. It heralded, too, the bomber as the main aerial striking force. For the campaign which Bomber Command waged against Germany during the Second had its genesis in the First World War.

In 1914 an onlooker recorded that 'a few BE 2cs and Avros staggered across the Channel' to support the armies in France. These were flimsy general-purpose biplanes, expected to carry out reconnaissance, spot for the artillery, fend off hostile aircraft and undertake rudimentary bombing, which initially consisted of tossing grenades or canisters filled with petrol over the sides of open cockpits.

Second Lieutenant Patrick Huskinson, an air commodore in 1942, recalled that 'in those days you sat behind a tiny windscreen literally *on* the aircraft and not, as now, snugly within it. A chilly business on the warmest day.' His experience in a single-engine, two-seater BE 2c underlined the hazards of bombing a train from 200ft. The sparse bomb load exploded instantaneously on impact, 'flinging me high like a jack-in-the-box. My wings . . . were nothing but a blur of flapping fabric, what I could see of the fuselage too closely resembled a sieve'. To make matters worse, anti-aircraft guns from both sides of the line opened up as he made his way warily back. 'My aircraft, when I landed, fell gently to pieces.'

Advances in airframe construction, engine capacity, bomb loads, bombsights, bomb-release gear and, crucially, operating range soon led to the development of more substantial, specialised bombers. The twin-engine Handley Page (HP) 0/100 could carry a crew of three or four, depending on how many of the maximum six machine-guns were mounted, and a bomb load of 2000lb. at 95mph. The de Havilland (DH) 9, although a single-engine twin-seater, flew over 120mph, carried three machine-guns and up to 1000lb. of bombs in racks under the wings and fuselage. With aircraft like these, the Royal Flying Corps and Royal Naval Air Service (later merged into the fledgling RAF) launched raids into western Germany from bases on the Continent, as similarly the Germans hit Britain from across the Channel.

Attacks by enemy airships and aeroplanes quickened the evolution of large bombers capable of aggressive retaliatory action. Two daylight raids on London by twin-engine Gotha machines in June and July 1917 provoked a public and political clamour verging on hysteria. As a result, Lieutenant General J. C. Smuts carried out an investigation into the whole future of air power, which concluded: 'The day may not be far off when aerial operations with their devastation of enemy lands and destruction of industrial and populous centres on a vast scale may become the principal operations of war.' A legend had been born.

In June 1918, an Independent Bomber Force, stationed in eastern France and tasked specifically to attack Germany, was created. Five months later, on the eve of the Armistice, three four-engine HP v 1500 bombers stood by in Norfolk to hit Berlin. With a wingspan of 126ft, length of 62ft and top speed of 97mph, they each carried machine-guns in the nose, amidships and tail, thirty 250lb. bombs and a crew of five. Dubbed 'gargantuan', they were a far cry from the wobbly machine flown by Huskinson and underlined the major role which the bomber now fulfilled.

No bomber crew, though, was yet a truly coherent body. Essentially, in the different positions the airmen carried out their own duties with very little coordinated help. Communication was the main problem, the electronic intercom of later years not even a pipe dream. Once aloft the crew could contact one another, albeit with difficulty, through the Gosport tube, simply a hollow length of rubber developed at the Hampshire air station. Freddie West, a VC winner in 1918 piloting a two-seater machine, explained that communication with his observer was difficult to the point of impossibility. To use the Gosport tube, 'you had to yell loudly against the noise caused by the slipstream and rat-tat-tat of bullets. I soon gave that game up. I didn't fancy being permanently hoarse.' So he and his observer took to using hand signals and pointing in good silent movie fashion, a system difficult to work with more than a two-man crew. Physical conditions in the air tended to preoccupy individuals. Crews often suffered from frostbite in their open positions, despite donning heavy leather clothing and fleece-lined boots. Sometimes members used whale oil or vaseline to protect their skin, not always successfully. There was no oxygen supply, which occasionally caused problems, although bombers did not officially fly high enough for it to be necessary.

Brigadier General P. R. C. Groves confidently declared that existing aeroplanes 'are toys compared with the machines which will soon be in use'. And, reflecting on the evolution of bombers in the First World War, the Chief of the Air Staff (CAS), Major General Sir Hugh Trenchard, prophesied 'there can be no doubt that we must be prepared for long-distance operations against an enemy's main source of supply'.

'Imperial policing' encouraged the belief that bombers could not only win a war but were a practical and attractive way of avoiding slaughter in the trenches. In 1922 the RAF took responsibility for maintaining law and order in Mesopotamia (modern Iraq) which had come under British control as a League of Nations mandated territory. Squadron Leader A. T. (later 'Bomber') Harris, commanding 45 Squadron, explained how 'the truculent and warlike tribes' were checked: 'When a tribe started open revolt we gave warning to all its most important villages by loudspeaker from low-flying aircraft and by dropping messages, that air action would be taken after twenty-four hours.' If the rebellion did not cease, bombs 'destroyed' the villages and air patrols discouraged inhabitants from returning until 'they decided to give up, which they invariably did'. In the wake of post-war cutbacks, purpose-built bombers were in short supply. So, as one of Harris's flight commanders, Flight Lieutenant the Hon. R. A. Cochrane, explained, the Squadron converted its transport aircraft which called for intensive crew retraining: 'We cut a hole in the canvas fuselage of our Vickers Vernons and taught the bomb aimers how to release their bombs from a prone position.'

Harris was not alone in asserting that bombers would henceforth be 'the predominant weapon'. A wide range of writers, including several former officers, were busy refining the 'theory of strategic bombing' – Trenchard's long-range aircraft striking at the heart of an enemy's war industries from distant bases. In short, offence was seen as the best means of defence. And, during the 1920s, the further concept of such an 'aerial knockout blow', delivered before or immediately after war broke out, gained momentum.

Countdown to Conflict

In 1932, a Cabinet minister, Stanley Baldwin, heightened faith in this prospect by exclaiming, 'the bomber will always get through'. Two years later, he declared: 'The old frontiers are gone. When you think of the defence of England you no longer think of the chalk cliffs of Dover, you think of the Rhine. That is where our frontier lies.' Reference to 'the Rhine' reflected rising concern about Germany, where an Air Ministry had been formed in 1933, the year in which Hitler signalled Germany's aggressive independence by withdrawing it from the League of Nations.

Worse was to come. In 1935, the Luftwaffe formally came into being and Cabinet ministers Sir John Simon and Anthony Eden returned from Germany to report Hitler's boast that by March 1937 it would number 1500 aircraft. Their findings caused something approaching official panic with plans quickly being drawn up for a rapid expansion of the RAF's aircraft and aircrew.

Despite Air Staff warnings that the existing training organisation would be overwhelmed, a recruitment drive was initiated and 'shadow factories' using car manufacturers' facilities were created to help produce a planned 1736 aircraft by spring 1939. Specifications for new four-engine 'heavy' bombers were issued, which would lead ultimately to the Stirling and Halifax and, indirectly, the Lancaster. Then Deputy Director of Plans in the Air Ministry, Group Captain A. T. Harris was closely involved with this development. A vast increase in storage depots, gunnery and bombing ranges and training schools was set in motion; fifty-two airfields in 1934 became 138 five years later. More widely, international tension mounted after March 1936 when Germany sent troops into the Rhineland, demilitarised under the Treaty of Versailles signed after the First World War. Four months later the cumbersome organisation Air Defence of Great Britain was replaced in the cause of 'specialised

9

efficiency' by separate Bomber, Fighter, Coastal and Training commands. The contemporary RAF War Manual declared: 'The bomb is the primary weapon of air power. The bomber is the means of conveying it to its target.'

Bomber Command quickly recognised the paucity of the numbers and the shortcomings of the aircraft it inherited, all of which had open cockpits. The two-seater, single-engine Hawker Hart with its 500lb. bomb load carried externally beneath the wings and fuselage had come into service in 1930. Another two-seater biplane bomber, the Hawker Hind, reached squadrons in 1936, a modified version of the Boulton & Paul Sidestrand biplane the same year. In September 1938, Robert Allen stood by to fly his open-cockpit HP Heyford to attack the Ruhr industrial region in western Germany if Neville Chamberlain's negotiations with Hitler at Munich failed. His and other crews were advised that they would have insufficient fuel to reach base again and were advised to bale out over Holland.

As the likelihood of war crept closer, in 1937 the Air Staff had drawn up thirteen detailed plans, known as the Western Air (WA) Plans, to deal with Germany. All relied on the assumption that bombers flying in daylight would locate, bomb and destroy selected targets. WA 5 foresaw neutralising the whole of the Ruhr's armament industries by attacking forty-five individual power and coking plants with three thousand sorties over a fortnight. Success, it was hoped, would be achieved for the acceptable loss of 176 aircraft.

The ability to attain this level of achievement depended not only on effective machines but practical crew preparation. Guy Brisbane, a navigator who began his war service as a sergeant and by the end had risen to acting group captain with a DSO, DFC and DFM after two operational tours, expressed serious doubts about the 'unrealistic' training provided. Too much emphasis was placed on pilots to the detriment of other crew positions. Day navigation exercises at 2–3000ft used 'large towns and coastal features as turning points'. Navigation, relying on good weather and visual sightings of landmarks, was by dead reckoning (DR), wireless telegraphy (W/T) bearings being 'regarded with the gravest suspicion'. These flights, Brisbane thought, were 'more in the nature of a pleasant aerial tour of the British Isles than serious training for war'.

Nor was Brisbane impressed with 'the most unrealistic' bombing exercises. The standard format required a crew to climb to bombing height and establish the speed and direction of the wind before 'the solemn trek across the range . . . straight and level with five miles run-up to the target'. Few crews took part in a live bombing exercise before the war began. As a result Brisbane claimed 'many bombs were dropped "safe" or not at all during operations, due to the unfamiliarity with the bombing equipment'.

Gunnery training was no more satisfactory, being undertaken on ranges without any attempt at fighter affiliation. Hence 'air gunners had no idea how to judge range or deflection accurately against a rapidly moving target'; defensive tactics were not properly worked out. 'Crews were merely told that the correct tactics to adopt if attacked by fighters were to close formation and shoot it out.'

Brisbane was scathing about the lecture programme, which he dismissed as mostly of the 'Beware the Hun in the Sun' variety and 'not good enough'. There was a lot about the number and size of flak guns, but 'no information' on how they were likely to be deployed 'to defend a vulnerable point or the volume and accuracy of the fire to be expected'. Annual exercises to test the defences of Britain were 'the nearest approach to true operational training'. Bombers were sent out to sea before turning to mount a mock attack inland, as fighters went up to intercept them. 'I was never lucky enough to be in a formation which was intercepted and attacked,' Brisbane mischievously observed. More 'realism' should have been arranged with all bomber formations attacked by fighters and 'bomber crews required to make "first time" attacks on unfamiliar targets'. Flying Officer Guy Gibson independently noted that, in the summer of 1939, he twice took part in similar exercises in which he saw no 'enemy' fighters and on one occasion his formation flew on theoretically to 'flatten' RAF Abingdon, near Oxford. Born in India in 1918, Gibson had been educated at St Edward's School, Oxford, where he developed a keen interest in the workings of cinema organs and learning how to fly. Tradition has it that his first attempt to join the RAF failed because, being only 5ft 6in. tall, his legs were too short to reach the rudder bar. Nevertheless in January 1937 he did secure a short service commission, backdated to his entry in November 1936.

In retrospect, Gibson would be among many caustically to condemn front-line aircraft available in 1939. But there is no doubt that the twin-engine, monoplane Blenheim, Hampden, Wellington and Whitley, each with enclosed crew positions and an internal bomb bay, were far superior to biplanes like the Hart, Hind and Heyford. The Whitley's top speed was 220mph, that of the other three around 250mph. Except for the Blenheim with 1000lb., their bomb loads totalled 4–7000lb. All had multi-machine-guns, though only the Wellington and Whitley were equipped with rear turrets. They were, admittedly, slower by at least 100mph than the more manoeuvrable Messerschmitt Bf 109 which caused alarm by its performance with the German Condor Legion during the Spanish Civil War (1936–9). But, as Brisbane sceptically pointed out, if a force of bombers were to close up in formation, supposedly its massed machine-guns would drive off any fighters. Paradoxically, too, destruction of the Spanish town of Guernica by German aircraft in 1937 appeared to support Baldwin's contention that bombers could not be stopped.

This gloomy scenario was hardly brightened by official predictions that within a fortnight the Luftwaffe would drop 100,000 tons of bombs on London, each ton causing up to fifty casualties. Gas was a particular dread. From the Opposition benches Winston Churchill chillingly reminded Parliament that the capital presented 'the greatest target in the world, a kind of tremendous, fat, valuable cow, fed up to attract the beasts of prey'. Better, therefore, to wreak havoc on the enemy before any of these fears could be realised at home.

The weakest of the bombers with which Britain went to war was the single-engine Battle: crew of three, speed 250mph, 1000lb. bomb load, only two machine-guns. While in training, the Canadian Donald Bruce described it as a 'very strong aircraft structurally, underpowered but flying light without a bomb load quite fast and very manoeuvrable' – a distinct drawback for an aircraft whose primary role required it to drop bombs. Overall, Bruce painted a bleak picture of the bomber: 'The observer's compartment was rather restricted and one sat on a small step, below the gunner, with feet dangling in the well below, which was the bomb aiming position. Sitting on the step one had a petrol tank about a foot in front of one's head.' From this position, Bruce could see outside the aircraft only 'through the sliding hatch where the Course Setting Bomb Sight was situated'. The means of communicating with the pilot was not by any electronic system, as in the other RAF bombers, but the crude First World War Gosport tube. In the Battle this was 'clipped so short that one had to get right down over the bombsight to plug the tube in and as the pilot's seat was on the other side of a bulkhead that shut the cockpit off and was way above the bombsight one sometimes got the feeling one was shouting up his a***hole, particularly as on most occasions little heed

13

seemed to be taken of what you were telling him'. As Freddie West had discovered many years earlier, the only means of amplification using this contraption was 'a strong pair of lungs'.

When bombing, the pilot used 'some sort of deflector shield' to cut off engine heat from the bombsight. If a 'forgetful' pilot omitted to operate this, 'one's chinagraph pencil would dissolve in a pool of wax on the glass surface of the bombsight making it impossible to obtain a three-course wind speed and direction'. Bombing exercises did not go smoothly for other reasons. Bruce once flew when the officer commanding was the pilot, a 'shorta*** and full of bull'. On this occasion, an ex-Guardsman was being put through his paces: 'So conditioned to bull that he looked upon a corporal as being three ranks higher than the King . . . [he] was lying to attention in the bomb aimer's position whilst the wing commander poured invective down the Gosport tube to him for getting a 400yd bombing overshoot.' 'In retrospect,' Bruce later reflected, this episode was 'even funnier, thinking how we dropped bombs on Germany, if and when we could find the target'.

He was not impressed with the gunnery arrangements in the Battle either: most gunners chose to stand rather than sit on the 'bicycle saddle type of seat' provided. The machine-gun operated from the rear of the long cockpit, effectively amidships on top of the fuselage, was 'mounted on a collapsible tripod arrangement that stowed away flat in a streamlined fairing'. 'To erect it one operated a trigger attached to a cable and heaved up on the gun and it then all seemed to click into place and could be swung to either side of the cockpit.' The rear of the cockpit 'hinged up' to give some protection from the slipstream, which was lost if the operator stuck his head too far over the side. Then 'you were clear of the hood and with the roar of the slipstream in your ears and blowing the water out of your eyes if you weren't wearing goggles and the gun thudding and bucking away on its free mounting'. The result might be exhilarating but did not make for accurate gunnery. Moreover, when firing downwards, 'electrical cut-outs were not unknown . . . and one only needed to hit a bump at the crucial moment and a few rounds had gone through one's own tailplane'. The gunner had no means of communicating with the pilot, who waggled the wings as a signal to stop firing. On one occasion during training, Bruce's gun continued to fire when he released the trigger. He did not think of simply removing the ammunition pan; instead he hung on to the 'bucking' machine-gun 'with my lower jaw resting on my flying boots with amazement whilst it continued to blaze away the whole pan of ammunition, and the waggling of the wings became more violent, spraying lead all over the sky'. 'The pilot said a thing or two when we landed,' Bruce admitted. Gerald Dickson, who also trained on Battles, reinforced one of Bruce's major criticisms. If the aircraft were manoeuvring and therefore not level, a careless gunner could easily shoot the tail off. Moreover, whether in formation or not, there was little prospect of the Battle coping with Bf 109s. Nonetheless, it remained an integral and numerically strong component of Bomber Command in 1939 with almost double the number of Wellington squadrons in service.

Despite its obvious superiority over the Battle and recent biplane bombers, Gibson was one of many to complain about cramped conditions in the Hampden, particularly for the pilot. Unable to leave his seat to perform natural bodily functions, he was provided with a bottle or flask. When that filled, a rubber tube leading through a gap in the fuselage was available. It was scurrilously alleged that, if a pilot and his ground crew were at cross purposes, a knot would unaccountably appear in the tube, to the discomfort of the pilot.

Vigorous, if belated, efforts were made to prepare Bomber Command for war. Recruitment to reserve organisations like the

Air Training Corps, Auxiliary Air Force and the newly formed Royal Air Force Volunteer Reserve (RAFVR) was stepped up. Seduced by the thrill of watching air displays, Yorkshireman Tony Iveson wanted to fly, and in the wake of the Munich crisis in September 1938 was accepted into the RAFVR, which entailed training at weekends (pay 1/- (5p) an hour) with promise of a £25 bonus after one year if he attended summer camp. He received 1d. ($^{1}/_{2}$p) per mile when driving his car on official duty, a sum which advanced to $1^{1}/_{2}$d. (1p) with a passenger. Petrol cost 10d. (4p) a gallon. Iveson went solo in January 1939 and by the outbreak of hostilities had amassed seventy-five flying hours.

During March 1939, in Peterborough, Ted Wass saw an advertisement: 'Fly with the RAF. Join the RAF Volunteer Reserve'. He promptly enlisted, flew a few circuits as passenger in a draughty Hawker Hart then had his hopes dashed. His entire part-time unit was informed that, after all, the RAF had no more aircrew vacancies and that they must remuster as ground crew. Five years later, Wass would finally realise his dream when he joined Iveson's Lancaster bomber as rear gunner.

This sort of frustration occurred, as the Air Staff had warned, because expansion had taken place in too much of a hurry. Harris was one of many commentators to pour scorn on political and financial constraints, which held back RAF development and preparation, particularly the ruling in 1924 (annually renewed until 1932) that no major war could be expected for ten years. Churchill flamboyantly referred to 'the years that the locusts have eaten'. But the backcloth of the Depression, high unemployment and revulsion at the very thought of another war, demonstrated by persistent international attempts to gain a limitation on weapons (arms control) or total disarmament, was not conducive to effective rearmament. That is, until Hitler upset the balance.

Countdown to Conflict

Shortly after 11.15 a.m. on Sunday 3 September 1939, the Prime Minister Neville Chamberlain announced in an historic wireless broadcast that Germany's failure to promise withdrawal of her troops from Poland, which she had invaded two days earlier, meant 'consequently this country is at war'. The following day, King George VI signalled the RAF that its 'gravest' responsibility 'will be safeguarding of these islands from the menace of the air'. In this, Bomber Command, through the doctrine of aggressive action against an enemy's source of military power in the cause of national defence, would play a pivotal role. On the crews of its front-line bombers, therefore, a heavy burden lay.

CHAPTER 2

Phoney War, September 1939–May 1940

'Gentlemen, we are at war with Germany'

Recently returned from Palestine, Air Vice-Marshal A. T. Harris considered Chamberlain's broadcast 'as stirring as a schoolmaster confirming the fact that mumps had broken out in his school'. The Prime Minister's delivery might have been flat and factual, lacking the flowing language and inspiring rhetoric of his successor, Winston Churchill. But the message was unequivocal, awesome and decisive. As he spoke, the Secretary to the Cabinet opened a meeting in Whitehall with the words, 'Gentlemen, we are at war with Germany'.

Hitler's so-called 'final demand' for control of the Sudetenland area of north-west Czechoslovakia at Munich in September 1938, in the wake of absorbing Austria earlier that year, had proved a false dawn for European peace. In March 1939, the remainder of Czechoslovakia fell under the Nazi jack-boot and subsequent months of further negotiation were still-born. British attempts to secure agreement with the Soviet Union failed, with tension immeasurably heightened by the announcement of a non-aggression pact between Germany and the USSR on 23 August. Ignorant of its secret clauses, which allowed for the two countries to carve up Poland, two days later Britain and France guaranteed Polish integrity – in practical terms, an empty gesture. Neither had the ability to interfere militarily in eastern Europe.

At dawn on 1 September 1939, the German Army crossed the Polish frontier, and by 6 a.m. Luftwaffe bombers were pounding the capital, Warsaw. Refusal to cease this aggression and to withdraw from Polish territory brought the Anglo-French declaration of war on 3 September.

By then, the RAF's final preparations were well underway. On 23 August, following signing of the Soviet-German pact, regular units had been ordered to a war footing. Officers and men were forthwith recalled from leave, the Auxiliary Air Force and RAFVR mobilised.

Enjoying a pleasant family sailing holiday at the Hampshire resort of Lymington in August 1939, Air Vice-Marshal Charles Portal prepared to return to the Air Ministry, telling his civilian neighbour, 'I'm afraid there's going to be a war.' Adding that he must depart for London immediately, he asked: 'Would you mind putting up my boat for the winter?' Perhaps, like the optimists of August 1914, the Air Member for Personnel thought that this conflict, too, would be over by Christmas.

As an RAFVR member, Tony Iveson reported for service on 1 September to find himself sleeping on the floor of Hull civic centre. Two days later, he sat listening to Neville Chamberlain with other recruits in a nearby hotel. They were all then sent home to await a summons, which for Iveson took six weeks to arrive, to the temporary relief of his mother. During the First World War she had suffered the agony of waiting for her wounded husband to return. Soon three of her four sons would be involved in another war. As her eldest son remarked, for her as for many more families 'the whole bloody thing had started up again'.

Bomber Crew

When he returned to 83 Squadron at RAF Scampton, Lincolnshire, on 1 September, Flying Officer Guy Gibson found laden bomb trailers emerging from the ammunition dump, tractors hauling bombers to their dispersal points, sand-bagged gun emplacements in the throes of completion and gas alarms being tested. Amid this organised confusion, bomber crews waited to take off at short notice. They did not know that their scope for action, and execution of the pre-war Western Air Plans, would be severely curtailed by an Anglo-French decision policed by a joint Supreme War Council that the two countries 'would not undertake air action against any but purely military objectives in the narrowest sense of the word . . . objectives attacks on which would not involve loss of civil life'.

On 3 September, Gibson and other members of A Flight listened to Chamberlain in their flight commander's office. After the Prime Minister finished, with studied understatement Pilot Officer A. O. Bridgman suggested 'there will probably be a job for you to do'. The Scampton crews were beaten into the air, however, by Flying Officer A. McPherson. Shortly after noon, he took off in a 139 Squadron Blenheim from RAF Wyton to reconnoitre the German fleet in Wilhelmshaven. Flying at 24,000ft the wireless froze and no results were therefore known until the crew returned at 4.50 p.m. The entry in the Squadron Operations Record Book (ORB) read: 'Duty successful. 75 photos taken. The first RAF aircraft to cross the German frontier.'

McPherson's evidence gave Gibson his first taste of operations. In company with five other Hampdens from 83 Squadron, each carrying four 500lb. bombs, he took off from Scampton at 6.15 p.m. A total of eighteen Hampdens and nine Wellingtons would make for the German fleet in the early evening. In keeping with the Anglo-French political agreement, they were briefed to bomb the warships but strictly forbidden to hit 'civilian establishments, either houses or dockyards' on pain

20

of 'serious repercussions'. The crews were warned, discouragingly, that poor weather was likely in the target area, which was known to bristle with flak and balloons. Moreover, to avoid bombs bouncing off the armoured decks of large ships, they should be lodged in the superstructure – which required an incredible degree of accuracy. With an eleven-second delay fuse, the crews were confidently assured that their bombs would explode after they had passed over.

As predicted, the cloud base in the target area was down to 100ft and, although gun flashes could be vaguely seen through the murk, the 83 Squadron aircraft turned back without attacking. They were unsure of position and acutely aware of the stern warning not to attack shore-based installations. By the time Gibson reached the English coast it was dark, and his formation floundered around completely lost until the moon rose. The Hampdens then picked up a canal leading to Lincoln, which allowed them to find Scampton 5 miles north. 'What an abortive show, what a complete mess up,' Gibson wrote after touching down at 10.30 p.m.

Headlines in the *Daily Herald* on 4 September confirmed, 'War Declared By Britain And France'. Readers were assured, 'The Fleet In Position', and that the King believed it 'Unthinkable We Should Refuse The Challenge'. Harris admitted 'we all expected violent fighting to start at any minute'. Nevertheless, when he took command of 5 Group in Lincolnshire on 11 September, Harris found only 'a skeletal formation . . . I had come to make bricks and there was no need for my predecessor in the Command to advise me of the lack of straw'.

The Air Ministry later confessed that 'during the first weeks of the war it was rarely possible to act on the information obtained by air reconnaissance, for the ships of the enemy remained too close to their bases', thereby putting civilians at risk from stray bombs. So attacks on naval targets got off to a fitful start. As they did, crews quickly discovered the difference between hostile skies and the peacetime bombing range.

On 4 September, fifteen Blenheims and fourteen Wellingtons from five squadrons set out to hit the naval base of Brunsbüttel at the western end of the Kiel canal and warships in nearby Schillig Roads. Rather dramatically and fancifully, gunners were warned, 'don't shoot till you see the whites of their eyes'. The aircraft quickly encountered heavy rain and low cloud, as Flight Lieutenant K. C. Doran, a Blenheim pilot who would win a DFC that day explained: 'Soon after crossing out over the North Sea we ran into the bad weather. The Met. forecast was only too accurate, a solid wall of cloud seemed to extend from sea level to about 17,000ft. We obviously had to keep below it to stand any chance of finding our target.' At the scheduled time, Doran's section turned over what it hoped was Heligoland towards Wilhelmshaven, when suddenly the coast loomed up. 'After a bit of feverish map-reading', the crew decided that 'by an incredible combination of luck and judgement we were right on track'. As the cloud base lifted to 500ft, the pocket battleship *Admiral Scheer* came into view, 'anchored in shallow water, near the bank and protected from the landward side by a "pin-cushion" balloon barrage'. They decided to attack the ship on a fore and aft axis, before turning sharply to port to avoid the balloons.

'We climbed as high as we could, which was about 500ft, and made our attack in a shallow dive. As we approached, we saw the matelots' washing hanging out around the stern and the crew idly standing about on deck. It seemed as though we had caught them, literally, with their pants down.' The flak gunners were more alert, and the bombers had to negotiate a hail of fire from ship and shore. Three of Doran's squadron attacked the *Admiral Scheer* amid rain squalls. German records later revealed that the 500lb. bombs which struck the deck failed to penetrate it and bounced overboard, as the crews briefed on 3 September had been warned. Blenheims from another squadron bombed more ships in the German flotilla, but only one of them survived. The Germans paid tribute to the 'reckless gallantry' of the crews, as five of the ten Blenheims went down, a truly dreadful loss rate. The final five Blenheims, from the fifteen which set out, failed to find the target and returned to base without attacking.

Meanwhile, fourteen Wellingtons made for Brunsbüttel. No discernible damage was done there and a further two aircraft were lost. A total of seven bombers had therefore failed to come back from the twenty-four which left base. 'With this the war began,' the Air Ministry proclaimed.

When, on 14 September, he took over 107 Squadron at RAF Wattisham, Norfolk, which had lost the four Blenheims out of five despatched ten days earlier, Wing Commander Basil Embry found his new command comprised sixteen aircraft organised into two flights of eight each under a squadron leader, and a maintenance flight led by a warrant officer. The Blenheim, he noted, had 'a specially long nose', which housed the bombsight and bomb-release gear and was large enough for the navigator to lie prone in his dual role as bomb aimer. There were two machine-guns: one fitted into a wing with a fixed line of fire and operated by the pilot, the other mounted in a power-driven turret manned by an air gunner, who also acted as wireless operator. Embry selected Corporal Thomas Whiting as his observer (navigator/bomb aimer) and Aircraftman 1 (AC1) Geoffrey Lang as his air gunner/wireless operator. 'I chose them', he wrote, 'because I liked the look of them and I was not disappointed.'

Embry's crew quickly discovered itself over Germany, where bombing was forbidden but reconnaissance flights freely took place. On 25 September, it was detailed to photograph 'road and railway communications in North-West Germany'. Opting to cross the North Sea and approach the Ruhr via Emden in the north, Embry took off shortly after 8 a.m. and climbed through cloud to 18,000ft. 'Photography was a matter of team work . . . Whiting and I were confident in our ability to work well together, and we set out on our mission full of optimism.' Embry confessed to being 'a little apprehensive' before takeoff on his first operation of the war, but soon the butterflies vanished as the clouds dispersed to leave ideal photographic conditions. Conscious that his gunner occupied a detached position which 'might create a feeling of loneliness', Embry made sure he spoke to Lang regularly over the intercom and encouraged him to keep a sharp lookout for fighters.

After fulfilling his orders unmolested, Embry turned for home with him and his crew elated. Prematurely, it transpired. Suddenly, near Leer, Lang yelled that two fighters were closing in from the rear. Almost immediately a burst of firing pelted the fuselage and tore a large hole in one wing. Embry desperately put on full power and dived for the sanctuary of clouds 10 miles away. As he did so, 'a metallic crash' announced that the second fighter had opened up, its bullets smacking into the armoured back of the pilot's seat. Amazingly, at that precise moment Lang was bending down to fix a fresh magazine of ammunition, otherwise he would have been killed. Instead, he suffered a scratched nose from the shattered Perspex of his demolished turret. Making steep turns to throw of his tormentors, Embry finally entered the enveloping cloud and safety.

Afraid of a damaged undercarriage, Embry decided on a belly landing, with the undercarriage retracted and not using flaps. As he did so, the Blenheim swerved violently to the left and one wing tip barely cleared the ground. On examination, Embry found that a tyre had been punctured during the fighter attacks, every petrol tank had been holed and the fuselage perforated. 'It was our lucky day,' he mused. But the crew had successfully completed its task by bringing back 'a most valuable overlap consisting of twenty-six photographs covering the whole of the northern portion of the Ruhr'. Squadron records showed that 'this was the first occasion since the outbreak of war on which photos of the Ruhr had been taken by British aircraft', complimented Whiting on his photographic skill and 'exceptionally accurate' navigation and Lang for driving off the two fighters.

More active bomber operations, too, were being flown against the German fleet. On 29 September, eleven Hampdens, divided into two formations, attacked enemy destroyers in Heligoland Bight, where fighters appeared in force. The first formation of bombers went in at 300ft, but in the face of heavy flak failed to inflict worthwhile damage. The Air Staff concluded that the lesson of 4 September had been underscored: 'a level attack on heavily-armed naval vessels was likely to prove a costly undertaking'. The entire second formation, which lagged behind the first, was shot down by the shore-based German aircraft, which had been alerted by a line of flak ships situated 70 miles west of Heligoland. The Bight was now dubbed 'The Hornet's Nest'. One airman wrote that 'the German fleet was a very grand sight . . . [but] when they shot at me it was like lightning flashing in daylight all about me'.

Concentration on the German naval forces was eminently sensible in the light of developments and had been provided for in pre-war plans. By the end of October, capital ships like the aircraft carrier *Courageous* and the battleship *Royal Oak*, as well as the passenger liner *Athenia* packed with evacuee schoolchildren, had been torpedoed. Furthermore, surface raiders, including the pocket battleships *Admiral Graf Spee* and *Deutschland* (later renamed the *Lutzow*), were at large threatening merchant vessels which provided Britain with vital food and fuel. By the close of 1939, 130 merchantmen would have been lost in the Atlantic.

In the meantime, the menace of bombers on land had been cruelly emphasized. On 27 September, Warsaw fell after suffering repeated attacks by the Luftwaffe. Yet still Bomber Command was denied positive action against German territory. When called on to authorise setting fire to German forests, a horrified Secretary of State for Air, Sir Kingsley Wood, replied: 'Are you aware it is private property? Why, you will be asking me to bomb Essen next.'

Armed reconnaissance flights continued during the autumn and into the winter, when weather permitted. Gibson might complain that the war was proceeding 'at a snail's pace', but there were some very nasty shocks. On the morning of 3 December, twenty-four Wellingtons took off for Heligoland Bight to attack the enemy fleet from the safer height of 7–10,000ft with armour-piercing bombs. Encouragingly, several hits were claimed and one minesweeper sunk. 'No damage was done by anti-aircraft fire from the ships.' Even more pleasing was the report that 'of the few fighters which appeared only one pressed home its attack and this was quickly shot down', accounted for by rear gunner Leading Aircraftman (LAC) J. Copley whose first intimation of trouble occurred when a bullet lodged in his parachute harness. None of the bombers was lost, and the comforting conclusion was that Wellingtons flying in formation for mutual protect from their massed machine-guns could easily see off enemy fighters.

Flying over Schillig Roads on an armed reconnaissance mission on 13 December, twelve Wellingtons were engaged by guns from warships and nearby flak vessels. When fighters appeared, during a running battle five Wellingtons were lost. However, a subsequent inquiry in England decided that all of these had actually fallen victim to flak not fighters. On the other hand, one German aircraft had undoubtedly been shot down in the mêlée. 'The maintenance of tight, unshaken formations' remained the recommended, apparently successful, tactic.

Five days later that myth was finally dispelled. With clear weather forecast over northern Germany, twenty-four Wellingtons set off from East Anglia for Schillig Roads and Wilhelmshaven on another armed reconnaissance. After two returned early, the remainder went north to skirt the line of flak ships before flying south to the east of Heligoland. There enemy fighters, warned of their approach, struck. Despite their attention and fire from flak guns on the warships and ashore, the Wellingtons completed their reconnaissance, pursued for 80 miles out to sea as they withdrew. The Germans adopted a new tactic – attacking not from the rear but from above on the flank. This neutered the Wellington's two turrets, which could not traverse to cover that arc: the single-engine Messerschmitt Bf 109 and twin-engine Bf 110 fighters caused havoc. Ten bombers went down in flames, two more ditched on the way home and three crashed on landing. One squadron lost five of its six aircraft and, overall, only ten out of the twenty-two attackers got back, three so badly damaged that they were write-offs.

The Germans praised their gunners for 'excellent shooting': four fighters were lost, though the British claimed twelve with six more having 'probably suffered the same fate' – an early example of exaggerated claims which would plague intelligence officers throughout the war. The bombers were criticised for sticking 'rigidly to their course', which the Germans were unaware had been their orders. 'It was criminal folly on the part of the enemy to fly at 4000 to 5000 metres in a cloudless sky with perfect visibility.' Despite 'a tightly closed formation', the greater speed of the Bf 109 and Bf 110 'enabled them to select their position of attack'. What the Germans did not reveal, nor the British realise, was the existence of a Freya coastal radar station which had alerted the enemy fighters. Even when a report was received via Oslo that such a device could detect incoming aircraft at a range of 75 miles, the RAF was not convinced. In December 1939 eight Freya stations were operational along the German coast.

Although unaware of this particular development, the British had recognised 'the vital necessity of fitting self-sealing tanks to all bombers', and also understood the inherent peril of the new German fighter tactic. 'Wellingtons cannot defend themselves from a beam attack from above', because such an approach had never been envisaged 'in view of modern speeds and the consequent deflection shooting involved'.

Elsewhere, the dangers of daylight operations were independently exposed. On 2 September, ten squadrons of Battles had been sent to France to join the Advanced Air Striking Force and undertake reconnaissance sweeps across the German border. On 30 September 1939, five ran into fifteen Messerschmitts near Saarbrücken and four were shot down, thus vindicating pre-war reservations about the Battle's operational effectiveness.

From the first week of the war, night raids of a sort had been carried out. Bombing of Germany might be strictly off limits, but the dropping of leaflets (codenamed 'Nickel' and often termed 'white bombs' or 'bomblets') was not. Optimists considered that the morale of Austro-Hungarian troops had been undermined in 1918 and pointed, too, to the perceived success of 'imperial policing' which made widespread use of this tactic to unsettle rebellious tribesmen. There was evidence, as well, that during the First World War factories stopped work once enemy aircraft were detected. It was felt that this would happen in Germany even if aircraft did not drop bombs. In any case, with the recognised lack of night training pre-war, flights into Germany would sharpen the navigators' skills and allow crews to become more efficient through cooperation under wartime conditions. In retrospect, these arguments may seem thin; at the time they were not unreasonable.

The bulk of the leaflet campaign fell to Whitley bombers, whose first excursion occurred during the night of 3/4 September 1939. The weather rather than enemy fighters or flak proved the greatest problem then and in ensuing months. Over Berlin on 1/2 October at 22,500ft the oxygen supply in one Whitley partly failed, causing two of the crew to pass out and the mechanism of the rear turret to freeze trapping the gunner inside. The navigator dragged one of his unconscious colleagues to a portable oxygen bottle and despatched two-thirds of the leaflets through the adapted flare chute before himself collapsing. Clear of the German capital, the pilot descended to 9000ft, the rear turret unfroze and the unconscious crew members came round. Order was restored, but the crew now knew that unpleasant emergencies on leaflet flights could happen without any enemy interference.

Towards the end of the month, on 27/28 October, Whitleys dropping leaflets in the Ruhr ran into difficulty in temperatures of minus 22–32 degrees centigrade, which officially 'caused much amazement, when it was realised that aircraft in such a condition of "icing-up" could still be controlled'. When a 6in. layer of ice formed on the wing of one aircraft, it went into a dive from which both pilots struggled to recover at 7000ft. They then found that the rudder and elevators would not move. The wireless operator's equipment was iced over, so he could not request a fix. At this point the Whitley's flight had been stabilised, but the port engine had stopped, ice could be seen sticking out of the cowling, the windscreen was covered with ice and the aircraft losing height at 2000ft a minute. With a crash seemingly inevitable, the pilot ordered the crew to bale out. When neither acknowledged, he discovered that both the front and rear gunners were unconscious, so he cancelled the order to abandon the aircraft. With the Whitley still losing height, the side windows and top hatch in the cockpit were opened in an attempt to see where the aircraft was going. At that point, the aircraft emerged from cloud in heavy rain at a mere 200ft. One of the crew afterwards described the scene: 'All we could see was a black forest with a grey patch in the middle, for which we were heading; the second pilot pulled the aircraft over the trees, brushing through their tops, and the aircraft dropped flat into a field, travelled through a wire fence, skidded broadside on and came to rest with the port wing against the trees on the further side of he clearing.' Clambering out, the crew saw that the starboard engine was in flames, which the wireless operator doused with an extinguisher after clambering on to the cowling. 'We ascertained that all members of the crew were safe and unhurt', and they decided to spend the rest of the freezing night inside their damaged Whitley. At daylight, they were relieved to find they had landed in France.

Early in 1940 the range of aircraft engaged in leaflet dropping increased with availability of refuelling facilities in France. Having topped up the aircraft there, a crew sent to Warsaw completed its task but, battling into a headwind on the return flight across Germany, the bomber ran short of petrol. Believing that it had reached friendly territory, the Whitley put down in a convenient field. Failing to make themselves understood by nearby civilians and with their suspicions rightly raised by the approach of a detachment of armed cyclists in uniform, the crew dashed back to the aircraft and hauled it into the air, pursued by a fusilade of rifle shots. With the tanks reading empty, they just managed to make the right side of the Franco-German border.

Only from the haven of hindsight do these happenings seem even mildly amusing. At the time they pointed to dangerous inadequacies in Bomber Command's ability to wage war. Whatever the merits of the leaflet campaign, not only did many Whitley crews suffer extreme discomfort and outright danger from the weather, but an unacceptable 6 per cent were lost. Staff officers held that improved navigational aids, better provision for crews at high altitude and more efficient procedures for emergency landings came from lessons learnt during this pamphlet war. Harris remained pugnaciously sceptical of its worth. In his view, the only achievement was 'to supply the Continent's requirement of toilet paper'.

The Air Officer Commanding in Chief (C-in-C) Bomber Command, Air Chief Marshal Sir Edgar Ludlow Hewitt, drew attention to the serious deficiencies in his force, emphasised that a daylight campaign against Germany as foreseen pre-war was out of the question, and paid the price. On 4 April 1940, Air Marshal Charles Portal replaced him. The new commander had only thirty-three operational squadrons at his disposal. Almost exactly half had Battles or Blenheims, leaving just seventeen with Wellington, Whitley and Hampden 'heavy' bombers with which to attack the German war industries.

In a determined effort to clear the log jam of applicants and to improve the training organisation overall, on 17 December 1939 the Empire Training Scheme had been agreed for aircrew to attend courses overseas (for example, in Canada, South Africa, Southern Rhodesia, India). Ultimately, more than two hundred thousand would be trained in this way, in addition to fourteen thousand in the United States. In March 1940, however, this scheme had not yet got underway, as a twenty-three-year-old customs officer from Southampton discovered. Dudley Heal, officially in a reserved occupation and not therefore liable to be called up, volunteered for aircrew for somewhat negative reasons: he did not fancy the 'cold steel' of the army nor seasickness in the Royal Navy. He made his way to Uxbridge with a fellow customs officer, armed with valuable advice. A friendly squadron leader had warned that 'the medical examination for aircrew included having to blow into a tube and hold a bulb of mercury at a certain point in the tube for a full minute'. All straightforward, except that Heal was asthmatic. Forewarned, he had daily practised holding his breath for the required time. Now the real test was at hand.

When the critical moment arrived, 'uttering a silent prayer and taking a very deep breath I blew the mercury up the tube to the required point and stood there, watching it as the seconds ticked slowly by. Then I could hold it no longer and the bulb sank to the bottom of the tube. I looked at the MO. He looked at me, paused, then indicated that I had passed. I believe it was touch-and-go.' Heal was then sent home and not recalled to Uxbridge until 8 May 1940. Even then, aircrew training still lay a long way off.

'One got the impression that the RAF didn't know quite what to do with us at this time. We found ourselves at Hendon, for example, looking after the coke boiler in the airmen's quarters. I remember it particularly,' Heal later reflected, 'because of that Saturday afternoon when we were so unpopular because we'd let it go out and nobody could have a bath.' Square-bashing, bayonet drill and cross-country running at various camps followed, capped by a spell as a Service Policeman – guarding the dock gates at Southampton, where his quest to join the RAF had started. Eventually, Heal began aircrew training at Newquay a year after joining up. Not until May 1942, though, would he begin the final phase of his preparation for operations as a navigator and almost another year passed before, in February 1943, he went on a raid to Germany.

Gerald Dickson had a similar experience. As a member of the RAFVR, he duly reported to Uxbridge, where he was attested and told to go home again. So he resumed his job with London County Council, which involved filling sandbags and making sure that designated rest centres for anticipated victims of bombing had supplies of sugar, tea, etc. He was not recalled until May 1940, though his progress towards being a navigator was swifter than Heal's. Moving via Hastings and Torquay, where his whole course had to dive behind a convenient wall as a lone intruder machine-gunned the seafront, and Canada, his first operational flight would be in September 1941.

Phoney War

The whole strategic scenario altered swiftly and dramatically on 9 April 1940 when German troops invaded Norway and Denmark. Leaflet operations were immediately suspended. Bomber Command had already been carrying out 'gardening' operations (dropping of mines at sea) to hamper German naval activity in the English Channel and North Sea. Now it made a strenuous effort to mine the seas off northern Germany and southern Norway. Between 7 April and 9 May 1940, Bomber Command lost thirty-one aircraft in carrying out 782 sorties. The First World War veteran Marshal of the Royal Air Force Lord Trenchard believed these operations misguided and wasteful. He remained wedded to the concept of concentrating on enemy industry, as he explained to Portal on 2 May: 'I am sorry you could not use it [Bomber Command] where I and others think it probably would have ended the war by now.' Ever the optimist.

Trenchard's aggressive adherence to the rubric of strategic bombing, developed by armchair theorists over the past twenty-five years, ignored the painful lessons of bomber vulnerability and the design faults so recently exposed. The Hampden, for example, had grave drawbacks, far in excess of its lack of toilet facilities for the pilot. In Harris's words, the bomber 'failed to meet many requirements of the normal specifications'. Flying one at an OTU, Sergeant Bill Townsend thought it no better than a flying coffin. The aircraft was structurally strong and mechanically reliable, but it lacked effective defensive power, 'with a single gun on top and a single one underneath, manned by a gunner in a hopelessly cramped position, together with a gun firing forward which, as it was fixed, was of no value at all'. Furthermore, 'the mounts of the two moveable guns were rickety and had a limited traverse with many blind spots'. In the words of another critic, the bomber was 'woefully underarmed . . . a bit primitive'. Small wonder, then, that Hampden crews found themselves vulnerable to fighter attacks even when flying in formation.

The so-called Phoney War, during which the bombing of Germany was prohibited, in every sense provided a wake-up call. The severe loss rate among Blenheims and Wellingtons, plus the obvious inadequacies of the Hampdens when faced with enemy fighters, sounded the death knell for the belief that bombers, whether in formation or not, could 'always get through' in daylight. The feeling that night operations were the way forward, despite the difficulties experienced by Whitleys on their leaflet raids, began to gather pace.

Guy Brisbane, in his later analysis, noted that much less attention had been paid to training for night operations during pre-war training or during the months immediately after the declaration of war. He also raised specific doubts about the credibility of the methods so confidently described by the Air Ministry at the time. Astro-navigational techniques were rarely taught and too much reliance was placed on the W/T 'fixes', which did prove effective over the North Sea but would be far less useful over the European mainland. The training process had been 'stereo-typed', with little differentiation between day and night requirements. Only on moonlit nights was the spotting of landmarks feasible. And, even if an aircraft reached the target area, in poor conditions target identification would be 'practically impossible', the 'limited number of flares' in each aircraft and 'the very primitive mechanism' available for their release 'vastly reduced' their utility. Moreover, the glare of searchlights had been too easily discounted.

Larry Curtis, a future wireless operator, had different misgivings. During training at RAF Yatesbury, Wiltshire, he received his only instruction in the use of a parachute. He was ordered to climb on to a five-bar gate and jump off. On hitting the ground, he should count to five before drawing his hand across his chest

to simulate pulling the ripcord. This was, he felt, less than adequate preparation for saving his life in an emergency. Nor did he
recall at any stage of his service being told how to leave a
stricken aircraft, for example, which exit to make for. 'Every
man for himself,' he said, when the time came, which may
explain why wireless operators who did bale out reported leaving either through the forward exit in the nose or the rear door
by the tail. There was no consistency in the procedure. The
only relevant advice Curtis remembers receiving was being told
to join the navigator sitting with his back to the main spar for
landing. Two navigator aircrew, Gerald Dickson and John
Langston, confirmed that they had no opportunity to practise
parachuting, not even Curtis's luxury of using a five-bar gate.
Both agreed that they were simply told to count to five after
baling out before pulling the ripcord.

For all the weaknesses in aircraft, equipment, tactics and
training which had been revealed during the Phoney War, the
importance of the interaction and cooperation between members of bomber crews had been vividly portrayed, not least
when a damaged aircraft with wounded men on board had
been safely brought home. Those qualities of individual efficiency, determination and comradeship were about to be put to
an even sterner test.

On 10 May 1940, German armoured and infantry columns
poured into France and the Low Countries under a protective
Luftwaffe umbrella. Objections to the air assault on Germany's
industrial centres, her sources of military power, envisaged in
the Western Air Plans were now removed. At last the strategic
bombing of the Reich could begin.

CHAPTER 3

Over Germany, 1940–41

'Bomber Command will allow no pause, no breathing space'

Having instructed it to deal with enemy troop concentrations, marshalling yards and oil plants in the Ruhr, the Air Ministry exclaimed that henceforth 'Bomber Command will allow no pause, no breathing space'. Bombing of Germany's armament factories was not yet a priority, though. Stemming the immediate advance of enemy columns either directly or through disrupting their movement and fuel supplies remained of paramount importance.

Two days after German troops violated the borders of neighbouring countries, on 12 May Battles of the Advanced Air Striking Force in France and Blenheims from England attacked the routes along which infantry and armour were driving westwards. Their vulnerability in daylight was once more heavily underlined.

Shortly after 8 a.m., with his normal crew (Whiting now commissioned, Lang a corporal) Embry took off in the van of 107 Squadron Blenheims. They were part of a formation bound for road bridges on the Albert canal and the Meuse river.

Over Germany

Each bomber carried two 250lb. and a dozen 40lb. General Purpose (GP) bombs. The outward flight at 4000ft was uneventful; until the aircraft started the run-in to their target, when 'a tornado of fire' burst around them. Embry had time to reflect that a low-level attack was 'suicidal' but unavoidable. To him, 'the whole earth seemed to be erupting'. As shell bursts, interlaced with colourful tracer, blackened the sky, the bombers were continually buffeted by the impact of shrapnel and near misses. Embry saw five Blenheims shot down, as Whiting in the bomb aimer's compartment calmly issued instructions to his pilot until 'bombs gone' came over the intercom. The post-operational summary would refer to 'accurate bombing' and 'excellent results', despite being 'subjected to heavy AA fire for a distance of 15 miles from the target which increased to an intense barrage over the target'.

The volume of flak caused the formation to break up leaving the target area, allowing fighters to shoot down one Blenheim. When the ground fire slackened, Embry ordered his remaining aircraft once more to close up in 'tight formation'. During the next 20 twenty minutes one enemy fighter was accounted for and another 'probable' claimed. Of the twenty-four Blenheims which set out, however, seven had been lost. Two others crash-landed, one in friendly Belgium. The other made it back home with a badly injured navigator lying in the bomb-aiming compartment as the aircraft made a belly landing. Hacked out of the nose, Sergeant Innes-Jones made a full recovery.

Independently Battles stationed at Amifontaine attacked another bridge over the Albert canal at Maastricht. With only 250lb. bombs available, like Embry's force, an attack had to be made at low level. Stressing that the target 'was to be destroyed at all costs', the Officer Commanding 12 Squadron called for volunteers. Every three-man Battle crew stepped forward, and six were chosen by lot. One aircraft and the reserve machine each suffered a mechanical failure, though. So only five took off. 'As anticipated,' the post-operational report ran, 'exceptionally intense machine-gun and anti-aircraft fire was encountered, and the bridge area was heavily defended by enemy fighters. In spite of this the formation successfully delivered a dive-bombing attack from the lowest practicable altitude and British fighters in the vicinity reported that the target was obscured by the bombs bursting on it and in its vicinity'. The bridge had been breached, and a French general signalled their squadron, '*Messieurs, je vous remercie*'. However, success had been achieved at a truly dreadful cost. The leading bomber, piloted by Flying Officer Edward Garland with Sergeant Thomas Gray as his observer, LAC E. Reynolds the wireless operator, and three others did not return. Only one badly damaged Battle survived the carnage, the pilot and wireless operator receiving the DFC and DFM respectively. For their 'coolness and resource' in leading the attack, Garland and Gray were both posthumously awarded the VC, the only time two members of a bomber crew would be so decorated on the same operation.

Two days later, on 14 May, thirty-four out of sixty-seven Battles were shot down; the same day German bombers virtually destroyed Rotterdam with a fearsome display of aerial might which prompted the Netherlands to sue for peace the very next day. Passing over the smouldering ruins an RAF pilot smelt the smoke of the fires burning 7000ft below and 'was shocked seeing a city in flames like that. Devastation on a scale I had never experienced.'

Bomber Command continued to hit enemy lines of communication, although the unsuitability of the Blenheim in this daylight role was further demonstrated by the loss of eleven out of twelve despatched on 17 May. Despite Bomber Command's best efforts, German forces moved relentlessly forward to reach the Channel coast at Abbéville on 21 May.

British, French and Belgian troops were then cut off from Allied formations to the south. As the military situation deteriorated, 338,000 troops were rescued from the beaches of Dunkirk between 27 May and 4 June as Bomber Command valiantly tried to delay the tightening belt of enemy forces. In spite of serious losses, the urgency of giving close support to the hard-pressed troops meant that the risks had to be taken in daylight.

However, night operations had also begun inside Germany. On 11/12 May, thirty-seven Hampdens and Whitleys attacked road and rail communications at Mönchen-Gladbach, the first bombing raid on German soil. Four aircraft were lost. Succeeding nights saw further raids on associated targets with few bomber losses. Ninety-nine Wellingtons, Whitleys and Hampdens set out for sixteen different locations in the Ruhr on 15/16 May. Eighty-one reported bombing their primary or alternative targets. No bomber was lost over Germany, although one crashed on the way back. Bearing in mind that twelve other bombers struck enemy lines of communication in Belgium that night, only one bomber was therefore lost out of 111. Successful raids on transportation centres in the immediate vicinity of the battlefield raised hopes of similar turmoil being caused in the German domestic railway system. An RAF officer, who had been shot down and subsequently escaped, described the encouraging results of a raid on a marshalling yard near the Somme river. 'Trucks and engines had been lifted bodily off the track, and the tenders on their sides . . . The general appearance was of utter chaos and confusion.'

Commitment to supporting the army on the Continent and the Royal Navy off north-west Germany and Norway demonstrated that, from the beginning of the war, 'the Reich' covered all aspects of enemy targets within range, not just the strategic bombing of the German homeland.

Basically, the idea for a night raid at this stage of the war was to stretch it over a long period to extend and exhaust the defences, a practice condemned by Harris as 'vague'. Gibson illustrated its practical shortcomings when ordered to attack part of the Hamburg docks on 17 May 1940. At briefing, cautioned that the moon was in the south-west and the recommended line of approach therefore from the north-east, crews were told that they could attack from whichever height suited them. Moreover, they might fly in and out via any route they wished, so long as they bombed between midnight and 4 a.m. Incredibly, as Gibson and his navigator wanted to see a film in Lincoln that evening, they decided to take off late and bomb after 3 a.m. Once airborne, planning to fly at 8000ft and bomb at 2000ft, Gibson found that his crew had not brought oxygen bottles with them; then over Hamburg the aircraft had a hangup of bombs in the bomb bay, requiring him to take the Hampden round again amid a barrage of colourful language. Diverted to Abingdon on return, damage to the aircraft was discovered 'due to colliding with a German balloon cable'. 'These early raids were haphazard,' Gibson rightly observed.

On 20 June 1940, the Air Ministry modified Bomber Command's instructions: 'the primary offensive' must be to achieve 'the most immediate effect on reducing the scale of air attack on this country'. A list of factory targets and equipment depots was appended. Attacks on marshalling yards in the Ruhr, aqueducts on the Dortmund-Ems canal and mining of other canals were to continue, as were 'gardening' operations off the coast. 'Oil plants and stocks in Western Germany and in German-occupied countries' were to be targeted 'as opportunity arises', justified by the rubric of strategic bombing theory. 'As stocks of oil available to Germany decrease the problems of distribution will cause increasing difficulty in the deployment and operation of the German armed forces.'

All of this presumed an unrealistic degree of accuracy.

Over Germany

Looking back, Harris castigated those who still believed that small targets could be eliminated and, further, dismissed the inadequacy of available bombs. 'In 1940 the Ministry of Economic Warfare was in its glory, planning a campaign against German synthetic oil plants, together with factories making aluminium, and aircraft works'. The idea that the 250lb. bomb ('a ridiculous missile') could break the fuel lines of power plants and pumping stations, which incendiaries would then ignite, was simply ludicrous.

Despite these reservations, Harris maintained that the bombing of Germany was 'an entirely practicable method of beating the enemy provided only that we got on quickly enough to keep ahead of his counter-measures'. A critical caveat. Speed was the essence and, for a variety of reasons, development could not be achieved at the pace Harris wanted. In a morale-boosting visit to the HQ Bomber Command, King George VI was more upbeat: 'The matchless spirit that has shown so clear an ascendancy over the enemy makes the final victory of the Allies doubly sure.'

Even after the last man had been lifted from the Dunkirk sands with Belgium having been defeated on 28 May, Bomber Command continued to attack German lines of communication in support of French forces in the field. That was why Leonard Cheshire hauled himself through the underbelly hatch into a Whitley bomber as Pilot Officer Long's second pilot just before 8 p.m. at RAF Driffield on 9 June 1940. Cheshire had graduated in Law from Oxford, where he enjoyed a colourful social life, learnt to fly in the University Air Squadron and joined the RAFVR in which he was mobilised. He would never lose his sense of fun, but would become a dedicated and brave airman, an effective if unorthodox leader who inspired loyalty and affection.

On his first operation to and from the target at Abbéville,

Cheshire took the Whitley's controls and remained impressed by the navigator's ability accurately to predict turning points and prominent landmarks below. As the flight lengthened Cheshire was struck by the fact that all 'the others seemed to know what they were doing'. For the attack, Long resumed the pilot's seat, an awkward physical interchange which Cheshire quickly mastered. Cheshire was dazzled by the multitude of flares from theirs and other aircraft which speckled the sky and startled by near collision with another Whitley. The operation was relatively uneventful, despite having to go round again before the navigator in his second role released the bomb load. When the rear gunner confirmed that they had hit the target, Cheshire 'felt happy from the infection of their high spirits'. On the way home, the wireless operator had difficulty in raising base and, leaving Cheshire to fly, the pilot went back to help him, another example of his leadership and crew cooperation. These were early days and significantly neither flak nor fighters had disturbed them. Breezily Cheshire summarised the operation: 'Took off after dinner and flew via Abingdon and Hastings and then direct to target . . . [which was] located without difficulty – dropped two sticks – one on southern bridge and one on north bridge from 4000ft. . . . Ground strafing of German troops on return journey. Landed back at dawn. No engine trouble or damage to aircraft.' The strain of repetitive, more dangerous operations deep into enemy territory had yet to come.

Within hours, the military situation immeasurably worsened with Italy's entry into the war, and during the night of 11/12 June RAF bombers carried out the first of many raids over the next four years south of the Alps which would drain resources away from German targets. Then, on 25 June, France capitulated, leaving the United Kingdom fighting alone in Europe. On 8 July, Churchill declared that 'an absolutely devastating, exterminating attack by very heavy bombers from this country upon the Nazi homeland' was the best way to defeat Hitler.

The fortunes of Paddy Denton, who had joined Bomber Command through subterfuge, suggested that such a convincing campaign was still far off. His father had been opposed to his joining the RAF after leaving Shrewsbury School because his mother's favourite brother had been killed in the Royal Flying Corps during the First World War. Denton, therefore, officially opted for Air-Sea Rescue but persuaded the recruiting sergeant surreptitiously to note his preference in the appropriate file. Hence, in July 1940 he found himself training as a pilot in Scotland.

'It is an indication of how ill-prepared for war we, as a nation, were', he wrote, 'when there was some sort of threat of attack, presumably from the sea . . . [and] some of the more serviceable Tiger Moths were fitted with bomb racks and tiny little bombs, about 3lb. I would have thought. These appalling threats to an invader were released without benefit of bomb-sight or anything so sophisticated, by a neat Heath Robinson device of little levers in front of the intrepid aviator.' Fortunately, these contraptions were not put to the test, but 'the experience did make me ponder about the possible outcome of the war'. Not, therefore, so confident as the King.

Even as Denton was expressing his doubts about Tiger Moths holding off an invasion fleet, further south the Battle of Britain was about to begin and Bomber Command to launch a lesser-known, associated campaign. On 4 July 1940, the Battle of the Barges commenced. That day, the Air Ministry declared: 'It is now considered desirable *as a first priority* [*sic*] to intensify our attacks on enemy ports and shipping against the threat of invasion.' An estimated three thousand of these vessels capable of crossing the Channel under their own power and a great many more needing to be towed were ready to transport German troops and their equipment to the shores of England. Bomber squadrons were detailed not only to hit specific ports but designated basins within them. 'Antwerp [was] a pistol pointed at the heart of England', the Air Ministry explained, with 'smaller and less important ports which still had a considerable part to play'. Calais, centre of the menacing crescent, lay 21 miles away; Flushing, Zeebrugge, Boulogne and Cherbourg among ports within sailing distance during a late summer's night.

The danger of attacking targets in Germany was sharply demonstrated during an operation on the Dortmund-Ems canal. This was a critical waterway for the passage of military matériel to and from factories and had been singled out for attack by the Air Ministry on 20 June. The intention was to breach either one of its vulnerable viaducts or an embankment running through low-lying land. On 12 August 1940, eleven Hampdens from RAF Scampton were ordered to hit one of the viaducts with a collection of 250lb. and 500lb. GP bombs. Three failed to reach the target area. Of the remaining eight, three made diversionary attacks while five attacked the main target at a mere 150ft. Flight Lieutenant Roderick Learoyd was the last of the five scheduled to attack. Circling at 4000ft, he watched his four predecessors go in, noting 'scores of searchlights and anti-aircraft batteries along both banks of the canal'.

When his turn came, Learoyd descended to attacking height and made sure that the target was silhouetted by the moon. But 'Jerry had got our range to a nicety'. As he flew through the glare of searchlights, his observer (Pilot Officer John Lewis), now in the bomb-aiming position, used the intercom to guide him. Learoyd sensed that lumps were being torn off the aircraft by flak. Suddenly, Lewis released the bombs and as Learoyd pulled up and away, the wireless operator, Sergeant J. Ellis, yelled that the viaduct had been broken. The crew realised the hydraulic system of their Hampden had been severely damaged so that the undercarriage could not be lowered and there was no guarantee that the back-up compressed air bottle would work. Having managed to coax the aircraft successfully through enemy territory and across the North Sea, Learoyd arrived over Scampton shortly after 2 a.m. He circled Lincolnshire for almost another three hours until daylight allowed him to make an emergency landing. The Squadron ORB simply recorded that Learoyd had 'successfully attacked and bombed' the target, and his aircraft had been 'severely damaged'.

For his feat Learoyd received the VC, and the citation was altogether more expansive. Paying tribute to his 'high courage, skill and determination', it explained that 'to achieve success it was necessary to approach from a direction well known to the enemy, through a lane of especially disposed anti-aircraft defences . . . and the most point blank fire from guns of all calibres . . . The reception of the preceding aircraft might well have deterred the stoutest heart.'

Throughout the summer, Bomber Command was guided by the directive that 'the destruction of Germany's oil resources remains the basis of the main offensive strategy directed towards the reduction and dislocation of German war potential'. On 1 September, Churchill praised the crews 'engaged in the recent long distance attacks on military objectives in Germany', which had been 'so sharply smitten'. These precision raids he contrasted with German airmen who 'vented their spite upon the defenceless watering-place and town of Ramsgate'. He believed Bomber Command's achievements to be 'another sign and proof that the command of the air is gradually and painfully, but nonetheless remorselessly, [being] wrested from the Nazi criminals who hoped by this means to terrorise and dominate European civilisation'. The Prime Minister's words so impressed Leonard Cheshire that he preserved them in a notebook.

Bomber Crew

Closer to home, in direct defence of British shores, the assault on the assembled barges reached a crescendo. On 15 September 1940, the very day on which Hurricanes and Spitfires fought the decisive day battle with the Luftwaffe on the approaches to London effectively to close the Battle of Britain, wireless operator and air gunner Sergeant John Hannah took off from Scampton in a Hampden piloted by Canadian Pilot Officer Connor. After successfully hitting barges at Antwerp, Connor was on the way home over Belgium when the aircraft was 'subjected to intense anti-aircraft fire and received a direct hit from a projectile of an explosive and incendiary nature', which burst inside the bomb bay. 'A fire started which quickly enveloped the wireless operator's and rear gunner's cockpits, and as the port and starboard petrol tanks had been pierced, there was grave risk of the fire spreading.' Hannah 'forced his way through the fire to obtain two fire extinguishers' and found that the rear gunner had baled out.

He could have followed him. Instead, Hannah fought the fire for ten minutes with the extinguishers and when they were empty beat the flames with his logbook. 'During this time thousands of rounds of ammunition exploded in all directions and he was almost blinded by the intense heat and fumes, but had the presence of mind to obtain relief by turning on his oxygen supply.' The inrush of air through the vast holes torn by the flak shells fanned the flames into 'an inferno', despite Hannah's efforts, 'and all the aluminium sheet melted on the floor . . . leaving only the cross bearers'. Despite these appalling conditions, Hannah managed to quell the fire, in the process sustaining 'severe' burns to his face and eyes. Crawling forward, he found that the navigator had also baled out and managed to pass his maps and log to the pilot, enabling Connor to get the bomber back to base. The official report referred to 'a hole in the fuselage large enough for a man to crawl through . . . The rear gunner's cockpit and half the interior of the fuselage were charred ruins. There were holes in the wings and in the petrol tanks.' '. . . no one who has seen the condition of the aircraft can be otherwise than amazed at the extraordinary presence of mind and extreme courage which Sergeant Hannah displayed in remaining in it', wrote the Group commander in recommending Hannah for the VC.

As the immediate threat of invasion receded, on 21 September the Air Ministry drew up a list of 'airframe and engine' factories and 'submarine building yards' for attack, in addition to the communication bottlenecks and oil resources in Germany already notified. 'Electricity and gas plants' in Berlin should be targeted 'from time to time when favourable weather conditions permit' as well. But by 30 October oil had again assumed primary importance with an additional emphasis on 'heavy material destruction' in urban areas, where 'as many heavy bombers as possible should be detailed for the attack, carrying high explosive, incendiary and delay-action bombs with perhaps an occasional mine'.

Flight Lieutenant Ken Batchelor went to one of the urban areas (Cologne) on 27/28 November as second pilot in a 9 Squadron Wellington, and recorded his impressions in his diary. 'My first operational trip. Lovely one too. Dark night, cumulus cloud and stratus haze over Holland. Searchlights and flak from Turnhout. Ran in and found the Rhine OK dropped flares and found Hohenzollern Bridge, the target, perfectly.' Curiously, Batchelor knew Cologne well, having lived there after the First World War when his father was serving in the Army of Occupation.

His wife Doris (always known as 'Micky') was not so relaxed about the raid. The Batchelors were lodging with other RAF couples at the Red House in the isolated Suffolk village of Livermere, three miles from RAF Honington and six miles from Bury St Edmunds with its welcome cinema. They shared a sitting room and dining room, where communal meals were served, only having to themselves an 'extremely cold' bedroom, with a 'very dim light' provided by a noisy and smelly outside generator which often malfunctioned. The room was 'small and stuffed full with . . . furniture all made of polished wood which, together with a small window, made the room look even more depressing'. Nor was the food inviting: 'We had custard and fruit for every sweet and the other course was usually cold meat, rabbit, cottage pie, or some wholesome but equally dull dish.' While her husband was at Honington, Micky 'just slept late and knitted and walked' waiting for Ken to come back in his car at about 5 p.m. That is, until the afternoon of 27 November.

'I don't think I shall ever forget that first night by myself', she recalled. 'Ken phoned at 4.30 p.m. to say that he was taking off soon, but didn't tell me anything more over the phone and I was left with my imagination. The whole household knew he had gone as soon as I hung up and they all immediately tried to cheer me up saying "He'll be back soon – don't worry, my dear" . . . I escaped to bed as soon as I possibly could and after shedding a few tears I felt better and tried to read. But the print kept on blurring and I found myself thinking – thinking, surely they must be home soon – was everything all right – was Ken wounded – or in the bitter cold sea – or a prisoner? And then suddenly, far away, I heard the throb of an engine. Was it a car or a plane – and as it grew closer my heart just leaped as the steady drone became louder and louder and then after going directly overhead faded towards the camp. To me – it was just like a message going ahead to say the others were coming. And soon after they were all overhead and around the sky – too many at once to count the separate engines and, praying that Ken was amongst them, I fell asleep. He woke me at 3.30 a.m. – cold and tired – but still a little excited and full of his first taste of enemy action. I could have wept again on such a big relief.'

48

Over Germany

Two nights later, 29/30 November, Pilot Officer Jack Wetherly took another Wellington to Boulogne, a traditional 'makey learn' initiation for new crews according to his second pilot, Pilot Officer Ian Lawson. The navigator, Sergeant N. F. Walker, agreed that this was 'the first step towards building up a relationship which was continually strengthened for the next three months, during which we completed fourteen sorties together'. Lawson reflected that 'new crews had to learn fast. Six lives depended upon each crew member knowing his job thoroughly . . . A proficient navigator, in particular, was essential.' Wetherly was 'horrified by the thought of flying deep into the heart of the Continent with a navigator who had never seen a sextant, and a wireless operator whose experience in his sphere of activity was equally limited'. So-called 'milk-runs' to nearby targets were, therefore, in every sense critical to 'crew bonding', in modern parlance.

Batchelor went to Düsseldorf on 7 December with Pilot Officer Whitehead 'on my second stooge trip', and again wrote with the enthusiasm and naivety shown by Cheshire when he began flying operationally: 'A very successful time was had by all, to put it in the vernacular. Dark night, icing and cloud in and out. Incendiaries triangulated targets perfectly. The first raiders had done their job well. Stooged around and had a good view. Heavy flak but little worried us.' His pilot elaborated: 'I did a couple of circuits after bombing to see results. It was well worth it too. Planes had bombed from all directions and I could make out the lines of the various sticks quite plainly. Even before the attack had ended, the place was just a mass of flames', the last phrase providing the headline for the *Daily Telegraph*'s account of the action.

Micky Batchelor had another stressful night with an unexpected further worry. 'The phone rang at 4.30 p.m. just as I was going to walk out a little way to meet Ken . . . They were flying at five – no time to talk – couldn't tell me where they were going – would be back late – "*au revoir*". I said "goodbye", not thinking, but was brought back to the seriousness of it when Ken said "Don't say 'goodbye' – just '*au revoir*.'" Micky had to post a letter after tea. She heard the bombers 'warming up' then saw them 'taking off, circling overhead and then they straightened out on their course and made a beeline for the coast'.

She dozed fitfully until 11 p.m., then went to sleep. 'I was woken suddenly by the sound of a telephone ringing downstairs. I just couldn't move and lay there while it was answered' by another RAF resident. 'It seemed ages before he came up and knocked on my door – my mouth was so dry I couldn't say a word. He shoved his head round the door and said, "Kenneth is back and will be home tomorrow morning as he had some work to do tonight". I can't remember if I thanked him – the relief was so great. Great tears rolled down my cheeks and I didn't try to stop them.' When Batchelor did return, his eyes were 'red and sore and bloodshot and his whole manner was jumpy'. He explained that they had all been waiting for a missing aircraft to appear, but there was no sign of it. He apologised for ringing at 1.30 a.m. His watch had stopped and he thought it was two hours earlier.

Despite worsening weather, raids did not pause during December 1940. In the second week of the month Cheshire flew to Mannheim, where 'ice rattled off the propellers and lay like white lead on the wings, the Perspex [of the cockpit] and the navigation table'. A blizzard closed in (10/10ths snowstorm, minus 30 degrees centigrade), so Cheshire and the crew were relieved to get back safely. Two days later, they set off for Duisburg only to be recalled after a mere twenty minutes. On 15 December, Cheshire went to Berlin, where he found the snow, ice and dense cloud obscuring the target more perilous than flak. His youthful exuberance had now been tempered by experience.

During 1940 several innovations had been introduced, not all of them successfully. The Course Setting Bomb Sight had not proved ideal for night bombing. It was superseded by an automatic device, but Guy Brisbane noted in his post-war summary that this was even less satisfactory and 'most observers' got the old sight back. Air gunners had received little or no 'night vision training' and this situation was rectified quickly. Other operational drawbacks emerged, too. Due to the inadequate heating, aircrew suffered frostbite and guns froze, so that they could not be fired. And Brisbane complained that 'one early oxygen mask developed the unpleasant fault of allowing ice to build up in the oxygen delivery tube, thus slowly asphyxiating the wearer'.

Brisbane himself learnt a sobering lesson from an operational error. After flares had been released to identify the target, the pilot decided on a low-level attack. In his 'excitement', Brisbane forgot to readjust the release mechanism. The bombs therefore exploded instantaneously on hitting the ground 1000ft below the aircraft. By 'good fortune' the 'catastrophic' effect did 'no great damage' to the Whitley, but the rest of the crew never let Brisbane forget the error, which might have cost them their lives.

In the opening months of war, the German defences had been relatively weak. By the close of 1940, there were uncomfortable signs that this was about to change. In the middle of the year, the coastal Freya radars had been supplemented by shorter-range Würzburg sets deployed inland, able to direct flak and night fighters. On 17 July 1940, Colonel (soon Major General) Josef Kammhuber was appointed to coordinate the night defences. By the end of the year he had organised a searchlight belt from Schleswig-Holstein to Belgium to illuminate bombers for flak batteries, backed up by night fighters alerted to their approach by Freyas and directed towards them by Würzburgs. These stronger defences were a concern. As a Wellington crew member explained: once caught in searchlight beams, 'all hell broke loose . . . The only way to escape was to dive, to pick up speed as quickly as possible, and get clear of the area.'

Even as the campaign on the Continent intensified, there were worrying signs that events in the Atlantic were not moving in Britain's favour. The fall of France had made her valuable west coast ports available to Germany. From there 'wolf packs' (concentrations of U-boats) attacked merchant convoys, reinforced by surface raiders like the pocket battleship *Admiral Scheer* and the heavy cruiser *Hipper*. During 1940, 1,059 merchantmen were sunk, 50 per cent of food imports lost. Bomber Command could not ignore this menace to the United Kingdom's lifeline.

Nevertheless, from the British point of view, 1941 started promisingly over Germany. *Daily Telegraph* readers learnt that, facing thick cloud, snowstorms and high winds, without loss RAF bombers struck Germany's 'greatest seaport after Hamburg' – Bremen – on the opening night of the year. The bombing offensive, they were assured, had not slackened. Shipbuilding yards, oil refineries and the railway centre were attacked, fires being seen by pilots of later aircraft from 120 miles away. The newspaper implied that night fighters were toothless: 'one or two enemy aircraft were seen wandering ineffectively over the town'. The impression of impotence was heightened by the report of a Junkers Ju 88 opening fire on a bomber from 800yd. 'The British rear gunner replied with a short burst, and the enemy then banked into a cloud, but just before the enemy entered the gunner fired another burst.' Two minutes later, the German fighter came out of the cloud 'belching clouds of smoke'.

Ken Batchelor flew his own Wellington on this raid. When

the 9 Squadron aircraft got back to base at around 1.30 a.m. on 2 January, comparing their notes and looking at the target maps the crews discovered that they had hit an aircraft factory producing the long-range Focke-Wulf 'Condor', which was being used to track convoys and guide U-boats towards them. So Batchelor was late back to the Red House 'full of excitement at this discovery only alas to find me [Micky] rather disgracefully in tears. Stupid of me, I know, but it was then 4.30 a.m. and I hadn't been able to sleep and therefore was tired and easily upset. I had heard them come back at 1.30 a.m. and when he was still not home by 4.15 a.m. I had filled my brain with so many stupid ideas of what had happened, and was so certain that he had not returned that the sound of the car coming down the road was such an enormous relief that I couldn't keep the tears back. I'd often heard of people crying with joy, but this was the first time I had ever done it myself and I felt ashamed.'

During January 1941, emphasis yet once more moved to oil targets. The Germans had overrun Romania in October 1940 to secure control of its refineries, but 'destruction of the German synthetic oil plants alone would bring about a crisis' of supply. These totalled 'only seventeen', of which nine accounted for 80 per cent of production. Ken Batchelor went to one plant at Gelsenkirchen on 9/10 January in a force of 135 Wellingtons, Blenheims, Hampdens and Whitleys. Flying south of Rotterdam in bright moonlight, his bomber met no opposition but clearly saw activity at the Eindhoven fighter station 25 miles away. Encountering patchy low cloud as it approached the Ruhr, the Wellington 'fanned out over the target area for one hour' without seeing anything. Hitting single targets remained elusive. Batchelor's aircraft bombed the alternative target of coking ovens at Duisburg, where visibility was better. On the way back, the wireless failed and the pilot descended below 1000ft over the North Sea as the clouds thickened.

Crossing the coast, the crew suddenly realised that one of the 500lb. bombs had hung up and Batchelor headed back out to sea to get rid of it – in vain. It would not budge. Once more crossing the coast, he saw snow-covered fields below as the wireless operator struggled to pick up a radio beacon flying at 500ft in dense fog. Frustrated, Batchelor yet again turned towards the coast where visibility was marginally clearer. As he avoided dangerous balloon cables, the crew tried to identify landmarks and confirm that they were in the Harwich area. The clouds seemed to be getting lower and lower as the supply of petrol drained away. Suddenly, through a break the moon illuminated the ground and, 'hedge-hopping at 0 feet', the Wellington flew inland, still uncertain of its precise position. To the crew's relief, a beacon bearing was picked up south of Cambridge. They were off track, but at least now had a runway to make for: RAF Stradishall. As the Wellington landed, the bomb fell off. Batchelor's wife, Micky, justifiably described this as 'a most unpleasant trip'.

Three Stirling four-engine bombers returned safely from a raid on oil-storage tanks in Rotterdam on 10/11 February, the first operation by this type of new machine. Few were yet in service, but high hopes of intensifying the bombing onslaught were immediately raised. On 11/12 February, Batchelor went to Bremen in a force of seventy-nine Hampdens, Wellingtons and Whitleys. After bombing, his Wellington ran into 10/10th cloud and 'got pasted; could hear 'em [flak shells] bursting as we got shaken up. That crump above the engines is not exciting.' Batchelor was concerned because there should have been no such flak on the planned track. 'Kept jinking all over the place for about twenty minutes but they kept our height nicely!' An unexpected, brief appearance of moonlight revealed the Rhine and the realisation that they were 'miles off course down south near the Ruhr'. Unable to obtain a fix – 'too much congestion' with so many other aircraft seeking assistance – Batchelor settled on a course of 300 degrees, having decided that a massive change in the speed and direction of the wind had caused the problem. On the way back, negotiating 10/10ths cloud over the North Sea, the pilot found that bad visibility prevented him from landing at base. Diverting to Newmarket, the crew discovered other Wellingtons 'milling around' in the rain and low, drifting cloud. Batchelor thought that they were lucky not only to find the aerodrome but to land safely.

The following morning, reports of all Wellingtons which had landed away from their base were collected: eleven had been lost, eight of them after running out of fuel. 'What a night,' Batchelor mused. 'Met.,' he added, 'should have looked out of the window as we took off in daylight. Thick sea fog could be seen coming in over the coast', and that persisted all the way to the target. Not for the first nor last time, forecasters got it wrong. The press were economical with the truth about the fifty-fifth raid on Bremen: 'An Air Ministry communiqué states that fires and explosions were caused among industrial targets.' No mention of the weather. Furthermore, readers learnt that 'three of our aircraft are missing', unaware that crashes after crossing the English coast were routinely not counted.

Micky Batchelor recorded a disturbing incident concerning a Czech airman and his wife, who had briefly stayed at the Red House. The airman failed to return from a raid on Boulogne on 6/7 February. A reconnaissance photograph later that month revealed a Wellington half-submerged in Boulogne harbour. This may have been the Czech's aircraft and, therefore, possibly, he was in captivity. But Micky observed: 'Unfortunately the Germans seldom take Czechs prisoner, but shoot them as traitors, so there is little hope for him. She [his wife] is extraordinarily brave and will not believe he is dead.'

Five weeks later, Ken Batchelor recorded his account of a

raid on 12/13 March by seventy-two bombers on Berlin: 'At last! I suppose one couldn't resist a thrill at the prospect of a chance of a bit of retaliation for London quite apart from the military importance of the target. That quite outweighed the fact that it is one of the hottest areas one could wish for with exceptionally accurate heavy flak'. Crossing the Dutch coast near the island of Texel 'on a perfect night, full moon and visibility almost as clear as day', as they 'forged on . . . diverse woods and occasionally railways and roads' could 'quite distinctly' be picked out. Ignoring a dummy town of red decoy lights north of Amsterdam, Batchelor's Wellington pressed on alone and undisturbed. After correcting for a variation of wind, which took it south of Hanover, the Wellington was back on track at Magdeburg, where flak opened up and two more dummy locations were ignored. Picking up a railway line south of Berlin, the bomber followed it to the target area, where 'a warm reception' waited. After bombing successfully, Batchelor's aircraft made its way home unscathed.

Micky wrote down her reactions while he was away. 'It is now 11.30 p.m. on Wednesday March 12. Ken took off about four hours ago to bomb Berlin. He said it was a nine-hour trip so I suppose he is over his target now . . . It is a lovely night – no clouds and a full moon but a strong wind. Pray God he comes back safe to me. It is awful just sitting here thinking, with nothing to do. Everyone else has gone to bed but I'm afraid to yet as I cannot sleep soundly when he is out. I keep waking, listening, and wondering where he is, or what time it is and if he is overdue as I always have a rough idea of the time he is due back. The doctor gave me a sleeping tablet, but I'm afraid to take one in case the phone rings and I don't hear. My one fear is of waking in the morning with no news of him. I don't think I should ever have the courage to ring up the Camp.' 'Well, my fears, as usual, were unnecessary,' she concluded.

Over Germany

Micky Batchelor noted 'a horrid fright' on Friday 21 March. 'I was dreaming that the phone was ringing and suddenly woke to find it was. At 5.30 in the morning it could only be for Ken. He rushed down in the dark, trying to find a match – and was told to report to Honington by 6 a.m. I shall *never* [*sic*] forget that awful morning. We thought the invasion had started – it was very foggy weather and just right – and we had visions of not seeing each other for weeks – or maybe never again. Ken dressed quickly, telling me what to expect, and what he might be doing and then he just stood around not knowing just how to say goodbye. It was awful, and when he had gone, I just lay in bed listening to the engines warming up at the 'drome and waiting for them to take off. But it was all one big scare for nothing. Ken phoned me at 10.30 a.m. to say I needn't worry.' They had been standing by to attack the battle cruisers *Scharnhorst* and *Gneisenau* off Bordeaux, but the operation was cancelled.

The fluctuating situation in the Near East, Mediterranean and southern Europe dictated that bombers had to be sent there rather than be committed to northern Europe. Ejection of the Italians from Abyssinia had been balanced early in 1941 by the arrival of German troops in North Africa to stiffen Axis resistance. In April, the Germans invaded Yugoslavia and Greece. A month later both had fallen and Allied forces had also been driven out of Crete.

The bombing campaign in north-west Europe received a boost in April, however, with reports of 'a new type of bomb, which appears to have devastating results'; a 'veteran of thirty raids' described its explosion creating 'a gigantic arc welding flash, blinding white'. During an attack on Emden, on 31 March/1 April, one pilot declared that 'houses took to the air', and imaginative leader writers embellished the scene: 'Masses of debris flying through the air were outlined against the glow of fires.' The novel weapon was dubbed a 'blockbuster' or 'cookie'.

Batchelor went to Berlin in a force of eighty bombers on 9/10 April, enthusiastically noting that three four-engine Stirlings were among them. Over the German capital, Batchelor saw five aircraft go down in flames in rapid succession and suddenly his Wellington was caught by a searchlight. 'Immediately about thirty searchlights' coned the bomber while Batchelor was running on towards the target. Fortunately, the storm of flak which came up at the Wellington did no damage, but, as Micky recorded: 'They were thoroughly shaken that night – frightened and scared stiff for the first time. To make it worse they lost [Pilot Officer] Sharpe and his crew and this shook them horribly.' Six parachutes had been seen coming out of one of the aircraft shot down, so there was a faint hope they had survived. There was a depressing postscript, too, Micky explained:

'Mrs Sharpe was down for Easter on her first trip to Honington to see her husband and she rang up the Camp not knowing he was missing as she had left her house near London before the Air Ministry wire had arrived. Poor girl. To hear over the phone like that. We went to see her later on as she wanted to meet us. I hope I shall be as brave as she it if should ever happen to me. She will not believe he is dead – has too much faith in his good flying . . . He did not believe in wives being near operational camps so she was never with him much. She had just become an [WAAF] officer and was going to tell him as a surprise for Easter.'

There was, though, a postscript of good news. Despite all Micky's fears, after eight weeks his wife had heard that the Czech missing from the Boulogne raid in February was a prisoner of war. 'God I wish this war would end. All the homes and happy lives broken up and what can we ever gain from it except a better land for the children we may never have.'

Over Germany

On 17/18 April, Batchelor flew to Berlin yet again, this time in a force of 118 aircraft, a 'more quiet' raid than eight days previously. Nevertheless, there was intense cold. Ice formed on aircraft wings and, according to newspaper reports, 'crews could hear it crackling faintly even above the noise of the engines'. To and from the target, over enemy territory, the flashes of flak shells 'shone through frost on the windows'. The press exclaimed that 'Berliners had a taste of the RAF's new bombs, which were dropped on their city for the first time. They have five times the blasting power of any bombs previously dropped.'

The *Daily Telegraph* penned a significant addendum. This was Berlin's 'heaviest raid, twenty-four hours after London had had its worst raid of the war'. Maintaining domestic, civilian morale was crucial to the war effort. An account of the shooting down of an enemy fighter apparently illustrated the growing power of the bombers: 'The captain banked to port and so did the enemy, making a perfect shot, I gave him a hundred rounds at point-blank range. He never had a chance to reply, but dropped in a sideslip and then went hurtling down.' The implication was that with the new bomb, four-engine bombers and such effective gunnery, the RAF was getting on top and that Berlin and other German cities would be hit harder and harder.

During the evening of Monday 28 April, Micky Batchelor watched her husband's Wellington among those setting off for Brest. She 'was amazed to see them taking off one after the other in a steady steam, coming from behind the trees from Honington and rising up into the clouds – and getting smaller and fainter . . . There was a lovely sunset and the quiet peace of the countryside now so green with spring, and the pheasants in the field and the birds singing so beautifully just made my eyes water as I thought of the destruction that was being done in the world.' She thought particularly of 'all those machines with six men on board', who might not come back. This week, she admitted, would be 'the longest I ever knew. We were so near the end now that I couldn't believe we'd get through safely.' After this operation, Batchelor had three more to do to complete his tour, and Micky could not know that would take more than a week.

He did return from Brest the following morning, but bad weather set in until Saturday 3 May when the French port was again the target. The intervening period had been a strain. Each day the crews stood by until 'about teatime', when operations were cancelled. 'Ken always came home in the afternoon of an "ops" day as his work really begins about four or five o'clock when they brief them – and after that nobody can leave camp again even if they didn't take off until midnight. So from lunchtime onwards I was listening for the car, hoping it wouldn't come, and when it did arrive and had returned to the camp I was listening for the phone to ring, telling me when they were going – or when the car was coming back.' Then news came via the Red Cross that Sharpe and his crew had all been reported dead: 'I simply *cannot* [*sic*] forget his face and how nice he was and the whole station has been affected by his loss.'

Suddenly, it was all over. At 7.30 a.m. on 9 May, Micky was woken up by Ken Batchleor, who had just come back from a raid on Hamburg. 'Get up! We're going on leave on the 9.30 a.m. train. And off we went'. Batchelor had completed thirty operations. The couple left the Red House on 29 May, in Micky's words 'after the longest six months I have ever known, most uncomfortable, I felt I was leaving prison . . . I can only thank God for sparing Ken.' Now a squadron leader, Batchelor had been given a ground appointment at a nearby Czech base. He would survive the war and retire as a group captain. Batchelor and his wife would raise the family which Micky, in her darkest moments during that tour from RAF Honington, feared Fate would prevent them from having.

Over Germany

Strenuous efforts were now being made to increase Bomber Command's strength and efficiency; not always smoothly. In April 1941, Wing Commander S. O. Bufton took command of 76 Squadron which had begun flying the four-engine Halifax. Unfortunately, when the undercarriage was lowered, it tended to burst into flames, and Handley Page had to act rapidly. While the crews were grounded for modifications to be carried out, 'as a matter of conscience', Bufton thought, the firm 'took everybody out to lunch'. New stations, as well as new aircraft, were needed too. At the end of May 1941, Bufton moved to Pocklington, in the West Riding of Yorkshire, with orders to establish a bomber base, which meant founding the entire administrative and operational set-up. Such was the urgency of the war situation that in six weeks 405 Squadron was off on its first raid.

Not all the administrative creases had yet been removed from the recruitment process. Two young BBC employees, Doug Radcliffe and Bill Wright, were anxious to see active service in 1941. Initially they were attracted to the Royal Marines because they rather liked the idea of wearing smart trousers with a red stripe down the side. Rebuffed in this quest, they made their way to Adastral House to try the RAF. Rejection looked likely there, too, until the interviewer discovered their place of employment – 'You'll be ideal for wireless operators' – unaware they had nothing to do with radio equipment. They omitted to enlighten him, reasoning that somebody at Broadcasting House would explain the intricacies to them. Unfortunately, nobody they knew could help. Nevertheless, both duly became operational wireless operators. H. F. C. 'Jim' Parsons and Dennis Langford also joined the RAF after their route into another Service had been blocked, in their case the Royal Navy. As shipwright apprentices in Portsmouth Dockyard, they were only permitted to volunteer for pilot or observer training.

61

Freddie West, who won his VC in the First World War for completing a critical reconnaissance despite a severely injured leg (which subsequently had to be amputated), self-deprecatingly remarked that he had been 'lucky'. Others had performed greater feats and not been so rewarded. The fate of Wing Commander Roy Arnold seems to support this thesis. Leading four 9 Squadron Wellingtons in a daylight raid against German shipping off the Dutch coast on 9 June, he lost his life in heroic circumstances described two months later by the *Daily Express* under the heading 'Captain Oates 1941'. The newspaper's account was based on a letter from one of the four survivors in his PoW camp: 'He [Arnold] ended his life as a truly gallant gentleman. In every way he was a fine man. His deed was deliberate. Our aircraft was set on fire and we baled out before the machine broke up . . . The Wing Commander went down with the aircraft. By holding it steady for us, he left it too late for himself.' Every year his widow would place a commemorative notice in *The Times*, underlining the depth of her personal grief. His crew and his Squadron were perplexed that, once the facts were known, Arnold did not receive the VC or any other recognition. Touchingly, five days before his death Roy Arnold had written: 'The minds of the living are the / Souls of the dead. Only then is / Immortality achieved.'

On 22 June, when broadcasting on the BBC, Winston Churchill rather optimistically promised, 'we shall bomb Germany by day as well as by night in ever-increasing measure . . . This is not a threat only, it is a statement of fact.' For the crews the operations were neither so straightforward nor triumphant. The bulk of the bombing was still being carried out by the twin-engine aircraft in service at the beginning of the war. Paddy Denton recorded his feelings as he approached the Dutch coast in darkness at the controls of a Whitley: 'Then you saw the stomach-retching lights of the flak belt and the incredible firework display and knew that this was what you had to surmount, like an Olympic ski jumper just after he has started his run. No going back.'

Tales of heroism remained manna for newspaper editors and provided the opportunity to demonstrate that the crew of an RAF bomber often came from far-flung parts of the Commonwealth. On 7/8 July, with forty-eight others bound for Münster, the Wellington of Canadian Squadron Leader Reuben Widdowson had three New Zealanders on board: second pilot Sergeant James Ward, the navigator/bomb aimer and rear gunner. The front gunner and wireless operator were British. This sort of combination was not unusual. After bombing the target in good visibility without encountering trouble, Widdowson was well on the way home when without warning at 13,000ft over the Zuider Zee a Messerschmitt Bf 110 raked the bomber from below 'with cannon shell and incendiary bullet'. The rear gunner was wounded, the starboard engine faltered, the wireless and intercom system were destroyed and the cockpit filled with fumes. Critically, 'fire then broke out near the starboard engine and, fed by petrol from a split pipe, quickly gained an alarming hold and threatened to spread to the entire wing. The crew forced a hole in the fuselage and made strenuous efforts to reduce the fire with extinguishers and even the coffee of their vacuum flasks, but without success.'

Widdowson warned the crew to be ready to bale out. 'As a last resort', Ward offered to attempt to smother the fire 'with an engine cover which happened to be in use as a cushion'. He was dissuaded from taking off his parachute to reduce wind resistance. The navigator helped him to clamber through the astro hatch, with the rope of the dinghy tied to him as an additional safety measure. The bomber's speed was cut back as far as possible, but still the wind pressure was strong. Ward broke the fabric of the Wellington to gain hand- and footholds as he descended 3ft to the wing, then another 3ft beyond the engine 'despite the slipstream from the airscrew which nearly blew him off the wing'. Several times, lying in a 'precarious position', he tried to push the cover into the hole and on to the leaking pipe. Each time it came out again and was eventually snatched away by the wind. By now Ward was exhausted, but the navigator firmly gripped the rope as he worked his way back. Still, brute force had to be applied to get him into the fuselage once more.

In fact, Ward's efforts stopped the fire from spreading. Although Widdowson had difficulty putting the Wellington down without flaps or wheel brakes, he did so safely. The crew owed their lives to Ward's incredible wing-walking feat. 'Sergeant Ward seemed to take what he had done as a matter of course, but in my opinion it was a wonderful show,' Widdowson concluded. The Air Ministry agreed: Ward was awarded the VC. Sadly, he would survive only another two months. On 13 September, piloting his own Wellington, he was shot down.

During July 1941, a determined effort was made to eliminate the menace of strong enemy naval forces in ports along the Atlantic coast of France. These targets had been highlighted in an Air Ministry directive of 9 March: 'The Prime Minister has ruled that for the next four months we should devote our energies to defeating the attempt of the enemy to strangle our food supplies and our connections with the United States'. Four-engine bombers (Stirlings, Halifaxes and RAF Flying Fortresses) were prominent in these operations, some of which took place in daylight. Twin-engine aircraft were not excluded, with friendly fighters able to provide protection for them to close destinations. Robert Allen recorded that, flying in a Hampden formation to bomb the *Gneisenau* in Brest on 24 July, Spitfires 'chased off' enemy fighters. Simultaneously, protected by more Spitfires, Blenheims were attacking Cherbourg. That same day, Brisbane was the navigator in a Halifax for the unescorted daylight attack on the *Scharnhorst* at La Pallice. Despite his aircraft being 'repeatedly hit by flak . . . the bombing procedure was carried out exactly as on a practice range'.

Although no warship was sunk, the performance of the heavy bombers boosted hopes that they would prove decisive once deployed over Germany in strength. The *Scharnhorst* suffered five direct hits, which caused so much flooding that she had to be moved to Brest for prolonged repairs. The Air Ministry could therefore claim that 'the attacks delivered by Bomber Command are steadily increasing in weight and severity'. The new bombers were 'the aircraft to deliver that overwhelming onslaught which will bring the enemy to his knees and then lay him prostrate in the dust of his own ruined cities'.

Another directive on 9 July, while acknowledging that naval targets must still be attacked, focused more sharply on the German homeland with a significant change of emphasis. The 'vital nature of the Ruhr-Rhineland industries' and 'dislocating the German transportation system' should be 'borne in mind', but 'the main effort of the bomber force' must aim at 'destroying the morale of the civil population as a whole and of the industrial workers in particular' – implicit authorisation to attack city centres or 'area bombing'.

Carrying out these instructions would involve human tragedies of which the campaign had already seen many. In July 1941, Paddy Denton failed to return from a raid on Hanover. As his parents waited for news of his fate, praying fervently that he had been taken prisoner, they corresponded with the relatives of other crew members, thus reinforcing the comradeship of their sons. To the Dentons' relief they learned that Paddy was indeed a PoW, but then encountered a formidable wall of bureaucratic obstruction. His father was told that his son's Morris 8 car could not be released without express Air Ministry permission. On 3 September, a communication from the RAF's Central Depository to Major Denton provided a list of Paddy's effects down to a half a pound of chocolate, but insisted that they could not be forwarded 'without the authority of the prisoner of war himself'. By return of post Paddy's father expressed his amazement at such a hidebound attitude, as he had received letters from his son asking for clothing to be sent, for which the Red Cross had already provided labels. With winter approaching, it was 'essential' that the clothes should be despatched immediately. 'If you cannot authorise this I shall have to take further steps,' he threatened. The administrators would not budge. Not until a card arrived from Paddy Denton in captivity, specifically authorising the release of his effects, were they forwarded to the family home at Wrexham on 6 October. Major Denton also conducted protracted correspondence with the Westminster Bank over a £10 deduction from his son's pay. Altogether an unedifying example of red tape, at a time of deep family distress.

In August came the unpalatable proof that, in spite of confident claims to the contrary, bombing accuracy was far from ideal. Mr D. M. Butt, a civil servant in the War Cabinet secretariat, produced an analysis of photographs taken during night operations over Germany. Only one in four of the aircraft which reported attacking their target had got within 5 miles (75 square miles) of it. In the Ruhr in good weather the figure was one in ten; in bad visibility a depressing one in fifteen. Harris admitted that Butt revealed 'the enormous possibilities of error in navigation at night'. The following month, he agreed that the thirty bombers which put 80 per cent of their bombs within two miles of the aiming point at Stettin were 'exceptional'. Shaken by Butt's revelations, Churchill lamented: 'It is an awful thought that perhaps three quarters of our bombs go astray.'

On 7 September, Gerald Dickson finally went to war in a 10 Squadron Whitley – on a short run to Boulogne. When he arrived at Abingdon Operational Training Unit from Canada in July 1941, his only navigational training had been in an Anson, and he had rapidly to learn the idiosyncrasies of the Whitley. It was, he found, a 'horribly cold' aircraft, and 'very uncomfortable', especially for the navigator. If someone in the front of the bomber wanted to use the chemical toilet in the rear of the fuselage, he had to fold up his papers to let him pass, 'a bloody nuisance, and when they'd done what they wanted to do, it started all over again'. In the Whitley, the navigator doubled as bomb aimer, but Dickson doubted the accuracy of the bombsight: 'I don't think we hit the target very often.' He was dispirited to think that the crew had achieved 'so little having flogged all the way to get to a target'.

The Whitley was not, Dickson felt, either a particularly reliable or safe aircraft, as his crew began to range deeper into Germany: to Hamburg, Stettin and Nuremberg. Twice they had to return early with engine trouble or an unserviceable (U/S) wireless. Although the ultra-casual approach of the previous year had been abandoned with aircraft now given designated routes and takeoff times, once bombing had been completed aircraft made their own way home. With longer trips this meant approaching the English coast at dawn, which the Germans soon came to anticipate. 'The Whitley had no prayer in a contest with a lurking Messerschmitt, and we lost a lot of aircraft because they were chopped down in sight of safety.' It was with a real sense of relief that, having picked up two extra crew at base, in November the crew began flying a Halifax without attending a Heavy Conversion Unit (HCU). For them, conversion training took place under the auspices of 10 Squadron and through a series of local and cross-country practice flights. Thus far, although he had absolute confidence in his crew and in particular the captain, Sergeant C. P. Peterson ('a bloody good pilot'), Dickson had been distinctly uneasy with the

Whitley as an operational bomber. Apart from its vulnerability to fighters, in practice, despite its manufacturer's claim, it could only manage a maximum 150mph and frequently even less.

Sergeant Ronald Neale, in correspondence with his family, was more upbeat while displaying a curious mixture of naivety and realism. On 28 October, he informed his brother that he would 'probably' be surprised to hear that he was a wireless operator/gunner on an operational squadron and had 'already paid a visit to the land of the Hun'. Because it might be 'suddenly cut short' Service life was different from civilian. There was no time for 'the petty jealousies and continual grumblings one finds so common in the world today'. 'I feel like a member of a big happy family,' he wrote. Despite the 'electrically heated fur-lined leather suit of trousers and coat and even with the hot air pipes provided in the plane, I felt bitterly cold'. After flying over the North Sea, the aircraft crossed the coast near Cuxhaven and followed the Elbe to Hamburg. From the coast inland, 'a terrific barrage of ack ack' went up and searchlights 'waved about' trying to locate it. 'A beautiful fire was burning, the largest fire I've ever seen' in the target area. 'Our heavy 1000lb. bomb dropped on a corner of the inferno and must have helped things along considerably.' As 'Jerry's attentions were becoming a little too close for our liking', the rest of the bomb load was released together with 'a few thousand leaflets' and the pilot turned for home. Neale felt excitement at seeing 'the good old English coast again' before landing at 2.10 a.m., 'very cold, tired and hungry, but satisfied that we had done a job and done it well'. 'I thoroughly enjoyed my first trip to Germany and I'm looking forward to my next sojourn.' He might have been writing about an outing to the seaside.

Less naively, on 10 November Neale wrote that he had been 'very busy lately'. Night flying was getting even colder, the German searchlights and flak 'uncannily' accurate. They had been to the Krupps works in Essen 'and left some very heavy calling cards. However, we did not exactly get away unscathed, since we landed with a kite full of holes and it was a marvel how the wings held, but they did and they got us back safely which counts above everything.' Neale, a devout Catholic, did not survive long, though. He was shot down and killed on 16 November.

With winter now imminent, on 13 November Bomber Command was cautioned to conserve 'our resources in order to build a strong force to be available by the spring of next year'. Except for 'vital operations', aircraft should not be 'exposed to extreme hazard' as the weather deteriorated. A month later, on 10 December, the importance of destroying enemy capital ships was emphasised, with calls for plans 'immediately' to carry out 'daylight bombing against the enemy cruisers [the *Scharnhorst* and the *Gneisenau*] in Brest'. Both ships and the U-boats remained a threat to shipping in the Atlantic, where 887 more merchant vessels were lost during 1941. Between 10 December 1941 and 20 January 1942, Bomber Command would expend 37 per cent of its effort on the French west coast ports.

Not least because of need to deploy its squadrons against so many other such targets, as 1941 drew to a close Bomber Command was far from striking a telling blow against German war industries, despite an Air Ministry publication referring lavishly to 'the bright colours of achievement'. Butt had exposed the shortcomings of existing navigational aids, and the bulk of the bombing was still being done from pre-war aircraft.

There were, nevertheless, grounds for optimism. Guy Brisbane paid tribute to the revised navigational procedures being devised at training units by instructors with recent operational experience. Undoubtedly not only had four-engine bombers seen action, but they were expected to be available in significant numbers in the new year. The A. V. Roe aircraft company (Avros) had produced a more advanced twin-engine machine, the Manchester. On the other hand, the German defences had been strengthened with the deployment of many more night fighters.

The Air Ministry accepted that 'the picture is sombre in places', while holding out hope of a more effective campaign over the horizon. It praised crews which 'plod steadily on, taking their aircraft through fair weather or foul night after night, and of late by day, to "the abodes of the guilty"'.

CHAPTER 4

Mounting Losses, 1942

'A serious deficiency of trained crews'

In January 1942, the old lack of accuracy remained all too apparent. Thirteen raids caused no significant damage to powerful naval units in Brest and St Nazaire and nor were twelve attacks on six locations in Germany any better. One against Wilhelmshaven by 124 aircraft was declared 'good'. In truth, due to a wide dispersal of bombs only 'light damage' and just six casualties were recorded by the Germans. From eighty-three bombers sent to Bremen on 17/18 January, a mere eight even claimed to have attacked the primary target.

On 14 February, the Air Ministry called for an 'offensive on a heavy scale . . . [to] enhearten and encourage the Russians' currently locked in battle with German forces from the Baltic to the Black Sea after Hitler's dramatic and treacherous invasion on 22 June 1941. The words of its 9 July 1941 directive were repeated: 'The primary objective of your operations should be focussed on the morale of the enemy civil population and, in particular, of the industrial workers'. Eighteen towns or cities were detailed for attack, Berlin and Essen in the van. The following day Air Chief Marshal Sir Charles Portal, who had become CAS in October 1940, made clear that 'the aiming points are to be the built-up areas, not, for instance, the dock-yards or aircraft factories'.

Tall and dark haired with a prominent beaked nose, Portal had a reserved manner and powerful intellect. Educated at Winchester College and Christ Church, Oxford, like Cheshire he had graduated in Law but never practised. In 1914, he enlisted in the Royal Engineers and subsequently became a pilot in the RFC and RAF, like Harris. Portal emerged from the First World War with a DSO and Bar. In 1934, having led a squadron and held several staff appointments, as a group captain he gained command of British forces in Aden, three years later returned to the Air Ministry, and as an air marshal took over Bomber Command for six months in 1940 before becoming CAS for the remainder of the war.

On 22 February, exactly a week after Portal's instruction on the nature of bombing targets, Air Marshal A. T. Harris took over Bomber Command and, like the CAS, would remain in post for the rest of the war. A stocky, sandy-haired man with an acerbic wit and prone to outbursts of temper, he had a powerful presence and was destined professionally often to disagree with Portal. From an early age, Harris displayed a stubborn streak of independence, emigrating, as a seventeen-year-old, after a family disagreement to Southern Rhodesia, where he drove bullock carts. Returning to England during the First World War, he became an RFC pilot, graduating to the RAF on its formation. After gaining bombing experience and leadership expertise during the 'imperial policing' of Iraq, he held several staff appointments at the Air Ministry, served as AOC 5 (Bomber) Group 1939–40, then was successively Deputy Chief of the Air Staff and Head of the RAF Delegation to Washington. Strongly influenced by Trenchard's views, Harris was convinced that bombers would be decisive in the present conflict. Shortly after reaching Bomber Command HQ at High Wycombe, Buckinghamshire, he declared in a newsreel interview: 'There are a lot of people who say that bombing cannot win a war. My reply to that is that it has never been tried yet.'

Harris was, as one pilot remarked, 'an airman's airman'. Incredibly hard-working (he took no leave during the war), he single-mindedly pursued the destruction of German cities laid down in the Air Ministry instructions which awaited him. He did not initiate 'area bombing', but he steadfastly pursued it. From this fundamental tactic he never wavered, despite receiving a stream of further directives which made adjustments to the target lists and priorities. He was decisive, never afraid to speak his mind and greatly respected by his subordinates. Arthur Travers Harris was a forceful leader at a time when Bomber Command urgently needed one.

For in February 1942, apart from fulfilling Air Ministry requirements, Harris faced another daunting task. He must prove that his new charge deserved priority in the delivery of aircraft over Coastal Command, in its fight to keep open the trade routes in the Atlantic (550 merchantmen would be sunk in the first quarter of 1942), and Middle East Command engaged in defending Egypt against General Erwin Rommel's Afrika Korps. Elsewhere, loss of Singapore and the news that German forces were poised to resume their advance into the Soviet Union after the spring thaw made depressing reading. Closer to home, the German battle cruisers *Gneisenau* and *Scharnhorst* had just sneaked up the Channel from Brest under the noses of the RAF and Royal Navy.

It was scarcely an auspicious moment to take post and Harris was distinctly unimpressed with what he found. There were merely 378 serviceable bombers, including just sixty-nine heavies as well as fifty Blenheim light bombers now used mainly for intruder, nuisance raids into enemy territory. Only an average of 250 medium and fifty heavy aircraft could therefore be relied on for normal operations. Available equipment 'was no more impressive than these numbers', with the result that 'at night the bomber crews were hardly ever able to find their targets'. It was 'glaringly obvious that the average crew in average weather could not find their way to the target by visual means alone'. A 'serious deficiency of trained crews' deepened Harris's concern.

With characteristic energy, he set about rectifying a situation whereby Bomber Command had done 'no more than scratch at the Ruhr in the previous two years'. Destruction of Germany's industrial base would be his main aim and, perversely, he argued that operations against ports like St Nazaire and Brest wasted resources better deployed against the Ruhr. There was a bonus, though. Harris found that the Senior Air Staff Officer at High Wycombe was his former flight commander in Iraq, now Air Vice-Marshal Robert Saundby. Harris had complete faith in Saundby, believing his views on bombing 'absolutely sound'.

Another major impediment to Bomber Command's success was the vastly extended and improved defences which Kammhuber had put in place by 1942. They now stretched from German-occupied Denmark to the Swiss border in a great arc. In-depth concentrations had been established around vulnerable targets and large cities; mobile flak guns mounted on suitable transport and trains. Immediately behind the coastal belt of radars Kammhuber created a series of overlapping defensive boxes approximately 20 miles wide. The so-called *Himmelbett* (four poster bed) arrangement then operated, with night fighters orbiting radio beacons for their instructions. A Freya would warn of an approaching bomber, the first of two Würzburgs would focus on that target and the second would guide the fourth element of the system (the night fighter) to within range of the bomber. Neither Kammhuber nor German scientists stood still, however. The older Freya coastal sets were being replaced by more effective equipment capable of determining height and bearing as well as range and effective up to 200 miles. Even more menacingly, the Lichtenstein airborne radar, with a 2 mile range, had been installed in many night fighters.

Quite apart from the challenges posed by this formidable array, Harris strenuously maintained, with transparent justification, that much more effective navigational aids were required and better bomb-aiming devices. A major new aid (Gee – Ground Electronic Engineering) did come into operational use against Cologne on 13 March, at once making the navigator's job easier and more complicated. He no longer had to rely predominantly on landmark identification or astro sightings, though these remained important. By using a 'box' installed in the aircraft to receive radio pulses sent out by three separate stations in England, he could now more accurately determine the bomber's position. This did not allow precision bombing, but it did enable the navigator to guide the aircraft to the target area. However, because this was a 'line of sight' device, signals were affected by the curvature of the earth, with the maximum range being 400 miles at an altitude of 20,000ft. The Ruhr and northern German ports like Emden and Bremen were therefore well within range, and Gee provided a boon to returning aircraft. Even those setting out for more distant targets could benefit from it over the opening part of their route. Eventually, the Germans would devise a means of jamming it (six months' grace was estimated; the first case actually being recorded on 4 August); in the meantime the new navigational aid would be invaluable. One immediate disadvantage, however, was that, with such a limited number of sets available, only a few bombers could be equipped with it. But they would mark the targets.

Bomber Crew

During March 1942 steps were begun to abolish the second pilot in Wellington and Whitley bombers and to discontinue the designation 'observer', which involved work as a navigator, bomb aimer and gunner. Division of these duties would lead to specialised navigators, bomb aimers and gunners in the four-engine bombers. Almost simultaneously, too, the Luftwaffe night fighters evolved a disturbing new tactic of attacking bombers from below, where RAF bombers lacked a gun position (attempts to install a ventral (belly) turret proved unsuccessful). This worrying development combined with no obvious progress in the bombing campaign against Germany, Harris thought, was making aircrew 'more and more depressed . . . they as well as the country at large needed the stimulus of some definite achievement'.

On the night of 28/29 March, therefore, 234 bombers set out for Lübeck, a Baltic port packed with wooden buildings. Two waves carrying incendiaries and high explosives destroyed much of the town. The operation was technically an overwhelming success, the loss of thirteen aircraft to fighters on a moonlit night less satisfactory. Patently, Gee would not solve the bomber's defensive problems. Harris never liked the 'inadequate' .303 machine-gun, which was outranged by a night fighter's cannon.

Delivery of increasing numbers of Lancasters to squadrons gave an opportunity to resurrect the dream of bombers flying in defensive formation in daylight. Thus, on 17 April twelve Lancasters in two groups of six set out at low level in daylight for the MAN (Maschinenfabrik Augsburg Nürnberg) diesel engine works at Augsburg. The Air Ministry admitted that 'the enterprise was daring, the target of high military importance. To reach it and get back, some 1000 miles had to be flown over hostile territory.' Seven aircraft were lost. Although the bombers crossed France as low as 50ft in places, according to one pilot keeping 'the tightest possible formation, wing tip to wing tip', enemy fighters hit them disastrously and only the Lancaster of the South African Squadron Leader John Dering Nettleton, whose rear guns had malfunctioned, and another Lancaster survived from one group of six. The raid was scheduled to take place as dusk fell at 8 p.m. Breasting a hill on the outskirts of Augsburg, Nettleton faced a barrage of flak, which he and the other Lancaster must penetrate to attack the targets studied so closely in pre-operational photographs. He came through, the accompanying bomber was set on fire by flak but managed to crash-land safely. With the fuselage of his Lancaster virtually a sieve, Nettleton persuaded it back to base at such a low level that en route it reputedly stampeded animals of an enemy horse-gun battery which, terror-stricken, vanished into the night still dragging their weapons behind them. Nettleton received the VC for his bravery. Due to the manner of its acquisition, fertile caption writers dubbed him the 'Roof-top VC'. Modestly, one of Nettleton's crew later wrote: 'I always felt we were credited with more courage than we deserved. We just went there and came back.'

Churchill referred to this as 'an outstanding achievement' because serious damage was undoubtedly done to the works which had been struck with such 'deadly precision'. Harris, however, acknowledged a 'prohibitive casualty rate': forty-nine of the eighty-four men who left England did not return, although some did become prisoners of war. This operation proved that even the four-engine Lancaster, Bomber Command's most formidable bomber, could not fulfil pre-war bombing theory. For Nettleton, there would be no happy ending. He was lost in July 1943 and never saw his unborn son, whom his widow named John Dering after his father.

On 5 May, the Air Ministry agreed that Harris's 'primary aim . . . must remain the lowering of the morale of the enemy civil population and in particular that of the workers in industrial areas', but wanted greater attention paid to areas containing aircraft factories. That month, bombers continued to attack German targets with mixed success. In Harris's view, the inability to muster a large force prevented significant results. Out of eighty-one sent to Hamburg on 3/4 May, only fifty-four claimed to have bombed accurately and five, including three Halifaxes, were lost. The following night, over the Bosch works in Stuttgart, 121 aircraft were foiled by heavy cloud cover and a clever decoy fire. Bombs were scattered over a wide area and the works remained intact. Only 'light' or 'moderate' damage was even claimed in operations against Warnemünde on 8/9 May involving 193 aircraft and Mannheim on 19/20 May with 197 aircraft. Rumblings about the ineffectiveness of Bomber Command led to renewed demands for the allocation of heavy aircraft to other types of operation.

On 20 May, Mr Justice Singleton, a senior judge tasked by the Prime Minister to evaluate current achievement and to forecast potential, produced an inconclusive report on the bombing of Germany, which scarcely helped Bomber Command in the short term. 'It ought not to be regarded as of itself sufficient to win the war or to produce decisive results', he wrote. 'If Russia can hold Germany on land', Singleton doubted whether Germany's 'war production, her power of resistance, her industries and her will to resist' would survive 'twelve or eighteen months' continuous, intensified and increasing bombing'. Very much a long haul, therefore, if at all achievable. Furthermore, 'recent results are not encouraging except in ideal weather conditions, and there are few nights in the month on which such conditions can be expected, and few targets on which a night bombing attack can be really successful'. Singleton concluded that 'great results' could not be expected for at least six months and then only if 'greater accuracy can be achieved'.

Mounting Losses

In the prevailing aura of doubt, not improved by Singleton, Harris believed that only a powerful demonstration of his command's capability would silence the sceptics. He decided on a thousand bomber raid, codenamed Operation Millennium.

This was planned for 27 May, but poor weather caused daily postponement until the evening of Saturday 30 May. Even then, broken cloud and occasional thunderstorms were threatened, a forecast which persuaded Harris that Cologne, not Hamburg, should be the target. It was a close call. This was the last suitable night of the present moon period. As Harris later reflected, 'the weather in those days had absolute power to make or mar an operation'.

By calling on his own training and conversion units and four aircraft from Flying Training Command, Harris launched 1046 bombers on the Rhineland city, 'the greatest attack yet made in aerial warfare'. Sergeant Bill Townsend from the Operational Training Unit (OTU) at Upper Heyford, Oxfordshire, had his initiation of fire on this operation. 'I found myself piloting a Hampden . . . before I'd had a second "dickie" trip with an instructor looking over my shoulder.' The risk of collisions over the target would be minimised with careful planning of a common route along which aircraft would fly at a prescribed height and speed to and from the target. At one pre-operational briefing, the prediction that only one collision would occur was greeted by a lone voice: 'Which two aircraft?' Amid the nervous laughter, the briefing officer replied quickly: 'A Tiger Moth and an Anson.'

The disparate array of Whitleys, Hampdens, Wellingtons, Manchesters, Stirlings, Halifaxes and Lancasters was divided into three waves. The force ran into cloud and icing conditions over the North Sea, but once across the enemy coast the weather gradually improved until bright moonlight over Cologne was interrupted by only occasional light cloud. There,

Gee proved invaluable for the leading aircraft, which ignited fires to guide succeeding waves to the target. Approaching Mönchen-Gladbach, 30 miles to the north-west, crews of the third wave were astonished at the vast glow ahead, some wondering whether the Germans had created an enormous decoy fire. The truth became all too obvious as they flew closer: Cologne was already ablaze.

Over ninety minutes, 868 bombers dropped 1500 incendiaries and high explosives to devastate 600 acres of the city and damage twelve thousand buildings. Despite the unprecedented concentration of aircraft over the city, as anticipated only two collided and forty in all were lost. Rear gunners reported still seeing the glow of fires over 100 miles from the target on the way home. At 5 a.m. a reconnaissance Mosquito reported a pall of smoke rising to 15,000ft, many fires still burning in the centre and suburbs of the city. In the context of the time, it was an awe-inspiring display of bombing potential. *The Times* exclaimed, with a tinge of exaggeration: 'Over 1,000 Bombers Raid Cologne. Biggest Air Attack of the War. 2,000 Tons of Bombs in 40 Minutes.'

Without this achievement, Harris believed 'we should never have had a real bomber offensive' in the years to come. In that sense, it was truly decisive. Furthermore, he insisted that, with Bomber Command's aerial threat now so apparent, the Luftwaffe had to withdraw support from armies in the field to provide greater defence at home. Use of a bomber stream, which would become standard practice, illustrated one weakness of Kammhuber's defensive box: it could be swamped by a large formation of bombers.

Leonard Cheshire, then instructing at a conversion unit, flew a Halifax during the Cologne raid in which twenty-one year old Flying Officer Leslie Manser gained the VC. Manser's experience underlines the danger of looking at overall statistics to discern the story of an operation. Only forty aircraft may have been lost, but, as Cheshire remarked on that first flight from Driffield in 1940, each of those contained a crew of five to seven men. Manser's Manchester bomber had seven. It was coned by searchlights and hit by 'intense and accurate anti-aircraft fire' as it approached the target, but the pilot pressed on to bomb, according to plan, from 7000ft. As Manser turned away, already heavily damaged, the searchlights and flak seemed to follow the aircraft despite desperate manoeuvring and descending to 1000ft. Eventually he shook off the defences, but by then the rear gunner had been wounded, the 'front cabin filled with smoke, the port engine began overheating badly'. At this point, 'the pilot and crew could have escaped safely by parachute'. Manser, though, was determined to get the aircraft home and 'stop the crew falling into enemy hands'.

As he climbed to 2000ft, the port engine burst into flames. Even though this blaze was put out, the engine was now useless and the aircraft's speed fell 'dangerously low'. Still Manser refused to order the crew out. 'Instead, with grim determination, he set a new course for the nearest base, accepting for himself the prospect of almost certain death in a firm resolve to carry on to the end.' Mysteriously, smoke was still getting into the cockpit and the aircraft began quickly to lose height once more.

The pilot now decided that the crew must bale out. As they did so, he wrestled with the controls to maintain the stability and altitude for them to jump safely. While they hung in the air beneath their billowing parachutes, the Manchester crashed with Manser inside it. He gave his life to save six members of his crew and was posthumously awarded the country's highest military honour. In a personal note to his father, Harris wrote that 'no VC was more gallantly earned' in rendering 'the last service to his crew'. The citation referred to his 'thinking only of the safety of his comrades'.

The second 'thousand-bomber' operation took place against Essen during the night of 1/2 June, but only 956 aircraft (including just two from Flying Training Command) were actually despatched, 278 of them four-engine types. Cheshire flew with the same HCU crew as on the Cologne raid, but like so many other pilots was frustrated by conditions in the target area. Cloud 5–10/10ths was encountered at 8000ft with another layer at 3–5000ft. Industrial haze further restricted visibility. Few crews clearly identified the target area, some bombed blindly using Gee, others carried out timed runs from the Rhine.

The concentration of Cologne could not therefore be repeated. Essen suffered very little damage, and many bombs were in reality dropped on eleven other towns in the Ruhr. The Germans did not recognise Essen as the target, reporting 'widespread raids over western Germany . . . especially Duisburg and Oberhausen'. Thirty-one bombers were lost. It was a blow to confidence that massed raids would always succeed.

The third and final 'thousand' operation of 1942 targeted Bremen on the night of 25/26 June. Gibson took on his first operation Australian Flight Lieutenant David Shannon, a twenty-year-old who would the following year join him at 617 Squadron for the celebrated Dambusters Raid. Of 1006 aircraft despatched, 899 came from Bomber Command, Coastal and Army Co-operation commands making up the rest. A weather forecast shortly before takeoff estimated that the 'chance of less than 5/10ths cloud is 50/50'. But it also promised a strong wind, which would 'favour a comparatively rapid passage of strato-cumulus across the target'. Not so, as it turned out. The wind neither cleared the sky over Bremen nor to and from the target area. Gee, however, allowed leading aircraft to mark Bremen with incendiaries. From Bomber Command, 696 aircraft reported bombing accurately, although German records held that only eighty did so. Greater damage was caused than at Essen, but less than at Cologne. Reconnaissance showed, though, that a Focke-Wulf aircraft factory had been wrecked, probably by a 4000lb. bomb. Overall the attack was deemed 'useful'. However forty-four bombers had been lost, and many twin-engine machines were still necessary to boost Bomber Command's operational strength. Of the sixty-five aircraft damaged, one Lancaster had been hit by incendiaries from another bomber.

Attacks on other targets in Germany were not neglected. Sergeant Donald Bruce described an excursion to Emden in a Wellington on 6/7 June in a force of 180 bombers. After breakfast the crew took up their machine to test the guns, automatic pilot ('George') and Gee. After landing an hour later, the members noted instructions to ground crew personnel chalked up on boards and, seeing 450 gallons ordered, speculated on that night's target, possibly 'Happy Valley' – the heavily defended Ruhr – or a 'cushy trip' to Paris. In the afternoon, after lunch, they sunbathed or tried to rest until called to briefing late in the afternoon when Emden was revealed as the target. Bruce, the navigator, set about 'preparing the Flight Plan'. The close organisation of the 'Thousand' raids was not yet extended to all operations. He recalled that 'at this stage of the war we were still given a certain amount of freedom in choosing our route and height at which we could bomb'.

Following 'another tense period of waiting', Bruce collected his 'bag of navigational instruments, a met. report and operational rations for the crew – chocolate, oranges or raisins, chewing gum and six thermos flasks, two of black coffee, two of tea and two of Bovril'. The crew then sat outside the Flights with their kit and parachutes waiting for transport to take them out to the aircraft where, in the sunny evening, they had 'a long wait'. Bruce had time to peer over a hedge to see a farmer studiously ploughing his field. He marvelled at the peaceful contrast with what lay ahead of him. 'Tense and nervous, we urinate against the wheels of the aircraft for good luck.' The first to climb aboard, Bruce found it 'strangely quiet compared to the noise of the aircraft outside'. He then 'set the detonators and diffusers on Gee and its map containers'. Alone, he looked round his compartment and wondered 'what it would be like with a hail of cannon shells from a night fighter ripping through the cabin'. His thoughts were interrupted by the rest of the crew joining him. The pilot started up the engines and from thereon he was too busy to let his mind wander.

The Wellington progressed round the perimeter track, maintaining strict wireless silence. The aircraft ahead of it began to move down the runway and Bruce's machine swung round 'to face up the takeoff strip' and await the green from the Aldis lamp signalling the Wellington away. 'No one speaks to the pilot, he must not be distracted, his aircraft is heavy and it takes all his concentration to get it off the ground . . . The heavy tail turret complete with gunner must be raised off the ground first so he jams on the brakes, pushes the throttles up to the "gates", the plane shudders and roars, he pushes the stick forward until it touches the control panel, slowly the tail lifts and when the nose is pointing slightly downwards he releases the brake and we trundle off.' Gradually the Wellington gathered pace and at 120mph left the ground. 'As I lift my hands off the log to note the time that we are airborne I see that the place where they were resting is damp with sweat. Takeoff with full petrol and bomb load is extremely dangerous.' Climbing out over the North Sea, the crew kept a wary eye open for coastal convoys which often opened fire at the sight of any aircraft, so that some RAF machines had been 'badly damaged in the past'. That danger having passed, the gunners received permission to try their weapons and 'the plane shudders as the guns open up and the reek of cordite pervades the atmosphere in the cabin, and we hope that no patrolling night fighter has spotted the one in five tracer'. As the Wellington approached the Dutch coast the 'armour plate doors' were unfolded 'ostensibly to protect the cabin and pilot's position from a rear attack'. With the aircraft continuing to climb, the wireless operator in the astrodome and rear gunner kept a special lookout for night fighters. 'The plane starts to weave gently from side to side as the pilot tries to uncover the blind spot below us for the gunners.'

At 10,000ft, 'cold but not unpleasant', the crew began using oxygen but the pilot had difficulty 'in getting the S Blower [the supercharger] in'. He eventually succeeded, otherwise the Wellington would not have gained more height. The pilot informed Bruce that he could not gauge the outside temperature 'because the needle has fallen off the dial'. He had also throttled back, afraid that the port engine might overheat. More trouble soon materialised. The rear gunner reported difficulty in operating his turret and Bruce discovered that 'the recuperator rams', which indicated hydraulic pressure, were 'flat' and the turret could only therefore be operated manually. The pilot as captain decided to press on, nevertheless. From 12,000ft the crew could make out the light of fires at the target, but 'apart from the odd flak gun pooping off miles out of range', the aircraft flew on undisturbed for a while. Bruce's calm was interrupted when the gunners began to 'shout warnings' over the intercom alerting the pilot of more dangerous pockets of flak around. 'We start to weave violently, I move forward to the bomb aimer's position, setting the course on the pilot's compass as I go past.'

Lying prone in the nose, Bruce saw the target well alight 'like a running red sore in the blackness of the night'. He concentrated on 'setting the rotor arm that will space the stick of bombs, removing the bomb release from its holder' and automatically fusing the bombs. 'I am lining the target up in the wires of the bombsight, the flak is heavy and the pilot weaving desperately, red balls of light flak start lazily from the ground, gaining in impetus, they are coming straight for my stomach. I suck my breath in, they have passed like lightning to one side of us and are arcing above us.' Catching a glimpse of the aiming point, amid this barrage there was 'no time for standard "bombing patter"', especially as the gunners were yelling for him to drop the bombs: 'they want to be away'. 'All is noise, confusion, flak, searchlights and a roaring, lurching aircraft', when Bruce finally released the bomb load and scrambled back to his table. Diving away from the target to increase speed, the Wellington reached the comparative safety of the sea. Flying parallel to the coast, the crew relaxed, although they must still guard against falling foul of a patrolling Ju 88.

As Bruce busied himself with navigation, the wireless operator poured coffee for all of them and took an empty milk bottle up to the pilot for him to relieve himself. The automatic pilot would not function, so he could not get back to the Elsan toilet in the fuselage. Not wishing to be intercepted by friendly fighters, approaching the English coast the IFF identification apparatus was switched on. Keeping a close watch for barrage balloons, after crossing the coast the crew located an inland airfield. Circling it, the pilot discovered that the undercarriage could not be lowered. The wireless operator called up 'Waggon Control' repeatedly, but received no answer. It dawned on him that, although he could pick up incoming messages, his transmitter had packed up. Then he heard another aircraft calling control and realised that their Wellington was over the wrong aerodrome. 'Panic for a while' until they worked out a bearing for Marham, the home base.

Reaching Marham, the bomber crossed the flare path at right angles firing the double green distress signal and flashing 'A' on

the 'downward identity light'. 'Waggon Control', their own controller, ordered other aircraft clear of the circuit and 'to cheer us
up they tell us that the Blood Waggon [ambulance] and fire
tender are standing by'. The pilot made a pass but overshot, and
'we are braced ready for a crash landing'. Second time round
they made a perfect landing. The undercarriage was down after
all but the light was not working. Climbing out, suddenly
Bruce's parachute harness seemed to weigh 'a ton'. 'A quick
debriefing with Intelligence and then cool, smooth sheets and
wonderful deep sleep' after five hours in the air. The end of
another operation completed through the cooperation and
interaction of the whole crew.

After completing ninety-nine night-fighter operations in
Beaufighters, Wing Commander Guy Gibson had returned to
bombers on 13 April 1942 to take command of 106 Squadron
at RAF Coningsby, Lincolnshire, then flying twin-engine
Manchesters. A short, solidly-built man, he proved a strict dis-
ciplinarian, insistent on close attention to rules and regulations.
He took over the squadron as Bomber Command expressed
concern about a tendency towards lax discipline on its stations:
rigid saluting and a proper dress code must be enforced at all
times.

For Gibson, 9 July proved a memorable day. He took off at
fifteen minutes past midnight for Wilhelmshaven on his first
Lancaster operation, part of a 285 aircraft force. After a practice flight, he had considered two members of his allotted crew
below par and had replaced them, yet another indication that
complete confidence in the ability of every member of a
bomber crew was essential. During a Manchester operation,
the bomb aimer had inadvertently put on the landing lights
and Gibson threatened to open the bomb bay doors and throw
him out if he did not quickly douse them. As the rear gunner,
Pilot Officer John Wickens, remarked, 'that man disappeared

from the crew pretty smartly'. On the other hand, when a visiting Air Ministry team declared Wickens too tall for the rear turret of a Lancaster, being above the regulation 5ft 11in., Gibson told them pointedly to forget the rules. Wickens was staying put in his crew.

After dropping five 2000lb. bombs on Wilhelmshaven in the face of 'fairly accurate' defences, Gibson declared the result 'a good prang', and landed once more at base exactly three hours after takeoff. There another unpleasant duty awaited him – having to visit the wife of an officer living close by to tell her that her husband had not returned. Later he recalled opening the gate and having to walk up the path to the cottage after glimpsing an ashen face at the window. She knew why he had come, opened the door and listened silently to what he said. He retraced his steps along the path extremely uncomfortable at seeing at close quarters a moving example of family grief. That incident stayed in his mind. Two years later, he used it to illustrate the strains of command to Flight Lieutenant J. C. Weller, a young pilot stationed at East Kirkby.

Four days after Gibson's trip to Wilhelmshaven, on 13/14 July Donald Bruce went to Duisburg, with a force of 194 bombers. Counting two North Sea sweeps, this would be the crew's thirteenth operation, but to avoid that unlucky number its members disregarded the maritime excursions. To them, therefore, this became the eleventh operation. At briefing in a crowded, hot room, Bruce fingered the lucky blue bottle top he always took with him when flying. That night he would certainly need it. As he took his place, he was thinking of the 4000lb. bomb they were to carry. 'Ugly, dustbin shaped with a protruding rim to prevent it penetrating the ground too deeply', it was designed for 'maximum blast effect' and 'studded with detonators'. Carrying this meant removing the bomb bay doors, because the bomb would 'bulge below the fuselage'. Minus

Handley Page V/1500. Four engine long-range RAF bomber, 126ft wing span, crew of five to seven, in service but not operational in 1918. Bombed Kabul during Third Afghan War (1919) and encouraged belief in 'strategic bombing' as a war winner. (*TRH Pictures*)

Hawker Hart. Single-engine two-seater bomber. In the early 1930s it could outpace every RAF fighter. Still used in training at the outbreak of war. (*Getty Images*)

Handley Page Heyford. Four-se 'heavy bomber' carrying up to 3,500lb bomb-lo: Ready to attack Germany if the Chamberlain–Hi Munich conferen of 1938 failed. (*TRH Pictures*)

Fairey Battle. Single-engine, three-seater, weakest of the RAF bombers in 1939. Suffered appalling losses before being withdrawn from operations. (*TRH Pictures*)

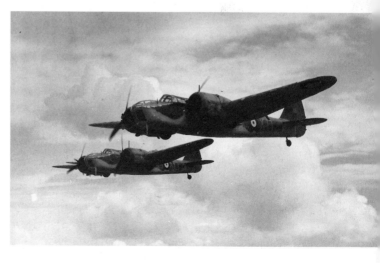

Bristol Blenheim. One of the new twin-engine monoplanes with which Bomber Command went to war. Crew of four, two machine-guns, 1000lb bomb-load. (*IWM*)

18-year-old Sgt John Hannah. Awarded VC for saving a burning Hampden on 15 September 1940, recovering from his injuries in hospital. (*IWM*)

Doris 'Micky' Batchelor. Wife of Flt Lt (later Gp Capt) Ken Batchelor, who stayed near RAF Honington and recorded her feelings about her husband's bombing tour, 1940–1. (*Taylor*)

Flying Officer Leonard Cheshire (centre), when a Halifax pilot with 35 Squadron, spring 1941. (*IWM*)

Sir Charles Portal, appointed Chief of the Air Staff October 1940, on a later tour of inspection. (*IWM*)

Sir Arthur Harris w staff officers plannir an operation. Harri: led Bomber Comma from February 1942 until the end of the Second World V (*IWM*)

Four-engine Lancaster bombers developed by Avro chief designer Roy Chadwick from th twin-engine Manchester. Could carry 22,400lb bomb-load. (*IWM*)

21-year-old Sgt Sam Beaumont, Blenheim navigator missing 21/22 July 1942, whose death was not confirmed until 11 January 1943. (*Griffith*)

Beaumont was buried by the Germans with full military honours at Lemvig, Denmark, on 11 September 1942. (*Griffith*)

New Zealander Flt Lt Les Munro (back row, left) with the crew which flew with him on 97 and 617 squadrons. (*Munro*)

Sqn Ldr H. M. Young, fligh commander on the Dambusters Raid, shot dow on the way back after makin the first of two breaches in t Möhne Dam. (*Owen*)

Möhne Dam. Reconnaissance photo of broken dam wall with signatures of 617 Squadron survivors. Presented to Barnes Wallis. (*BAC*)

RAF Scampton, 27 May 1943. (L ro R) Flt Lt D. H. Maltby (made second breach in Möhne Dam), Gp Capt J. N. H. Whitworth (station commander), Air Vice-Marshal the Hon R. A. Cochrane (commander 5 Group), Barnes Wallis, King George VI, Wg Cdr G. P. Gibson. (*IWM*)

Canadian F/Sgt J. W. Fraser escaped from a Lancaster shot down at the Möhne Dam during the Dambusters Raid and became a prisoner of war. (*Fraser*)

Missing in Action. The telegram received by Fraser's wife Doris, 17 May 1943. (*Fraser*)

Crew of American Sgt H. C. 'Nick' Knilans with 619 Squadron. Knilans, front row second left, went on to bomb the Tirpitz with 617 Squadron. Commissioned in the RCAF before joining the USAAF in 1944. (*Knilans*)

Australian Plt Off Les Knight (front, centre) with the crew that breached the Eder Dam during the Dambusters Raid and crashed attacking the Dortmund-Ems canal, September 1943. (*IWM*)

'most of its flotation bags to accommodate the bomb, the bomber will not fly on one engine or float in the sea because of these modifications'. 'The bomb we hate carrying', due to which **KO-K** would be one of the last aircraft over the target. The Wellington was scheduled to arrive after a lull following the main force, which it was hoped would convince the Germans the raid was over. The 'maximum blast' bomb was intended to disrupt the rescue services. Bruce heard the squadron commander say, 'go for the centre of the old town, boys, plenty of dry old timber there, it will burn well . . . after all they do it to our towns so we do it to theirs'. 'The old platitudes,' Bruce reflected, 'but how else can we argue?'

The outward flight proved 'uneventful'. 'We are becoming battle hardened, it is all "Old Hat", we have done and seen it all before.' Nonetheless, approaching the target at 13,000ft, the pilot cautiously circled the town. Seeing another Wellington about 500ft below making its run over the target and attracting a bevy of flak guns and searchlights he followed it in 'unmolested'. That is, until the other aircraft dived away leaving Bruce's Wellington totally exposed to the alert defences. Right over the target, it was coned by searchlights. Fortunately the bomb had already been dropped, but the pilot, for some reason not wearing his goggles, became blinded. The rear gunner, who had been wounded by flak once before, screamed over the intercom to get clear of the beams. 'Can't shake them off, they are hitting us, a sound like a stick rattling on corrugated iron, the port engine is hit.' In desperation, the pilot pulled the nose 'up and up'. 'There is the inert sensation before a stall then we are swinging over . . . he has stall turned the bomber', and the aircraft was now diving in the opposite direction. The searchlights had lost them, but Bruce wondered whether the aircraft would stand the strain as it plunged to 9,000ft. He desperately clung on to the navigation table, as 'accumulators, maps, nuts and bolts, pencils' floated past him. His eyes were riveted on the airspeed indicator.

The needle crept up to 350mph, and he remembered a red warning plate on the pilot's panel: 'This aircraft must not be dived at speeds in excess of 300mph.' Due to gravitational force, Bruce felt his hands, arms and feet like lead, himself pushed down into his seat, his eyelids begin to close. He could hear the pilot 'panting with exertion' over the intercom, as he struggled to control the aircraft. 'As suddenly as it began it is over, we are straight and level.' Moveable objects were scattered all over the floor; raisins from the burst ration case had showered the navigation table. Incongruously, in the dim cabin light Bruce noticed an earwig crawl out of 'the sticky heap'.

He gathered his maps and other equipment as the pilot strove to keep the port wing with its dead engine on an even keel. It was a losing battle, as the starboard engine began to overheat and the aircraft started rapidly to lose height. It would never reach the coast. Bruce and the pilot hurriedly consulted and decided that they must bale out. 'Jump, jump, rear gunner' – the command always repeated to avoid misunderstanding. No acknowledgement. Hearing the discussion over the intercom, the gunner had not waited for the order. He had already gone. After groping for his parachute which had been dislodged in the general chaos, the front gunner went out via the forward hatch, as the wireless operator frantically searched his compartment for his gloves. Having removed his intercom connection – 'liable to be strangled by the leads if they catch in the chute as it opens' – Bruce loosened his tie and fastened his parachute pack to the harness. He then kicked the wireless operator to get his attention and indicated that he ought to move forward, only to be motioned on. Bruce hesitated no more and went past the pilot who grinned and gave him the thumbs up; 'good old Delmer, he's a great guy, and then I am at the opening'. He remembered the words of an instructor at his OTU. 'When you have to go you should dive out head first but if you have time you will probably lower yourself by your hands'. Bruce decided he had time, faced the rear of the aircraft, with his back to the slipstream and hands holding either side of the hatch. 'Gingerly' he lowered his feet and legs, only to be caught in the slipstream and 'like a straw I am swept along the underside of the fuselage', as the parachute pack snagged against the edge of the hatch. Bruce desperately tried to free himself. Eventually his shoulders were caught by the slipstream and he was 'wrenched away into the night'.

He wrote dramatically of the next few minutes. 'It is so quiet, the air rustles past my face. Which way am I falling, am I looking at the sky or the ground? My knees fall towards my chest. I am falling head downwards with my back towards the ground. No sensation, almost pleasant except for the feeling in the stomach. The ripcord, pull the ripcord, you fool. My hand clutches the D ring, I pull, there is a sharp slither as the pilot chute tugs at the main fabric then a crack like a pistol shot as the cords holding the harness across my chest break allowing the harness to swing above my head. I have already turned my face to one side so that there is no fear of my nose being broken as the harness flies up and over my face. A terrific jolt, the umbrella of silk has opened above me and I am swinging into nothing . . . another terrible swing into blackness . . . another . . . the chute steadies. I feel so sick, I hang limply in the harness. Suddenly the noise of an aircraft, a terrible whining roar as it dives. Stupidly, I can only think of night fighters, a flare lights me up . . . they are going to shoot . . . I collect my senses, the noise was KO-K making her last dive, the "flare" is KO-K erupting into a blossom of fire in the void, the oxygen bottles burst in brilliant blue flashes, there is a rattle of exploding ammunition and rivers of fire spread with the spouts of petrol from the shattered tanks.

Alert once more, I peer at the ground, I can see nothing, then dim shapes begin to form. I am heading straight for a tree. I get into a sitting position with the chute trailing ahead in a light wind, brush the tree, swing into soft earth and graze my elbow. There is a farmhouse ahead, people standing watching scream and then there is no one. I have come down so silently that they did not realise that I was there and now thoroughly startled and frightened they have disappeared into the house. I stand alone in the darkness, in a strange country.' Years later he would learn that the farm dwellers thought he was a German airman and were afraid to be caught outside during curfew. At the time, he was captured by a patrol.

Although a prisoner of war, Bruce was considerably more fortunate than Sergeant Samuel Beaumont, navigator of a 114 Squadron Blenheim. On 22 July 1942, he failed to return from an operation against the German air base at Vechta, 30 kilometres south-west of Bremen. Like so many others in similar circumstances, his family desperately hoped that somehow he had survived.

Beaumont was a bright youngster, at the age of twelve top of the forty-four in his class, leaving Salford Technical College four years later with a testimonial from the headmaster and subsequently beginning work as a junior draughtsman. When called up he volunteered for RAF aircrew. After basic training, Beaumont qualified as an observer, all the time regularly corresponding with his parents and sister Mary. In February 1941, he proudly told them that he had passed all his exams with credit, been promoted LAC and hoped to qualify for a commission. He celebrated his twenty-first birthday on 16 October while on another course at RAF Upwood, Cambridgeshire. Three days after Christmas, Beaumont described a day of exercises starting 'at the crack of dawn' in bitter weather which chilled his bones despite being swathed in heavy clothing. Forced to fly through thick cloud, his aircraft emerged on course, a tribute not only to his navigational ability but to the pilot's 'skilful' flying on instruments. The hazards of training were underlined by his revelation that one bomber had just managed to glide in safely, another had been obliged to land at RAF Finningley in Yorkshire 'to ask the way'. The afternoon's exercise, involving live firing and bombing, was marred by one aircraft hitting 'sand flats', turning upside down and injuring all of the crew. 'It's been a bad day on the whole,' Beaumont observed mildly.

In April 1942, a letter from his sister Mary coincided with abolition of the multi-role observer: 'You would be a fool to accept an air gunner's job. It really would be a letdown. You would be better off on the ground staff. People would wonder what was wrong if you were still flying but in a lower position.' The crisis, though, passed and two months later Beaumont was serving as a navigator on 114 Squadron. The measure of the family's concern for his safety was shown in another letter from Mary: 'We do worry when we hear of these raids. I guessed that you would be in that raid last Thursday . . . Regarding prayers we all say them every morning and night and I call in church every morning and I hope you say prayers for yourself also.'

On 19 July, his father wrote: 'Dear Son, Pleased to hear you are doing OK. Mam was getting a bit worried when we did not receive a letter', emphasising how his parents relied on regular correspondence to allay their fears. Beaumont's father concluded with a touch of maternal care, indirectly underlining his son's youth: 'Mam will send your washing away tomorrow trusting you can manage until you receive it.' That same evening, the son wrote to his father that 'I found a pipe in my kit, so now I'm looking distinguished', and closed 'with the help of God I should be home on leave soon'.

It was not to be. His father's letter, concluding 'hoping to see you soon' and postmarked 10 a.m. on 22 July, was 'returned to sender under Air Ministry authority'. Sergeant Beaumont was already missing. Later that morning, the Beaumonts received the fateful telegram informing them that Sam had failed to return. His father immediately sent a heart-rending wire to the house in Blackpool where his daughter was on holiday: 'Sam met with accident. Please break news to Mary Beaumont.' Two days later a formal letter from the officer in charge of RAF records arrived, confirming that Sam was missing, with a gentle addendum: 'This does not necessarily mean that he is killed or wounded. I will communicate with you again immediately I have any further news.' The hope that Sam had survived a crash, become a prisoner of war or evaded capture, remained.

On 26 July, the Officer Commanding 114 Squadron sent a personal, five-and-a-half page hand-written letter. He, too, held out hope that Sam might have been captured, confirmation of which could take up to three months. Paying tribute to the 'courage and cheerfulness' which 'endeared' him to his colleagues, Wing Commander Poltard wrote, 'you have every reason to be proud of your son'. He concluded: 'Germany may be victorious on every battlefield but she will be beaten sooner or later by the repeated blows of Bomber Command.' Responding, Sam's father assured the OC of 'our pride in him as a dear son and brother', adding 'we are still hoping and praying that he is a prisoner of war and we long for the day when we will receive news from him'. To the parents of Sam's girlfriend Joan, Mr Beaumont repeated that 'we haven't given up hope and are praying that we will have better news soon'.

Weeks passed with nothing but administrative correspondence. On 18 August, the RAF Accounts Branch informed Mrs Beaumont that the 14/- (70p) weekly voluntary allotment from Sam's pay to her would continue until 18 November 1942. Six days after that date a telegram arrived, confirmed by letter the following day. Quoting German information, the International

Red Cross had reported Sam's body being recovered from the sea off Jutland on 9 September. All vestige of hope that this might be a case of mistaken identity vanished on 11 January 1943, when a letter from the Air Ministry revealed that Sam Beaumont's body had been buried on 11 September 1942, giving the precise location and number of the grave in Lemvig Cemetery. The final official leaf was turned on 8 April 1943, when the Beaumonts received notification that their son's personal effects would now be released by the RAF, almost nine months after the telegram announcing that he was missing. In truth, though, any realistic hope had evaporated in November 1942 after four months of agonising uncertainty. Sadly, Sergeant Sam Beaumont's story was by no means an isolated one.

His loss demonstrated that, although four-engine aircraft had taken over the bulk of strategic bombing targets, twin-engine machines like the Blenheim, Boston and Ventura would continue to carry out a variety of other tasks including intruder operations against enemy airfields, on one of which the young navigator lost his life.

By the end of July the impact of the thousand-bomber raids had begun to fade, as Rommel continued to threaten Cairo from North Africa, German formations renewed their thrust through the Ukraine towards Stalingrad, U-boat activity rose dangerously in the Atlantic and naval units led by the battleship *Tirpitz* lay menacingly in Norwegian ports. Yet once more pressure built to divert Bomber Command's resources to other areas. On 28 July, Harris addressed an aggressive plea personally to Winston Churchill. 'Those who advocate the break-up of Bomber Command for the purpose of adding strength to Coastal and Army Co-operation commands and overseas requirements are like the amateur politician who imagines that the millennium will arrive through the simple process of dividing available cash equally between all.' In a conclusion, which he no doubt calculated would appeal to the Prime Minster's bulldog spirit, he argued: 'One cannot win wars by defending oneself.'

So, despite the contrary pressures, the campaign against Germany continued apace. After three operations in five nights during the second week of August 1942, Wing Commander Gibson celebrated a night off in a local hostelry, standard practice for relaxing aircrew. On the night of 27/28 August he flew an operation against Gydnia naval base at Danzig, where German capital ships were anchored and the aircraft carrier *Graf Zeppelin* was under construction. Armed with six 1000lb. bombs and equipped with the advanced Stabilised Automatic Bomb Sight (SABS), Gibson's Lancaster was frustrated by thick haze in the target area. But that night it carried an unusual bomb aimer, Squadron Leader Richardson, a First World War veteran and expert on the new sight from the Armament School at Manby, Lincolnshire. The operation was remarkable for another reason: a touch of journalistic fancy. On the night that Gibson bombed Gydnia, Soviet bombers simultaneously attacked nearby Königsberg and imaginative leader writers next day referred to 'aerial arms shaking hands over Danzig'.

During August, Sergeant George Johnson joined 97 Squadron at Woodhall Spa in Lincolnshire. When his ambition to become a pilot had not been realised, he trained as an air gunner. Arriving at Woodhall, Johnson found the Squadron needed bomb aimers for its new Lancasters and agreed to be retrained. Meanwhile, he completed ten operations as a gunner with different crews. One trip with a single 8000lb. bomb underlined the twin problems of navigation and target identification. On this occasion his aircraft was piloted by a wing commander, who had the squadron navigation officer on board to carry out the navigating and bomb aiming in accordance with current practice. Arriving in the target area, the pilot noticed a concentration of explosions and fires away to port. He promptly blamed 'those bloody fools' for attacking the decoy target. Instead, he flew south and the bomb was dropped in the face of 'no opposition'. Johnson recalled that 'all hell was let loose when we got back. The Wingco. continued his tirade about everybody bombing the wrong area.' That is, until the photographs were developed, which showed that his aircraft had bombed another town 80 miles south. Johnson observed that they had been 'a little off course, as it were', adding semi-apologetically that 'the approaches to the target were very, very similar'. Shortly afterwards, American Flight Lieutenant Joe McCarthy arrived with his Lancaster crew from a training unit minus a bomb aimer. Johnson was recruited to fill the vacancy and never regretted it.

Aircraft fitter Ray Grayston similarly responded to a call for flight engineers principally needed to supervise the fuel system and engine power of a Lancaster. In that aircraft, the flight engineer had responsibility for shutting down ('feathering') a damaged engine and being prepared to assist the pilot to maintain speed at any time. His job was complicated by the fact that several of the dials, which he must check, were at floor level, requiring him to squat on the fuselage floor. After qualifying and being promoted sergeant, he was allocated to the crew of Sergeant Les Knight with 50 Squadron.

Grayston was impressed by how quickly the others accepted him: 'They were a wonderful crew, never a harsh word, never, no'. He thought himself 'dead lucky', because the bomb aimer, Pilot Officer E. C. Johnson, was also a trained navigator. With the pilot and the designated navigator, there were therefore three in the aircraft able to navigate. Grayston soon developed 'every confidence' in them, the two gunners and the wireless operator.

The bombing campaign as a whole was not progressing smoothly at this time and Grayston's ground crew colleagues were not unreasonable to question his sanity in applying for a flying transfer. Casualties were so heavy that a member of a bomber crew had only a fifty-fifty chance of surviving a tour of thirty operations. By now, too, as feared the Germans had begun to jam Gee. The time was ripe for innovation: the Pathfinder Force (PFF), which was introduced in the teeth of fierce opposition from Harris, who believed his best squadrons would be snatched from him. According to Group Captain S. O. Bufton, now Deputy Director of Bomber Operations, Harris was given an ultimatum: accept the Pathfinders or go.

One Sunday morning as Bufton pored over yet another lengthy paper full of objections from Harris in his Air Ministry office the Vice Chief of the Air Staff, Air Chief Marshal Sir Wilfrid Freeman, poked his head round the door and asked if everything was all right. 'No, sir. It's Bert [Harris].' Bufton went through Harris's argument that creation of this force would denude his bomber groups of their best squadrons. Freeman listened quietly, then took away the relevant file. An hour later he rang to add his support. The very next day the CAS sent for Bufton and pledged his support, too. On Tuesday, the CAS saw Harris, who had previously told Bufton the PFF would become fact 'over his dead body'. Indirectly, almost two years later, Harris confirmed this sequence of events, when he complained to Portal 'that his [Bufton's] ideas on Pathfinders, as on some other matters, have always been and still are rammed down our throats whether we like them or not'.

On 15 August, Air Vice-Marshal D. C. T. Bennett, 'a brash young officer' aged thirty-two, was given command of the new organisation. An Australian pre-war airline pilot and early in the war involved in ferrying aircraft across the Atlantic, Bennett had been shot down while leading his Halifax squadron to

Mounting Losses

Norway in an attack on the battleship *Tirpitz* at the end of April 1942. He was guaranteed to ruffle feathers but expected to get results. Post-war, Group Captain Guy Brisbane explained the rationale behind the Pathfinders. The thousand-bomber raid on Cologne had proved that 'with adequate navigational aids' aircraft could reach a target at night. However, despite the perceived success of the operation, for 'an effective raid' aircraft 'should be concentrated in time and space over the target'. Until the advent of the Pathfinders, Brisbane maintained this could not be properly achieved. The Pathfinders would mark the route to the target with coloured flares, illuminate the target and mark the aiming points with incendiaries in advance of the main force. Although 'remarkable' results were obtained from the outset, Brisbane admitted that adverse weather could still be frustrating, and controversy over the Pathfinders' performance would excite the more trenchant opponents.

Critics did have a good deal of ammunition to promote their cause. Brisbane's favourable conclusion was altogether too sweeping and apparently a case of selective memory. On the night of 1/2 September, for example, the Pathfinders set out to mark Saarbrücken, which 205 following aircraft reported bombing accurately. Unfortunately, they hit Saarlouis, 13 miles north-west of Saarbrücken but similarly on a river bend, which had been illuminated in error. This was an extreme instance of faulty marking, but by no means unique at this stage of the Pathfinders' existence.

Nor did the PFF always secure suitable aircrew. Another Australian, Flight Sergeant Rawdon Hume Middleton, was posted to it. After one early operation he was told that some of his crew did not come up to the required standard. He refused to lose them and went back to his original squadron with the crew intact, a striking illustration of crew loyalty. Three months later, although badly wounded, obviously in extreme pain and completely blind in one eye, Middleton would bring a heavily damaged Stirling back from Turin and keep it aloft long enough for his crew to bale out in sight of England. He earned a posthumous VC. The citation praised his 'fortitude and strength of will . . . [and] his devotion to duty in the face of overwhelming odds.'

However, cases of so-called Lack of Moral Fibre (LMF), refusing to fly or perform duties in the air, were not unusual in Bomber Command. In other ways a sympathetic and compassionate commanding officer, at 76 Squadron Wing Commander Leonard Cheshire ruthlessly rooted out aircrew suspected of this failing. He argued that swift action was necessary in the interests of the man himself and, more importantly, of others. 'That sort of thing could spread like wildfire, like an infectious disease,' he insisted. 'I could not afford to hesitate as soon as there was a hint of a problem.' Yet he is reputed to have taken a decorated man, suspected of LMF, in his own aircraft to give him a chance of redeeming himself.

The actor Denholm Elliott had a brief career on 76 Squadron, but for reasons not connected with LMF. When he arrived on the station at Linton-on-Ouse, he did not have a crew. As elsewhere, choosing one was quite informal. People were 'swarming around drinking beer in an enormous room, meeting each other and somehow crews got together'. He joined the crew of Squadron Leader Barnard. 'Oh dear. Well, the last wireless operator of K-King got a cannon shell up his backside,' a Squadron veteran greeted him. 'That didn't encourage me too much,' Elliott mused. On his third operation, over Flensburg, the aircraft encountered 'unpleasant' flak and 'enormous turbulence'. 'A shell bursting beneath you lifts the plane 50ft upwards in the air. You certainly find instant religion.' Caught in searchlights, with the pilot 'chucking the plane all over the sky, which with a four-engine bomber takes some doing . . . [and] is very, very frightening', the Halifax was suddenly hit and 'the port outer engine burst into flames'. All the lights went out and Elliott could not find the apparatus to send out the automatic SOS signal as the bomber went into a steep dive. He scrambled to take up the crash position with his feet braced against the main spar and hands behind his head.

In the early hours of 23 September 1942, despite fire having a firm hold on the port wing, Barnard managed to put K-King down in the North Sea. Elliott sustained only 'a tiny bruise on the back of the head'. That was a minor inconvenience. The aircraft was rapidly filling with water and they had to launch the dinghy, which with considerable difficulty was achieved. Knowing that German-held Denmark lay close by, the crew realised that it was hopeless to attempt paddling to safety and, with resignation, sent up a distress signal. In due course an enemy tug came out to get them. Elliott recorded the scene, which would have graced one of the post-war comedy films in which he appeared. 'We were met on dry land by a sort of picture postcard Nazi officer with a monocle and a long cigarette holder, who said, "For you ze war is over".' And it was. There was, though, a pleasant corollary. Because Elliot had been unable to send out an SOS from the Halifax, his mother assumed that he had been killed. When a card from him via the Red Cross signed 'In Vinculis' (in chains) reached her totally unexpectedly, she was in the bath. She 'practically drowned with surprise and joy'. Another actor, Donald Pleasance, had a similar, bizarre welcome to captivity. Also a wireless operator, in accordance with normal procedure he had been issued with a packet of condoms to protect important parts of the radio equipment should the aircraft ditch in the sea. His bomber was shot down over land. On being searched after capture, the protectives were duly discovered. 'You vil not be needing zeeze now', his captor triumphantly proclaimed.

Harris, as C-in-C Bomber Command, was right to highlight the shortage of bomber crews. Quite apart from the thousand-bomber raids, many at OTUs were sent on other operations, with predictable results. Three times in September, Sergeant Reg Lewis navigated a Wellington from Wing, Buckinghamshire, to Germany. Only two from the twelve crews on his course survived to be posted to an operational unit. Against Düsseldorf on 10/11 September, No. 16 OTU at Upper Heyford lost five of the thirteen Wellingtons it put up. During the bomber campaign as a whole, OTUs would lose 120 twin-engine aircraft on raids, the bulk of them in 1942.

In Canada, courtesy of the Empire Training Scheme, the former Portsmouth Dockyard apprentice Jim Parsons had at length settled on a role in the RAF, though hardly voluntarily. His hopes of becoming a pilot having been dashed, he planned to be a navigator. When the time came for specialisation, he was interviewed by the chairman of the selection board, curiously a former employee at Portsmouth airport. He would, however, show Parsons no favour. 'You're to be a bomb aimer,' he informed Parsons, who asked why not a navigator. The wing commander explained that his performance in the final examination had not been good enough, to which Parsons replied in that case nobody else would qualify as he had gained the top navigation marks. Cue for much shuffling of paper and a grudging admission that this was indeed so, followed by: 'Sorry, but we've decided you're to be a bomb aimer.' As it turned out, this suited Parsons better because in the nose of an aircraft he could see what was going on, instead of being 'cooped up' in the navigator's compartment.

October 1942 saw a number of daylight raids, many of them against Italy in the run-up to the American landings in North Africa the following month. Others were on targets in France. On 17 October, recreating the tactic used at Augsburg but this time skirting the west coast of France to attack the Schneider armaments manufacturing complex at Le Creusot and the nearby Montchanin transformer station, ninety-four unescorted Lancasters turned eastwards to fly inland between La Rochelle and St Nazaire, 'like being part of the Grand National', according to one participant. Bombing at relatively low level (maximum 7500ft) the force lost only one aircraft and claimed extensive damage. In reality, very little was done to the main target, although the transformer was put out of action for a considerable time. The deficiencies of bomb-aiming equipment were again exposed. For there was little flak in the target area, visibility was good and no fighters interfered.

Conditions were somewhat different over Germany. On 9/10 November, Pilot Officer Gordon Carter navigated a Halifax to Hamburg piloted by Wing Commander B. V. Robbins as part of a 213 aircraft force. Very heavy icing in thick clouds occurred in the target area, with 'St Elmo's fire, a visible form of static electricity, flickering all over the inside of the aircraft'. Visibility was nil. As Carter considered the unpromising conditions, 'thickly moustachioed Robbie's voice came over the intercom: "Navigator, I hope you're thinking".' Carter recalled: 'Frankly I wasn't feeling too proud or too sure of our whereabouts but I didn't let on.' The raid was not a success due to the weather, but Carter's aircraft did get back safely; fifteen others did not.

The airborne radar carried by enemy night fighters remained a puzzle. Until more details were known, no effective countermeasures could be fashioned. In the early hours of 2 December, therefore, a specially equipped Wellington from No. 1474 Special Duty Flight took off from Gransden Lodge near Huntingdon with extraordinary, and for its crew potentially fatal, orders to allow a night fighter to close in, all the time radioing information about its radar emissions and performance. Once this had been done, the crew could make its escape – if still possible. The Flight's ORB noted that 'the aircraft was engaged on the eighteenth sortie on a particular investigation, which necessitated the aircraft being intercepted by an enemy night fighter, and up to this sortie all efforts to get such an interception had failed'. Shortly after 4.30 a.m., near Mainz, the special radio operator, Pilot Officer Jordan, picked up faint signals, which increased in volume as a fighter came closer. He warned the crew to expect an attack and drafted a message for the wireless operator, Flight Sergeant Bigoray, to transmit, it being 'absolutely vital that this information' – and particularly the frequency of the incoming signal – 'should reach base at all costs'. 'Almost simultaneously the aircraft was hit by a burst of cannon fire. The rear gunner gave a fighter control commentary during the attack and identified the enemy aircraft as a Ju 88.' While the pilot, Sergeant Paulton, corkscrewed, although hit in the arm Jordan drafted another message confirming the frequency of the fighter's airborne radar. At this point, the rear turret malfunctioned and the gunner was wounded in the shoulder during a second attack in which Jordan was hit in the jaw. 'But he continued to work his sets and log the results and told the captain and crew from which side to expect the next attack.'

The front turret was then disabled and the gunner (Flight Sergeant Grant) wounded in the leg. As the wireless operator (Bigoray) went forward to help Grant, an exploding shell wounded him in both legs and he had painfully to return to his seat. The Ju 88 could not be shaken off, but Pilot Officer Barry (the navigator) managed to free Grant. Jordan now suffered an eye injury, and he realised that he could not continue with his work much longer. With his intercom connection shot away, he had physically to fetch the navigator to help him. However, Jordan was effectively blind and was forced to 'give up the attempt to show Barry what to do'. Meanwhile, Flight Sergeant

Mounting Losses

Vachon had moved from the useless rear turret to the astrodome from which he 'could give evasive control' until wounded once more, whereupon Barry replaced him. During all this chaos, the aircraft had plunged from 14,000ft to 500ft, with 'violent evasive action still being taken by the captain'. To his and his crew's relief, after an estimated ten to twelve attacks, the fighter broke away, leaving the Wellington heavily damaged and four of its six crew seriously wounded. Fortunately, the pilot was not one of them, but his aircraft was certainly in a bad way. The port engine of the twin engine machine had its throttle shot away, that of the starboard engine had stuck. Both engines were therefore misfiring, and both gun turrets were out of action. Added to these calamities, both airspeed indicators, the hydraulic system and the starboard aileron were useless. The prospect of reaching England looked decidedly slim.

Paulton did, though, nurse his perforated charge gently over the Channel, and at 7.15 a.m. the Kent coast appeared ahead. He decided that it would be unwise to attempt a conventional landing, so opted to pancake on the sea close inshore. Bigoray's injured legs were a problem. The wireless operator had the best chance of survival if he used his parachute, so Paulton flew over land before turning out to sea again. Bigoray duly made his way painfully to the rear exit, before he realised that he had not locked down the morse key so that the position of the aircraft could be traced. He went back to his post to do this before baling out with copies of his signals in his pocket in case they had not been received. Paulton put the damaged Wellington down on the water off Walmer. He and the rest of the crew then clambered into the dinghy only to find it so badly holed that they had to splash their way back to the wreckage and cling on until a small boat rescued them. The Flight report sparsely recorded: 'Aircraft sank. All crew safe'.

In the third week of November, flight engineer Sergeant

Edgar Childs had begun operations with 83 Pathfinder Squadron. 'This was a momentous time for me,' he wrote, 'and I found myself under close scrutiny from the other members of the crew being something of a novice at the job. This made me feel uncomfortable but fortunately I came through without letting the side down.' During his second operation, the mid-upper gunner called out: 'Skipper, we're on fire.' Childs was sent to investigate and found a canister of incendiaries 'still on board and burning fiercely'. On hearing this, the pilot made 'a rapid descent', the bomb aimer managed to jettison the blazing mass 'and all was well'. Childs flew only five times with this crew, which completed its tour on 9 December.

He was then assigned to Flying Officer Smith, who told him: 'While we are flying the engines are entirely your responsibility. I will handle the throttles on takeoff and landing. Any adjustments of power and the synchronisation of the propellers is up to you.' 'This set the tone for our cooperation,' Childs recalled. 'While flying together, I felt completely at ease.' He soon appreciated, too, 'the mutual respect of all the crew for one another'. Rather like Lofty Long's words to Leonard Cheshire in June 1940, Smith insisted that 'the safety of all the crew depends on each member keeping a good look out at all times and while over enemy territory he would weave at all times so as to afford the gunners a maximum view below'. Smith was superstitious. He hated to miss the comedian Tommy Handley's weekly *ITMA* show on the wireless and ritually tucked one silk glove into each of his flying boots when going out to the aircraft.

During the final weeks of 1942, several new devices appeared to assist RAF bomber crews. To combat cloudy conditions and imperfect visibility on the ground, the Pathfinders had begun to use coloured flares in the sky ('sky markers') to act as aiming points for the bombers. Perhaps the most important innovation at this time, though, was the blind-bombing aid Oboe. Like

Mounting Losses

Gee it had a device fitted into an aircraft, in this case linked to two stations in England. Unlike Gee, though, it relied on the pulses transmitted by the two ground transmitters being received by the aircraft and retransmitted to the originating sets. The Cat station kept the aircraft on track; Mouse signalled exactly when it should bomb. All calculations were carried out at the ground stations, but a high degree of competence was required in the bomber, too. Visual identification from the aircraft was not therefore necessary and the system could function in all weathers. It could secure a bombing error of just 300yd. There were drawbacks, however. Like Gee it was a line-of-sight device and so Oboe's range, too, was limited by the curvature of the earth. Furthermore, the stations in England could cope with only twelve aircraft per hour. Perhaps critically, the bombing run of an aircraft carrying Oboe must be straight and level for some distance, making it particularly vulnerable to flak or night fighters. (The name Oboe is supposed to have evolved during the experimental stage, when the transmissions from ground stations were thought to resemble the sound of the musical instrument.)

Given the limited number of aircraft which could carry it, Oboe could best be utilised by leading Pathfinder aircraft to mark the target, followed by others to drop back-up incendiaries. It was first used successfully against a power station at Lutterade in Holland on 20 December. Before the end of the month another navigational aid appeared in embryo form, as yet with only hazy pictures but capable of development and improvement: H2S. This was an airborne radar carried in the aircraft and not therefore dependent on ground stations at home, its range only limited by that of the aircraft in which it was fitted. Service folklore has it that choice of the name H2S, the chemical symbol for hydrogen sulphide which gives off a smell like rotten eggs, was a whimsical joke. A research scientist reputedly remarked that development of the device took so long that the process stank, so the original designation BN (for Blind Navigation) was altered. Whether true or not, H2S became generally known among aircrew as 'Stinky'.

Two further aids to bomber crews came into service in December 1942 and enjoyed a fair degree of success in the coming months. Mandrel, a device fitted to selected aircraft, jammed Freya radar emissions. Tinsel, also airborne, comprised a microphone which could be used by the wireless operator to block the frequency employed by German controllers broad-casting instructions to their fighters. By now, too, all bombers were fitted with aerial cameras, which allowed more compre-hensive operational analysis.

These various devices at different stages of development pro-vided a major boost to Bomber Command at the close of a period during which heavy casualties had been suffered. Between August and December, 520 aircraft (more than 3500 men) had been lost, almost 6 per cent of those flying on each operation. During these months, a further 879 machines had been badly damaged; overall, 1399 bombers were thus lost or damaged, 15.8 per cent of those despatched. With the new aids, however, 1943 should bring a welcome change in fortunes.

And there were other encouraging signs. An 8000lb. bomb had come into service, a considerable advance on the 500lb. one in general use two years earlier. When Harris took over Bomber Command in February, fifteen squadrons were equipped with four-engine heavy bombers; by December that figure was thirty-six. The twin-engine Hampdens, Whitleys and Manchesters had been withdrawn from front-line service. However, Harris argued that his force ought to have been even stronger: to his dismay sixteen new squadrons had been allocated to the Middle East or Coastal Command. The arrival of the heavy bombers did bring an inbuilt penalty: existing crews had to be retrained at HCUs, and new crews required up to forty hours special training. Hence the wartime navigator Brisbane in his later reflections believed, 'the result was that when a new crew went on their first operation, they had a much clearer picture of what to expect than their predecessors'. The downside of the lengthier training process was that the shortage of crews, identified when Harris took over, substantially remained.

1942 had undoubtedly seen the acquisition of greater potential. A further bonus was about to stretch the enemy defences. In January 1943, aircraft of the US 8th AAF Bomber Command based in England would join RAF Bomber Command over Germany. The first American bombing mission in Europe had taken place on 17 August 1942 against marshalling yards in Rouen. Referring to the name painted on the commander's Flying Fortress, Harris flamboyantly signalled: 'Yankee Doodle certainly went to town and can stick another well-deserved feather in his cap.' Between that date and 30 December, American four-engine bombers flew 1547 sorties over occupied territory for the loss of only thirty-two machines.

The fervent hope was that in the new year B-17 Flying Fortresses and B-24 Liberators, together with Stirlings, Halifaxes and Lancasters of Bomber Command, would make a tangible impact on targets in the German homeland.

CHAPTER 5

Fierce Combat, 1943

'Ready to start the real offensive'

Writing after the war, Marshal of the Royal Air Force Sir Arthur Harris declared, 'by the beginning of the year 1943 . . . I was ready to start the real offensive'. To assist his squadrons, Harris could count on a rising number of Lancasters (more than a hundred a month) coming off the production line and the promise of new equipment like Oboe and H2S. The entire bomber force now had Gee and, within five months, the improved Mark II version. More effective target indicators came into service as well: 250lb. light case devices which burnt at 3000ft and showered coloured balls over a target for approximately five minutes. 'At long last,' Harris concluded, 'we were ready and equipped.'

Declaration of the Allies' commitment to extending the bombing campaign offered timely encouragement. At a meeting between Churchill and President Roosevelt in Casablanca in January 1943, a combined aerial assault on Germany 'round the clock' was agreed with Bomber Command predominantly carrying on night area attacks, the Americans daylight precision bombing. On 21 January, therefore, Harris was formally instructed: 'Your primary object will be the progressive destruction and dislocation of the Germany military, industrial and economic system, and the undermining of the morale of the German people to a point where their capacity for armed resistance is fatally weakened.' This was the theory of strategic bombing rewritten for modern consumption.

The Casablanca Directive was not that simple though. Bomber Command must continue to target 'submarine bases on the Biscay coast . . . Berlin, which should be attacked when conditions are suitable for the attainment of specially favourable results unfavourable to the morale of the enemy or favourable to that of Russia . . . objectives in Northern Italy . . . important units of the German Fleet in harbour or at sea'. Harris was reminded that 'in attacking objectives in occupied countries' he had to 'conform to such instructions as may be issued from time to time for political reasons by His Majesty's Government'. Bomber Command still could not, therefore, focus its attention on Germany, despite it being the 'primary object'.

Surrender of the German 6th Army, which had been surrounded at Stalingrad, on 2 February 1943 led to another change of emphasis in a directive issued a fortnight later: 'Recent events on the Russian front have made it most desirable in the opinion of the Cabinet that we should rub in the Russian victory by further attacks on Berlin.'

A lanky, taciturn New Zealander, nicknamed 'Happy' by his crew, Flight Lieutenant Les Munro, flying with 97 Squadron from Woodhall Spa, took part in the Berlin raids. Munro was quite clear about how a crew should work. 'Irrespective of rank', the pilot must be in charge of a bomber. 'He was the leader, the boss, the director of what went on in the aircraft. The navigator was the next in importance after the pilot. Without him it might have been possible to find the way home on a daylight op but very difficult at night. The rest of the crew all had important roles to play at different times of an operation and I would not like to allocate a degree of priority to any of the positions over that of the others.' Munro learnt that many pilots handed over the controls to their flight engineer on the way home. 'This practice became more common as the risk of Jerry night fighter attack diminished. I must admit that it was a long time before I was prepared to hand over the controls to Frank [Appleby] and when I did he handled them quite well. When I was confident of his ability to stick to the course and height I would take over from the gunners in their turrets and get a feel for their contribution to the team effort.'

Munro flew his first operation on 2 January 1943 and experienced no great difficulty until his sixth trip – to Berlin, an unhealthy spot at which to hit problems. On 16/17 January, his whole high explosive and incendiary bomb load hung up and, after circling with flak providing a dangerous background cacophony, nothing could be done to release any of it. The very next night, they went back to the German capital. This time their bombs did release, but bad weather over Lincolnshire meant that they were diverted to RAF Harwell, Oxfordshire. Bound for Hamburg on 30 January, the crew had another sharp reminder of the unfriendly elements. Off the Dutch coast, the air speed indicator and the heating system failed in an air temperature of minus 46 degrees centigrade, and the rear turret malfunctioned.

In December 1942, a Canadian bomb aimer, Sergeant John Fraser, had written to his mother about two raids on Turin, when 'we gave them HELL', adding that 'the Alps are beautiful at night' and the moon 'did light up the mountains wonderfully'. With the enthusiasm of youth, he concluded: 'And so life goes on – plenty of thrills and excitement.' On 2 February 1943, another letter was more sombre. 'By now you will know Len [a good friend] is missing and dead, a sudden shock to me on arriving back from leave. To me and most of the other boys, perhaps we are hardened to it. To those back home – parents, sisters and brothers – it must be a severe loss. Not often do we think of them. And so to Len, he volunteered, he fought and died for his country – God Bless Him.'

Not until February 1943 was the former customs officer from Southampton, Dudley Heal, ready to fly operationally after almost exactly three years in uniform. Neither he nor Fraser could have imagined that they would soon be serving on the same squadron set to fly the Dambusters Raid. Heal's hopes of becoming a pilot had not been realised and, via Pensacola, in the United States, and Canada, he qualified as a navigator. In June 1942, he had reported to No. 3 Advance Flying Unit at Bobbington in Shropshire, where he came top of the course – something which would influence his immediate career. Heal moved on to No. 19 OTU at Kinloss on the Moray Firth, where he expected to join a crew. 'I had no idea how this crewing-up was done but I soon found out. A day or two after my arrival at the Station, I was walking through a hangar when three Canadians stopped me; a pilot, bomb aimer and gunner. "Your name Heal?" asked the pilot, a tall, well-built chap. "Yes," I said. "Then you're going to be our navigator," he said. I looked questioningly at him. "Who says so?" "I've just been to the Navigation Office", he replied. "You were top of your course at AFU so we want you to be our navigator." I looked at the other two, who were obviously in complete agreement with him. I liked the look of all of them and if I considered it at all my reaction would have been that here was someone who was interested in survival, which couldn't be bad. I agreed without further ado. His name was Ken Brown. We shook hands, he introduced the bomb aimer, Steve Oancia, and the rear gunner, Grant McDonald, and off we went to the Naafi for a cup of tea.'

Writing fifty years later, Heal reflected: 'I can honestly say that I never regretted that decision. We then acquired a wireless operator, Hughie Hewstone, and from that time on our being together as a crew was everything.'

At Kinloss, the five men perfected their skills flying a Whitley and moved on towards the end of October 1942 in the same type of aircraft to carry out anti-submarine daylight sweeps over the Bay of Biscay and the Atlantic attached to Coastal Command at St Eval in Cornwall. This posting, given that they were destined for Bomber Command, 'came as something of a surprise'. Brown and his crew were soon off to Wigsley HCU, though, where they learned to fly first the Manchester then its four-engine successor, the Lancaster. And they acquired a flight engineer and mid-upper gunner before joining 44 Squadron at RAF Waddington, Lincolnshire.

Like Brown and Munro, Gordon Carter (who in November 1942 had side-stepped his pilot's query about navigational accuracy) came from abroad. His was a less straightforward journey. An Englishman living in Bronxville, New York, he had enlisted in the RCAF as soon as he became eighteen in June 1941. The following year, he was posted to the Pathfinders shortly after their formation. A contemporary described him: 'Carter, the navigator, whom nobody understood, [was] tall, sleepy-looking, very dark, very handsome and very reserved . . . He was universally acclaimed the best navigator in the squadron.' Carter would have an eventful war. On 3 February 1943, he recorded: 'gun turrets frozen, compass U/S, undercarriage locked up.' The pilot executed a belly landing on a grass runway, which resulted in 'a long slide' from which, fortunately, the crew escaped unhurt. The very next night, in another aircraft, the guns again froze, 'the airspeed and rate of climb indicators' failed, the DR compass 'became U/S'. Once more, they survived.

Carter, however, was directly responsible for another

unpleasant episode. He inadvertently switched on the self-destructive device attached to the H2S set, which made sure that it exploded to prevent the Germans capturing it if the aircraft crashed. Carter's error meant that the equipment blew up in the air 'filling the aircraft with smoke and bits of bakelite and generally causing alarm and despondency among the crew'.

With many of the naval escorts withdrawn between November 1942 and April 1943 to cover the Operation Torch landings in north-west Africa, between 14 January and 6 April 1943 Bomber Command flew 3170 sorties against Brest, Lorient and St Nazaire.

Carter was involved in this mini-campaign. The crew of Halifax TL-B from 35 Squadron took off at 6.20 p.m. on 13 February 1943 to mark the naval base at Lorient in the van of 466 bombers about to mount the heaviest raid of the war there. Just after the target indicators had been released, Carter's aircraft was hit by flak and he saw the port inner engine catch fire. Thomas, the pilot, dived sharply to quell the flames. In vain. 'Bale out! Bale out! Bale out!' came the order. Carter snapped back his folding table and seat, clipped his parachute pack to the harness he wore and removed the escape hatch cover. Facing backwards, one boot was wrenched off in the slipstream as he sat on the forward edge of the hatch with his feet dangling in space. 'Navigator baling out', he said, and 'in the nick of time' remembered to take off his helmet with the attached intercom connection and oxygen supply tube, otherwise his head might have been ripped off as he fell. Gripping the ripcord handle in his right hand, he let go the left hand which was holding the rim of the hatch. His 'guts cramped with fear', and in his own words he 'vanished into 10,000ft of pitch black and void'.

As he left the Halifax, the tail fin flashed by and he pulled the ripcord. 'After a short moment of the worst anguish I have known in my life, I was suddenly totally delivered of it, swinging

115

softly and silently in the pale moonlit sky.' All of the crew initially survived to be picked up by members of the French Resistance. Unfortunately, though, the rear gunner, Flying Officer W. J. 'Bill' Freeman, was fatally injured when his parachute became entangled and he died shortly after midnight. Eventually, the pilot would reach Switzerland and be interned; the mid-upper gunner, wireless operator and bomb aimer got home via Spain. The flight engineer, however, was captured, and Carter endured a series of fairly hair-raising exploits.

Of this, his parents knew nothing. At 10.18 a.m. on 16 February in their Bronxville home they received a telegram informing them that Gordon Carter was missing in action. This was followed by standard advice: 'In the best interests of the possible safety of your son it is requested that you withhold any information from press or radio for five weeks from the date he is reported missing.' A large mirror had fallen and shattered in the family home on the day Carter was shot down, something which his mother had feared constituted a dreadful portent.

Over the following weeks, the families of the Halifax's crew exchanged anxious letter; the bomb aimer's mother wrote to the Carters: 'Though you are unknown and unseen I do feel that we together share a great burden.' Amid a number of official letters came one from the Air Ministry in London, enclosing a pamphlet, 'Advice to the relative of a man who is missing'. No doubt well intentioned, but somewhat impersonal.

In the meantime, Carter had been moving around northwest France by train, bicycle and on foot, his movements and shelter being orchestrated by the Resistance. Carter had one major advantage: having lived with his parents in Paris as a child, his French was fluent. So much so that he went to the town hall in Ploermel, claimed to have lost all his possessions during an Allied raid on Lorient and left with a replacement identity card in the name of Georges Charleroi, food and tobacco ration cards, clothing and shoe coupon books. Arrangements were made to take Carter off in a submarine, but they fell through. After an abortive trip to Paris, he then found himself back in Brittany in the care of Lucette Cougard and her husband Raymond in the village of Gourin, after a 20-kilometre cycle ride which would ultimately have a pivotal impact on his whole life. His companions and effective cover on that journey were Lucette's brother Georges and her younger sister Janine, 'an attractive blonde'. 'She was impressed by the fact . . . that I cycled at her speed and fixed her chain when it slipped.' Because the brother's introductions had been 'cursory', Carter was not sure which sister Janine was, 'but I was hoping against hope that she wasn't the married one'. His wish was granted, and 'so began a love affair and a companionship'.

For two weeks Carter stayed in Gourin, all the time wary about falling foul of the Austrian garrison. Carter went for long walks with Janine and when sitting on the grass to rest in the unseasonal sunshine on one occasion asked if he might kiss her. Her encouraging reply was that she was not used to being asked. When Janine went back to Carhaix, Carter risked capture to cycle there ('sheer madness', he later reflected), on one trip being stopped by a German soldier and asked the way to the military headquarters, which fortunately he knew. His time in Gourin was spiced up by the presence of the garrison commander being billeted across the street and having to greet him from time to time.

This was, however, a mere interlude in the business of war. A scheme was concocted to seize a new torpedo boat from Douarnenez harbour, with Carter disguised as an engineer. Janine was contacted and rushed back to Gourin by train, where Carter met her on the platform wearing a tie – their agreed signal that he was about to leave. Knowing that they might never meet again, as he left by car Carter's 'last glimpse

117

of Janine being of her leaning out of a ground-floor window with a wistful look about her'.

Instead of seizing a German motor torpedo boat, Carter actually sailed on 4 April aboard a small fishing vessel. It fooled the German harbour authorities, weathered a violent storm and was at length guided safely through a British minefield by a friendly fishing boat into a Cornish harbour. Two and a half months after taking off, Carter returned to RAF Graveley, Cambridgeshire, full of his new girlfriend whom, with a hint of exaggeration, he declared was his fiancée.

Back in the United States, Carter's parents had been waiting anxiously. On 22 March, the *New York Daily News* noted briefly that he had been reported missing and that same day another newspaper phoned his father and 'contemptibly told him that they had learned that I had been killed'. 'This was not the last despicable media call that my parents received', but they were buoyed by Carter's Service friends who wrote to them. On 10 April, a telegram arrived at the Carter home: 'Pleased to advise your son Flying Officer Gordon Henry Francis Carter has arrived safely United Kingdom.' The next day, a more personal one was delivered: 'Back again stop had a swell time sorry to have caused you grief happy birthday' (that of Carter's mother). On 19 April, the Casualties Officer wrote to Carter's father 'a kind letter', which ended 'joining with you and Mrs Carter in your joy in your son's safety'. As Carter remarked, 'the RCAF did things in style'.

While Carter criss-crossed northern France in March 1943, the bombing campaign had intensified. H2S had been used by the Pathfinders since January and on 1/2 March they took it to Berlin for the first time; four days later, Oboe was used against Essen, home of the vast Krupps armament works. Harris believed this raid to be 'easily the most important attack so far carried out by Bomber Command'. Led by thirty Pathfinders,

Fierce Combat

392 Lancaster, Halifax, Stirling and Wellington aircraft bombed; only fourteen were lost. Cheshire, who had completed sixty operations, had been given a ground appointment as station commander at Marston Moor, North Yorkshire, and did not take part. Nor did Gibson, but he agreed with Harris that the losses were 'incredibly small for the results achieved'. The *Sunday Express* was not so restrained: 'This was it. Three tons of bombs on Essen every four seconds for thirty-five minutes.' It concluded that this was 'the most outstanding show of the last six months and perhaps the heaviest and most concentrated air attack of the war'.

Harris declared the Essen raid of 5/6 March to be the beginning of the Battle of the Ruhr. The industrial complex, which sprawled around the junction of the Ruhr and Rhine rivers, had figured prominently in pre-war plans and been intermittently attacked for three years. Harris now determined to launch a coordinated assault against it. Between 5 March and 12 July, apart from Essen, Dortmund, Duisburg, Bochum, Mülheim and Wuppertal were among the targets against which individually up to seven hundred aircraft would be sent in a single night. However, the forty-three raids associated with this 'battle' were not confined to 'Happy Valley'; Nuremberg, Munich and Stuttgart, for example, were also visited. Partly this was to discourage the Germans from redeploying their defences to the Ruhr, if that were singled out for attention. Overall, 24,355 sorties were flown, costing 1038 aircraft with a further 2216 damaged or crashing in England.

By now, Bomber Command was aware that its new aids might not go unchallenged for long and of the need to be wary not only of interference but other more positive enemy countermeasures. What the Air Ministry scientist Dr R. V. Jones would dub 'The Most Secret War' basically involved stealing a march on the opposition and exploiting that advantage as long as possible. By spring 1943, the Germans had learnt to cope with Mandrel (aimed at neutralising Freya sets), though Tinsel (jamming ground to air communication) remained effective. Monica, a rear-facing radar mounted in a bomber to warn of an approaching fighter, unfortunately allowed the enemy aircraft to home in on its emissions; Boozer, a passive radar, did not have this disadvantage. An orange light showed up on the pilot's panel if a Würzburg gun-laying radar had locked on to the bomber, a red light if an airborne Lichtenstein had. However, not all fighters operating at night used radar and many which did switched them off when in visual contact with an incoming bomber. An unlit red bulb, therefore, did not always equal safety from interception. The Air Ministry's fear was that the enemy would sooner or later find one of the new aids in a crashed aircraft. On 2 February, the Germans had discovered an H2S set in a Stirling, but mercifully could not work out what it was. Otherwise, that piece of valuable equipment could have enjoyed a very short shelf life.

Les Munro, the New Zealand pilot, knew that many technical difficulties had still to be solved, despite the influx of new aids. Night operations were a lonely business and many might pass without another bomber being seen, nevertheless, 'when in the target area you knew and could sense the near presence of many other planes of the attacking force in your vicinity. On occasions their presence – particularly above you – would be signalled by the sight of bombs or incendiaries dropping around you.' Munro mused on the peril of such occurrences, recalling that once 'I had an incendiary go right though my fuselage without igniting – another case of Lady Luck being on my side during my operational career'. 'Strange as it may seem . . . even when major targets such as Berlin were badly hit and a mass of fires illuminated the sky it was not very often that I saw another one of our planes crossing the target area.'

Fierce Combat

Berlin was memorable, though, for more personal reasons. After releasing the bombs on one raid to the German capital, as the bomber turned for home Munro's wireless operator decided to leave his equipment and have a look at the proceedings through the astrodome. The sky behind was 'a mass of [flak] fire and searchlights waving everywhere.' He exclaimed 'to all and sundry': 'Jesus Christ! Have we come through that?' Munro observed this was a good example of 'what you can't see you don't worry about'. On 1/2 March a somewhat bizarre sequence of events occurred during another Berlin op, involving 302 aircraft. After bombing, Munro duly set the course given to him by his navigator, but immediately sensed something was wrong. This course would take him south-east of Berlin, whereas he remembered that the route given at briefing for the first leg after bombing was to the south-west. Twice he queried the direction as his Lancaster ploughed steadily onwards in splendid isolation towards Poland. Suddenly an apologetic voice came over the intercom explaining that the course was some 90 degrees out. It was the only mistake that Jock Rumbles ever made. Munro thought him 'a bloody good navigator', an integral and invaluable member of the crew: 'It never affected my confidence in his ability on all our subsequent trips together.'

The American bombing of Germany had not started smoothly. The low loss rate in 1942 had largely been achieved because fighters accompanied the heavy bombers. But the distances involved now meant that protection could only be given for a short while over enemy territory, roughly to the German border. Thereafter, the bombers were on their own until they reached the same area on the return trip. During February 1943 the 8th USAAF had lost twenty-two bombers from an average available strength of seventy-four crews, a most worrying figure. But on 18 March, first use of the Automatic Flight Control Equipment (AFCE), which allowed the bombardier (bomb aimer) to fly an aircraft during the bombing run, proved highly successful against Vegesack, where ninety-seven B-17s and B-24s caused 'extremely heavy damage' by bombing accurately and only two aircraft were lost. Major General Ira C. Eaker, commander of the 8th USAAF, declared that this was 'a successful conclusion to long months of experimentation in daytime, high-level precision bombing. After Vegesack comes a new chapter.' On 12 April, he drew up the Eaker Plan for the destruction of 'the three major elements of the German military machine: its submarine fleet, its air force and its ground forces, and certain industries vital to their support'.

During April, Bomber Command introduced an operational technique used in conjunction with Oboe which would be employed for the rest of the war. Pathfinder aircraft equipped with it would drop target indicators and illuminating flares, to be followed immediately by aircraft visually dropping more target indicators of a different colour. A third group of 'backers-up' would then release still further target indicators to ensure that main force bombers behind could quickly identify the target. Although it could be used for longer-range targets, H2S was never so accurate as Oboe, controlled as it was from ground stations in England.

Flying Officer Gordon Carter would be in one of the Pathfinder crews to follow this system. In April 1943, he was back in training with Flight Lieutenant E. W. 'Dipper' Deacon, an older, pre-war regular pilot. Apart from Carter, Deacon's crew were 'sprogs – green'. 'It says a lot for him, senior in so many respects as he was, to have agreed to place his life in our inexpert hands.'

Carter very nearly did not survive to return to operations, however. On 5 May he was detailed to check out a 'rookie crew' in a daylight target location exercise aimed at London. They arrived over the capital just as several batteries of anti-aircraft guns opened up on German bombers engaged in a nuisance raid. The pilot reacted swiftly, putting his machine into a steep dive. 'That the aircraft's tail wasn't wrenched off as we pulled out of the dive for all we were worth speaks well for the Halifax's airframe. So much for training flights over friendly territory.' On 23 May, Carter flew the first of twenty-three operations with Deacon's 'stalwart' crew.

That same month, Fying Officer Frank Blackman illustrated the hopes and thoughts of a navigator awaiting operations, when writing to his girlfriend Mary Mileham on 2 May. 'We are resting in a really beautiful garden this Sunday afternoon ready for a possible raid tonight, and I suppose somewhat naturally in such surroundings on such a lovely day, one's thoughts turn to the sweet things of life. Truly this moment is so peaceful that the prospect of the next few hours seems like an evil dream.' Everybody, he felt, needed 'some little dream tucked away in his mind. Without it existence for most of us would be a barren experience.' Blackman made clear that his dream involved 'somebody to idolise and love': Mary. She would figure prominently in his life and career in the coming months, their relationship typical of so many other wartime romances.

The most striking example of crew cooperation in 1943, and possibly the entire war, concerned the Dambusters Raid, carried out during the night of 16/17 May. No. 617 Squadron was formed in March 1943 specifically to drop Barnes Wallis's 'bouncing bomb' on seven German dams. Some of its original twenty-two crews – reduced to twenty-one during the training process – had flown together before, including those of Canadian Flight Sergeant Ken Brown. The flight engineer, Sergeant Basil Feneron, recalled that Brown was at pains to ensure the newcomers fitted in quickly and took every opportunity to run through drill and procedures. Posted to 44 Squadron, the crew had completed only six operations over the

Continent when Brown announced that they were moving to Scampton. 'I protested,' said Feneron; to no avail. The bomb aimer, Sergeant Steve Oancia, later recollected that he did 'not recall volunteering for this transfer'.

This crew had been assured at Waddington that it would be 'the backbone' of its new squadron. On arrival, the Cockney wireless operator and 'old man' at thirty-two, Flight Sergeant Hughie Hewstone, surveyed the assembly of experienced crews and turned to his pilot: 'If we're the backbone of this outfit, I reckon we're close to the a***hole.'

One of the crews Hewstone referred to was that of the Australian Flight Sergeant Les Knight, which had almost finished a tour with 50 Squadron. Knight's wireless operator, Sergeant Bob Kellow, summed up its reaction: 'The offer presented to us sounded interesting and with our faith in each member's ability, we made up our minds there and then that we would accept the offer and move over as a crew to this new squadron . . . We were a mixed bunch with implicit faith in Les, our pilot, and confidence in each other.'

Other crews had to be completed and in at least one case put together from scratch. Munro lacked a regular bomb aimer and his rear gunner declined to come, so he picked up the final two members of his crew when 617 Squadron assembled. Sergeant Bill Townsend's wireless operator similarly refused to come, and he got a replacement at Scampton, Sergeant George Chalmers. Unlike Francis Drake, summoned to face the Spanish Armada from a bowling green, Chalmers, a pre-war regular, was playing snooker at a conversion unit when informed of his posting to 617 Squadron. His pilot also reached Scampton in an unorthodox fashion. As a boy, he had 'the firm intention of joining the Indian Army', and donned khaki when called up in January 1941. He did not enjoy basic training and responded to a notice calling for volunteer navigators and pilots for Army Co-operation

Command. 'I never had a yen to fly. It just seemed a better proposition than route marches and square-bashing.' After qualifying as a pilot, Townsend did not return to the army. He had completed twenty-eight operations when the commanding officer of 49 Squadron asked him to join a new squadron for 'special duties'. 'I had a clue that the missions were likely to be difficult, because I was told that a tour with the new squadron would consist of five operations instead of the usual thirty'. He accepted the challenge, as did five of his crew.

Flight Lieutenant David Shannon, who arrived via the Pathfinders, was another pilot to complete his crew at Scampton, in an even less orthodox manner. Flight Sergeant Len Sumpter (a bomb aimer and former Grenadier guardsman who had retrained for aircrew) and Sergeant R. J. Henderson (a flight engineer) from 57 Squadron, whose pilot had been grounded for medical reasons, heard that 'an Aussie' on the new squadron was looking to fill those positions. So, in Sumpter's words, 'we wandered over to see him'. The meeting proved mutually satisfactory, and Sumpter would begin a long association with Shannon which culminated in flying as his bomb aimer/navigator in a Mosquito during Leonard Cheshire's later low-level marking operations.

The new squadron's commander Wing Commander Guy Gibson, veteran of two bomber tours and ninety-nine nightfighter operations, had to put together a completely new crew, although the wireless operator Flight Lieutenant R. E. G. (Bob) Hutchison had frequently flown with him on 106 Squadron. The navigator, Pilot Officer Taerum, was the Canadian son of an immigrant Norwegian farmer. His mother explained: 'When Norway was invaded by the Germans and reports began to filter through of the manner in which his father's people were being treated, Harlo enlisted in the RCAF'. Before joining Gibson, Taerum had completed a tour on Hampdens and instructed navigators in the art of operating Gee at an HCU. Writing home, Taerum explained: 'We got on to the Squadron. I'd never met Wing Commander Gibson before. So this was a new experience.' Gibson's front gunner was another Canadian, Flight Sergeant George Deering. Curiously, Gibson would later and quite unjustifiably refer to him as a 'sprog'. In reality, he had already completed a tour of operations, been an instructor at an OTU and, unknown in March 1943, been promoted pilot officer the previous month.

Unlike Munro, Flight Lieutenant Joe McCarthy (the giant, blond American who had joined the RCAF before Pearl Harbor) came from Woodhall Spa with his whole crew. Having completed a tour of operations, the crew members were due for leave, but they agreed to go to Scampton for one more raid. A domestic squabble, however, nearly spoiled the plot. His bomb aimer, Sergeant George Johnson, was due to be married, and his fiancée Gwyneth issued an ultimatum: 'If you're not here on 3 April, don't bother to come at all.' Diplomatically, McCarthy intervened and secured four days' leave for the entire crew.

The Johnsons would soon experience the difficulties of married life in wartime. Although a WAAF, Service regulations prevented Gwyneth from being posted to the same station as her husband, so she found herself instead at nearby RAF Hemswell. Occasionally, during the training period, they would meet in Lincoln, then catch their respective last buses back to the different airfields at 9 p.m. In theory. George mused, 'I seemed invariably to end up on the one from Lincoln to Hemswell, which meant walking back the eight miles from Hemswell to Scampton afterwards. What love does . . .'

Even those crews which had only recently been formed quickly developed camaraderie and keenness to excel. Munro explained that 'occasionally two or three planes would be arriving back from perhaps a cross-country flight, and before we knew what was happening, the pilots would be chasing one another. They'd see a plane arriving back in the distance and they would be trying to get on its tail . . . tight turns and high speed manoeuvres at low level.' Crews had to master a range of extraordinary techniques, with time the essence. The operation required moonlight. Its success also depended upon striking the dams before the water level in their reservoirs was too low for 'Upkeep' (the codename for Wallis's weapon set to explode 30ft below the surface) to be effective. The twenty-sixth of May, later amended to 19 May, was the last possible date for Operation Chastise.

Upkeep would have to be released a set distance from each dam wall and at right angles to it – with one exception, which required a different approach. Making use of the distance between two towers on the major dams, a triangular wooden sight was devised for bomb aimers. Looking through a peep-hole, they would release the weapon at the point where two nails at the extremity of the base coincided with the towers. This method was tried out against two cricket sightscreens mounted on the Wainfleet bombing range at the Wash and two canvas screens erected on the dam of the Eyebrook reservoir near Corby in Northamptonshire. At this point, crews had no inkling that they would be carrying a large garden roller (50in. in diameter, $59^7/_8$in. in length) which would be spinning before release. In practice, as the height of release was reduced from 150ft to 60ft, many bomber aimers found it difficult to hold the triangular sight steady in one hand at such low altitude amid the inevitable turbulence, while preparing to release the weapon with the other. Crew ingenuity took over. Navigators in some crews, including McCarthy's and Knight's, worked out a more stable system. Employing the same triangular method to determine the release point (450ft from the target with a tolerance of 25ft each side), they put two chinagraph marks on the clear

127

vision panel in front of the bomb aimer and calculated the length of string attached to the panel's retaining butterfly nuts. The bomb aimer simply held the string to his eye and dropped Upkeep when the chinagraph marks coincided with the two towers. Not every crew used this method; some retained the wooden sight. All crews, therefore, worked out the best way for them to achieve success, the result of discussion and cooperation between their navigator and bomb aimer.

Those two crew members worked together in another crucial way, and, again, different crews agreed on the method which suited them. The route to the target would be flown at a maximum of 100ft to avoid radar detection and fighter interception. Each bomb aimer, relieved of his normal duty to man the front gun during an operation, would be issued with maps to advise the navigator and the pilot of dangers such as high-tension wires, low hills and buildings ahead. In some crews, including Gibson's, the bomb aimer had his maps connected on a sort of toilet roll contraption. But Canadian Flight Sergeant Don MacLean in McCarthy's Lancaster was among those bomb aimers who reasoned that this would be dangerous if the aircraft strayed off track. He therefore opted for folded maps on which the route had been clearly marked.

The Lancasters would not only fly out at 100ft but be restricted to 180mph, because of the single, cumbersome 9250lb. missile dangling beneath the bomb bay. To gain the necessary 220mph ground speed for the attack, determined by the flight engineer during the bombing run, the pilot must dive from approximately 2000ft, something which had to be practised constantly over Scampton's grass runway.

Aldis lamps were fitted in the front camera slot (from which other equipment was removed) and in the rear of the bomb bay (whose doors had been taken off to accommodate Upkeep). They were angled to meet in a figure of eight in front of the leading edge of the starboard wing. It was the navigator's job to advise the pilot when their beams settled in this position, indicating that the aircraft was flying at 60ft. Furthermore, the weapon had to be backspun at 500 revolutions per minute ten minutes before the Lancaster began its attack run. The wireless operator, who, like the navigator, had by then left his normal position, used a gauge mounted on the fuselage floor and attached to a motor utilising hydraulic power usually employed to operate the bomb bay doors. With this, he ensured that the requisite number of revolutions occurred.

The cooperation of all members of each crew was thus essential for this unique, specialised operation, which one high-ranking German official would declare 'precision bombing of a high order' after its completion. At the Sorpe, where the attack took place along the top of the dam rather than at right angles to it, the bomb aimer had to make sure that the unspun Upkeep was dropped in the centre of the dam. It would then roll down the side of the earth support to the central concrete core on the water side and explode, as at the other dams, 30ft below the surface.

During the operation, three aircraft aborted due to mechanical problems. The rear turret of Flight Sergeant Cyril Anderson's Lancaster malfunctioned and Pilot Officer Geoff Rice flew so low over the Zuider Zee that he knocked Upkeep off, to the extreme discomfort of his rear gunner. He was swamped by a combination of water and the contents of the Elsan toilet, which poured down the fuselage as his pilot pulled up steeply. His mild expletive over the intercom – 'Christ, it's wet at the back here' – could be forgiven. More seriously, without the weapon Rice had no choice but to turn back soon after crossing the enemy coast.

Les Munro had a more difficult decision to make. His Lancaster was hit by enemy flak as he crossed the island of

Vlieland off the Dutch coast, but the extent of its impact did not become clear until well over the Waddenzee. The intercom had been put out of action, the master compass, rear turret and wireless equipment damaged. Munro decided that, on such a low-level operation, unable either to contact other aircraft or to receive flying instructions from his navigator, he had no option but to turn back. It was the captain's decision and, given the extent of the damage, inevitable, but he sought information from the crew before making up his mind. With mist swirling around the lakes and river valleys, approaching his Ennepe Dam target at 3 a.m. on Monday 17 May, Bill Townsend would consult his crew about target identification and, like Munro, base his decision upon the information they supplied. Sergeant Doug Webb, his front gunner, had unstinting praise for Townsend that night: 'The best pilot I ever flew with in every way. If it had not been for the absolutely superb flying Bill put in, simply by going lower and lower, we would not have survived.'

Eight aircraft were lost, two on the way home. In that of Squadron Leader H. M. Young, shot down as it crossed the Dutch coast tantalisingly close to the comparative safety of the North Sea, it was the thirty-third birthday of Sergeant Lawrence Nichols, the wireless operator. Two of the missing pilots, according to the testimony of survivors, and quite possibly two others, tried to save the lives of their crews when a crash became unavoidable. Evidently hit by flak and having struck power lines, Flight Lieutenant Norman Barlow appears to have attempted a pancake landing almost certainly because the aircraft was too low for the crew to bale out. The same may be true of Flight Lieutenant Bill Astell, whose Lancaster also came down after hitting power lines. Detached from the aircraft, Upkeep exploded some distance from the site of the bomber's crash. It seems feasible that Astell ordered release of the bomb prior to attempting to crash-land the Lancaster. When his Lancaster was fatally damaged at the Möhne dam, Flight Lieutenant John Hopgood valiantly struggled to get his stricken machine high enough for three of his crew to get out, two of whom survived. Pilot Officer Bill Ottey, who had chosen to join 617 Squadron with his crew from Pathfinders when he heard Gibson was to command it, ran into flak near Hamm. Like Hopgood he made every effort to gain height, but the last words his rear gunner Sergeant Fred Tees heard before the crash, which he survived with third degree burns, were: 'Sorry, boys, we've had it.'

Flying Officer Charles Williams, Australian wireless operator in Barlow's Lancaster, was not one of the three survivors that night. The account of his time with 617 Squadron, contained in correspondence with Gwen Parfitt, who worked for the Naafi in Nottingham, and his own diary, is both professionally revealing and personally moving. He had met Gwen (whom he addressed as Bobbie) while flying with Barlow from RAF Syerston, Lincolnshire. Williams reached Scampton at 1 p.m. on 7 April, Barlow's crew being one of the last to arrive on the station. 'Things are a bit of a mess here' with severe overcrowding and a gale blowing 'with dust flying everywhere', he wrote. Williams already knew that the Squadron would not be flying operationally for 'at least a month' and that 'quite a lot of practice' lay ahead.

The following day, 8 April, Williams wrote that he had not yet found his feet, but warned Bobbie not to ask any questions: 'They are very tough on security and one has to be very careful what one writes or speaks over the phone.' He realised that Barlow's crew was 'well behind' the others: 'We'll have to do more than our share to catch up.' Unfortunately, therefore, he could not guarantee to meet her if she travelled to Lincoln, because he never knew when the crew would be flying by day or night. 'Writing to you seems to relieve my feelings, and I do not feel so lonely when I have written a page or two.' He promised to try to ring the next day.

Williams was soon reporting that he had met another Australian, Flight Lieutenant Jack Leggo, who remembered her 'as a pretty kid'. 'I agree,' he added. He revealed the perils of flying 'fairly low', in noting that their aircraft had run 'into a flock of birds, some of which came through the windscreen of the plane and caused the pilot to lose control of the plane for a few seconds and we hit the top of a tree, but it did not do any damage and we were able to continue our journey'. On 12 April, Williams did manage to get to Nottingham to see Gwen, but she had 'a nasty cold'. Six days later, he announced that at last he had 'a decent room' and could unpack. The 'mess' he encountered on 7 April had been sorted out. Many aircrew composed poems for their loved ones, Williams being no exception. He ended this letter with one to Gwen.

Despite the unpredictable hours, discipline remained tight. On 22 April Williams admitted to being 'clipped' by his flight commander for not shaving. He had been late getting up after night flying and did not have the opportunity at lunchtime. Six days later, he wrote that he had put Gwen's good luck charm on his chain 'with the other gadgets . . . One brought me through one tour. I should have no trouble getting through the second one with two more added to the collection.' There had been 'quite a heavy storm' the previous night, with pouring rain and 'a lot of thunder'. Flying, he emphasised, depended very much on the unpredictable weather of an English spring. It did not prevent Squadron personnel having to do 'a lot of cleaning up' on the ground in preparation for a visit from the Group commander on 29 April. In the event, the parade for Air Vice-Marshal the Hon. R. A. Cochrane occurred on a frosty morning with no gloves allowed to warm frozen hands.

Fierce Combat

Returning from a forty-eight-hour pass, unbeknown to him the last he would enjoy, on 5 May Williams expressed a disturbing sense of foreboding: 'I feel deep, dark and depressed and distrustful. I certainly do feel thrilled and excited, and am looking forward to the day [of the operation], but when the day comes I shall most likely feel somewhat nervous, but I will have to overcome that.' He concluded: 'No one wishes that the war was over more than I do.'

On 6 May he informed Bobbie that the C-in-C Bomber Command, Harris, had visited the squadron, and the following day he had missed lunch, having to go to another 'aerodrome on the south-east coast', possibly Manston in Kent from which the final Upkeep trials would soon be flown.

Williams' letter on 11 May was, in retrospect, heart-rending. He had suddenly become free to go to Nottingham the previous evening, could not contact Gwen on the phone and had travelled to their usual rendezvous, the Nag's Head in the hope of seeing her. He sat there nursing a pint of beer, turning his head each time the door opened, only to be disappointed. Williams went back to Scampton 'like a balloon that had been pricked', and admitted to being reluctant to call at her house for some unexplained reason fearing her mother's reaction. He learnt, by return post, that Gwen had been at home all that evening. In his letter of 11 May, Williams explained that he had 'bad news' from home, a cable informing him his father was in hospital. That day the crew had 'rather a long trip' and he was therefore 'rather tired'.

Williams did not know that the Dambusters Raid now lay only three days away. He apologised for not being able to speak to Gwen when she phoned on 13 May; 'but I am away at all hours of the day and I can never say when I will be here'. 'Must go and work again', he signed off. On Friday 14 May, they did manage to make contact on the phone, the last time they would speak. In thanking her for ringing, Williams wrote: 'I will do my best to get in on Sunday. I am looking forward to having a day off.' He added that the weather was so warm that everybody was now in shirtsleeves. There was no further information about his father, so he assumed all was well.

At 5.30 p.m. on Saturday 15 May, Williams began his penultimate letter. He thanked Bobbie for an 'interesting and amusing long letter'. Clearly, though, there had been serious passages as well. 'It is certainly disgusting to hear of the bus drivers being on strike when everyone should be doing all they can to assist the war effort.' 'I will try and ring you tomorrow but I know there is no possible chance of my getting in.' He wrote that his pilot, Norman Barlow, was 'very thrilled' at being awarded the DFC after 'thirty-two successful trips'. Williams' letter contained sobering sections: 'What a strain we are under the whole time without the actual operations . . . our nerves are bad at times . . . [we] cannot help being depressed when some of them [friends] fail to return'. 'I can see that if I don't get in to see you soon you will forget me and find another one.'

The next day, Sunday 16 May, Williams learnt that the operation was on that night. Barlow's was destined to be the very first Lancaster to take off at 9.28 p.m. Double British Summer Time as the sun set after a boiling hot day. While he waited to leave, at 7.30 p.m. Williams wrote his last letter to Gwen, one full of doomed hope. He apologised for neither getting to Nottingham nor phoning her: 'I am almost sure I will be in Monday or Tuesday night, but will phone you and try to let you know.' When he did see her, he would explain why he could not get away sooner. For the past two weeks it had been 'absolutely impossible' to do so, except for the night when he failed to find her. There was 'quite a chance that I may get leave sooner than I expect . . . I will have a lot to tell you when I do see you.'

Fierce Combat

That promise would never be fulfilled. At 11.50 p.m., Barlow's Lancaster crashed near the Rhine 5 kilometres east of Rees on its way to the Sorpe Dam. There were no survivors. On 20 July 1945, in a rather macabre example of administrative lassitude, and more than two years after his death, Williams was awarded the DFC for his time with 61 Squadron, 'effective from 15 May 1943'.

On 20 May 1943, 617 Squadron adjutant Flight Lieutenant H. R. Humphries, in answer to her request, undertook to send Gwen Parfitt the address of Charles Williams' mother. Gwen later recalled 'in that fateful May of 1943' Williams had asked her to marry him and she had accepted. That is why, in an explanatory note attached to their correspondence, she is described as his fiancée. Fate decreed that she would not be in the Nag's Head on the last day he could have met her. Significantly, during their correspondence he enthused about the ability of his skipper, 'the same Norman Barlow' with whom he had flown so often and taken part 'in the big Berlin raid', and who appears to have made a final desperate effort to save his crew in the dying minutes of Sunday 16 May 1943.

Flight Sergeant John Fraser, the Canadian bomb aimer, survived Hopgood's crash at the Möhne Dam. Recalled from leave in April 1943 to join 617 Squadron, like George Johnson in McCarthy's crew, he managed to get leave to marry – in his case, just one day. On 15 April, he had written to his mother: 'And so the war goes on – just a year ago yesterday I landed on this foreign soil and first heard murmurs of pounds, shillings and pence over shop counters, saw cars driving on the wrong side of the road – today these differences plus hundreds of other oddities have become quite familiar.' He had just completed his tour of operations and was set to go on seven days' leave 'with Doris – she's going to get a few days off at the same time'. 'To leave the squadron now is just like leaving school after grade

135

12 – we all know the boys – the mess is just like home and to go away . . . [is] just like starting out on your first job.'

After their marriage, his wife Doris (née Wilkinson) from Doncaster did not see Fraser for two years. She received the formal telegram and follow-up letter after her new husband went missing, but not until a card arrived from him did she know he was alive. Thereafter, she wrote regularly and Fraser later told her that letters were censored by the Germans, with news of Allied victories in particular cut out. There was some practical compensation for Fraser's time in captivity. On release, he learnt that he had progressively been promoted to flight lieutenant, which meant a welcome rise in his expected back pay.

The family of Fraser's pilot, John Vere Hopgood, did not receive such encouraging news. He had perished in the crash near Ostönnen north of the Möhne Dam. After leaving Marlborough, Hopgood secured a place at Corpus Christi, Cambridge, to read Law, which he did not take up before joining the RAF. A cultured man, Hopgood played the piano and oboe, but the strain of operations became evident to his parents and two sisters. His nicotine-stained fingers disclosed an acquired habit of chain smoking, which worried his mother. Taxed about this by his solicitor father, he replied that it did not matter as he would not live through the war. His parents in particular were devastated by the loss of their only son; his sisters confirmed that Hopgood always had a high regard for his crew. Their brother's selfless action did undoubtedly save the lives of two of his crew, Fraser and the rear gunner, Burcher.

The Australian Pilot Officer Tony Burcher had grabbed a supply of malted milk tablets, sent by his mother from home, before takeoff that night. He heard the commotion in the cockpit over the intercom, discovered that he could not mechanically operate his turret so manually turned it to gain access to the fuselage and his parachute. His only exit then was via the rear door. Hopgood's last words, as Burcher reported that he was preparing to jump, were: 'For Christ's sake get out of here.' Burcher badly damaged his back on the tailplane and appreciated too late the official warning not to exit that way. As he lay immobile on his injured back, he quietly sucked the malt tablets while awaiting capture. He had been due to marry Joan Barnes in two weeks, and the wedding would now be postponed for two years until his release from prison camp. Of Hopgood, he said: 'He was a man out of this world, the way he chose to go on', referring to the pilot having been wounded and the Lancaster damaged on the way to the Möhne Dam. Of the crew, he opined, 'we weren't what you'd call buddies, but we did what we were sent to do', an example of off-duty socialising not being mandatory for an efficient crew.

Thirty-four of the Dambuster survivors were decorated, including Gibson who received the VC. Congratulatory telegrams had been sent from Harris to all the recipients, who were on leave, on 23 May. Suspecting a practical joke, Sergeant Doug Webb telephoned Scampton for confirmation, then found 'a shop round the corner' with a DFM ribbon. Dudley Heal opened the door to the telegraph boy at his parents' home in Alverstoke, Hampshire. Opening the buff envelope, 'I was flabbergasted. "Why me?", I thought.' It didn't stop him and his father visiting the Gosport branch of the British Legion to celebrate that evening. Taerum learnt of his award at Scampton, as he explained to his mother: 'One morning they woke me up and told me that I had been awarded the DFC. Later I had a ribbon sewn on my tunic. Can you imagine me strutting around town with it afterwards?' The citation for Len Sumpter's DFM contained a significant passage, which highlighted the role of the crew as a whole: '. . . with great skill and determination they succeeded in dropped their mine in exactly the right position. This was due to the excellent spirit and understanding of the crew.' It was significant that Heal, learning that he, the pilot and bomb aimer were to be decorated, recorded: 'We three were a little unhappy that the other members of the crew, who had faced the same dangers and done everything that was required of them had nothing to show for it.'

During the royal visit on 27 May, Taerum explained to his mother: 'I was really lucky as I was introduced to both the King and Queen. The Queen is most charming and gracious. It was really quite a day.' That applied especially to Australian Pilot Officer Lance Howard, whose pilot was indisposed. He therefore had to introduce the crew to Their Majesties. This was captured on camera and duly appeared in newsreel programmes. Back home his proud wife Marjorie, by her own admission, 'dragged my friends round every cinema to see Lance on screen'.

A painful illustration of what the loss of an airman from this or any other operation meant to a family was provided in the adjutant's office shortly after the casualties were known. The mother of a missing sergeant, 'a frail middle-aged lady, holding back her tears', explained that he was her only son and repeatedly posed an unanswerable question: 'Did he suffer?'

In an interview, Gibson's wife Eve admitted to being 'worried all the time when they go out on their raids. You don't know whether they are going to return or not . . . If my husband's efforts and all the boys in the Services with him can bring this war to a close quickly, so much the better.'

Harris considered the Dambusters Raid 'a major victory in the Battle of the Ruhr', an integral part of that effort. But it had significance far beyond this. At long last, as proved by the post-operational reconnaissance photographs published widely in the press, Gibson and his crews had demonstrated that RAF bombers could strike precision targets with accuracy. AVM Cochrane, AOC 5 Group, used the results to encourage all his squadrons to put the dark days of the Butt Report behind them and strive for such perfection. Ivan Whittaker, Flight Lieutenant H. B. 'Mick' Martin's flight engineer on the raid, agreed that it proved 'a great milestone in the standard it set'. James Robertson, a school contemporary of Gibson, summarised the feelings of many: 'a tremendous uplift after so many defeats'; an RAF Intelligence Officer, Flight Lieutenant G. E. Pine, thought it 'marvellous, terrific . . . just like Winston Churchill's speeches'. In an international context, both Stalin and Roosevelt expressed their delight at the outcome of Operation Chastise. Newspapers and wireless stations throughout the world, especially in the Commonwealth and United States, enthused about the raid. Speaking to the American joint Houses of Congress three days later, Churchill highlighted it to a standing ovation.

This success came hard on the heels of news that Axis forces had finally been defeated in North Africa; with control of the Mediterranean, the Allies were about to invade southern Europe and, after raising of the siege of Stalingrad, the Soviets were pressing westwards in strength to recapture the Ukraine. There were, though, still dark spots. In March 1943, 477,000 tons of shipping had been sunk by U-boats in the northern Atlantic and, as yet, only Allied bombers could exert direct pressure on Germany itself.

The conduct of the bombing campaign were therefore closely addressed in June 1943. Fully aware that, despite the bomber onslaught, German aircraft production had almost doubled in the preceding nine months and that command of the air had not yet been achieved, staff officers drew up the Pointblank Plan, which was communicated to Bomber Command in a directive on 10 June. Essentially, this was a refinement of the Casablanca Directive's overall aims, which the Air Ministry had outlined on 21 January 1943 and whose central thrust of undermining industrial production and civilian morale was restated: 'Unless this increase in fighter strength is checked we may find our bomber forces unable to fulfil the tasks allotted to them.' So 'the first priority' of British and American bombers in the United Kingdom 'shall be accorded to the attack of German fighter forces and the industry upon which they depend'.

Harris resisted attempts to force the RAF into attacking specific targets like aircraft assembly plants and ball-bearing factories, which, experience taught him, could not be picked out at night. He settled for Bomber Command's 'main aim' as 'the general disorganisation of German industry' with action 'designed as far as practicable to be complimentary to the operations of the [American] 8th Air Force'. This may have been a form of words crafted to authorise business as usual, but it did mean that Harris must at least appear to launch more attacks on targets connected with the aircraft industry.

During the night of 20/21 June, a raid by sixty Lancasters on the former Zeppelin factory at Friedrichshafen, which was now making Würzburg radar sets, saw two initiatives. Repeating the technique used by Gibson to direct individual aircraft at the Möhne and Eder dams, a 'master bomber' directed the operation in the target area. And to confuse the Germans further, instead of returning to England the bombers flew on to North Africa – the first shuttle operation of this type in the European theatre. No Lancaster was lost.

Questions of operational planning were far from the minds of individual aircrew. At a personal level, continuing his correspondence with Mary Mileham, Pilot Officer Frank Blackman fretted at both the length and nature of his continuing navigator training. He apologised for not always being 'at my best' during phone conversations, but expressed his gratitude to Mary for calling him. He felt better able to convey his thoughts and feelings in writing. Thus, in a letter of 10 June, he confessed to being 'not altogether looking forward to the next month. At these conversion units I believe spare time is negligible – and with no chance of leave for the whole month or so with the possibility of P. T. battle courses, lots of parades – in general the sort of fuss we thought we had left behind. Also somewhat naturally the kites are anything but new, which makes things even more of a lottery.' A week later, he complained that he had to wait two hours to use the phone and then could not get through to her.

Blackman's letter of 20 June opened with another dose of depression: 'This is one of those grey afternoons when having nothing to do, I can sit and think of peacetime and all the pleasant things I would rather be doing'. 'Not that this is such a good idea, perhaps', he went on, 'as not only does it make me resent the war, but fills me all the more with the desire to be with you.' He was acutely aware that they had not yet been to a concert with one another: 'To listen to good music together is one of the complete forms of communion', and he described part of his record collection, including a piece played by Yehudi Menuhin.

His mood of introspection continued in another letter ten days later: 'I have been trying to analyse my own state of mind,' he explained. 'Since you opened once again my eyes to such boundless happiness, I have hated this war more even than at any time since it began.' He hoped that 'almost all of us' might have a 'dream which one might try and fulfil but for this wretched, stupid war'. Not exactly the words of an intrepid warrior, but as he admitted 'those grey thoughts which one tries to keep in the background'. My 'fear is not of dying . . . but the fear of losing the good things of life', an illustration of the strain which war service could impose on a sensitive airman.

Australian Sergeant Jack Bormann, also under training in June 1943, underlined the importance of receiving letters, noting in his diary the number that came each day and from whom. On 20 June, after getting a 'letter from Dad', he visited London, finding the 'East End appalling' and going to the show *Random Harvest* before returning to his unit. Four days later, he wrote despondently: 'No letters today am disappointed.' Like Blackman, he did not find training invigorating.

The task of the bomber crews had been eased by the establishment of a third Oboe ground station in England, and eighteen aircraft carrying the device could now be put over a target in one hour. Harris had condemned the standard bombsight, which required an aircraft to fly straight and level for so long that 'the risk was altogether excessive'. The new Mark XIV sight he believed much safer, as it could be used to release bombs when a machine was climbing or turning. The irreverent dubbed it 'all singing, all dancing', but it was without doubt a positive acquisition. So was Window.

The thin strips of tinfoil were designed to neutralise enemy radar transmissions on which fighter controllers, flak posts and searchlight positions relied for guidance and information. The idea of Window had first been mooted in 1937, but its development took a long time and when it did become available there was reluctance to use it in case the Germans copied the tactic. However, Harris argued that: 'The Command has nothing to lose and possibly much to gain', estimating that losses could be reduced by a third. Eventually it was agreed that Window could be employed once the amphibious landings on Sicily (accomplished on 9 July) had taken place, when Churchill stridently overrode persistent objections: 'Let us open the window.'

On the night of 24/25 July 1943, therefore, in a cloudless sky with only a slight haze after a scorching few days, Window made its operational debut over Hamburg with spectacular success. Germany's second largest city lay 55 miles from the mouth of the Elbe, along whose banks were shipyards, docks, oil refineries and factories. Bomber Command believed that 'the total destruction of this city would achieve immeasurable results in reducing the industrial capacity of the enemy's war machine . . . [and] would play a very important part in shortening and winning the war'.

The defences of the German port, which had so far survived 137 raids without serious damage and was beyond Oboe range, were formidable; they included an estimated fifty-four flak batteries, twenty-four searchlight positions, besides smoke-generators, decoy fires and night fighters. All of this counted for nothing once Window had been deployed. Bundles were dropped at set intervals on the way to, over and away from the target. Intercepted radio signals revealed the extent of confusion on the ground ('I cannot follow any of the hostiles – they are very cunning') and in the air ('What's happening down there? I'm chasing my tail'). Searchlights could be seen weaving aimlessly as flak gunners hopefully pumped fifty thousand rounds of ammunition upwards without direction. Kammhuber admitted that 'the whole defence was blinded at one stroke'.

Operation Gomorrah involved 791 aircraft. Shortly before 1a.m. on 25 July, twenty Pathfinders using H2S dropped yellow, followed by others visually releasing yellow and still more green target indicators. From the main force, 728 then bombed for forty-six minutes and only twelve bombers were lost. In daylight on 25 and 26 July, American bombers carried out follow-up raids, and during the night of 25/26 six Mosquitoes further harassed the defences. Then 787 RAF heavy bombers attacked on 27/28 July, 722 of which dropped their loads on fires still smouldering from the previous raids. This time there was a difference: a firestorm engulfed 22 square metres of the city, creating temperatures estimated to be over 1000 degrees centigrade as the air sucked up by the conflagration caused a tornado of flame and smoke. Still more raids occurred on 29/30 July (777 aircraft) and 2/3 August (740 aircraft). Overall, 30 per cent of the buildings (including 580 factories) were destroyed, 6200 acres laid waste.

In the Battle of Hamburg, 24 July–3 August, Bomber Command alone flew 3095 sorties, dropping almost 10,000 tons of high explosive and incendiaries for the loss of eighty-six aircraft. Joseph Goebbels, the Nazi Minister of Propaganda, called it 'a catastrophe, the extent of which simply staggers the imagination'. Hamburg's police chief declared 'the damage was gigantic'.

H. C. 'Nick' Knilans, an ebullient RCAF sergeant, flew a 619 Squadron Lancaster during the first operation. His progress to this point had not been entirely orthodox. An American citizen, the son of a Wisconsin farmer, he had been drafted in his native country during 1941. He learnt, though, that only college graduates with degrees were being selected for the pilot training on which he had set his heart. With only a high school diploma he did not qualify. Telling his family that he was going on a short holiday, he crossed the border, enlisted in the RCAF and duly registered for pilot training. After a year he qualified with the sobering memory that two members of his course had been killed during the final week attempting an unauthorised dogfight. Knilans was offered a posting in Training Command or combat duty overseas, choosing the latter: 'I was upset by German submarines that were sinking British ships containing children evacuated to Canada.' He therefore joined 22,000 other Servicemen on the liner *Queen Elizabeth*, which steamed at 35 knots with no escort other than a hovering Catalina flying boat and relying on frequent changes of course to throw off potential attackers. Knilans and seventeen other sergeants shared a stateroom, equipped with triple bunks: 'not exactly a luxury cruise'.

Fierce Combat

During further training in England, he survived unscathed when a Bf 109 intruder strafed the parade ground at Bournemouth, 'killing and wounding several airmen'. Shortly afterwards, having moved north-westwards to train on Airspeed Oxfords, he suffered 'my only injury of the war' after crashing his bicycle following a visit to the Bass Brewery in Burton-on-Trent. Debonair, with a jaunty manner and matinee idol looks ('a Clark Gable double', according to an envious colleague), Knilans always had a full social diary.

On the train to an OTU on the Moray Firth, he acquired a wireless operator from Norwich. At Lossiemouth, aircrew were assembled in a hangar where 'a long bar with free beer was provided. Pilots stood along the bar awaiting those desiring to join their crew.' In that way, Knilans collected an Australian and a Scotsman for his gunners, and a 'jolly fat Canadian', Harry Geller, as his navigator/bomb aimer.

This five-man crew survived the OTU but not without hair-raising moments. During one exercise, Knilans noticed a build up of 'rime ice, a white granular condition' forming on the wings as he climbed beyond 10,000ft. Forced to dive to avoid a stall, the Whitley emerged from cloud at 2000ft to be greeted by a concerted barrage from the naval escorts of a coastal convoy. 'I could see blinding yellow dots as their deck guns fired at us . . . I found out later that the Royal Navy had claimed the right to shoot first and identify later.' On this occasion the gunners had a point. An aircraft, not dissimilar in profile to a German Dornier Do 17, had suddenly dived out of cloud towards them. Knilans' other moments of danger were less life-threatening. He was among a group to stage a mock gunfight and generally cause off-duty mayhem in an Inverness hotel, which resulted in their being 'asked to leave and never to darken those doors again'.

At Swinderby HCU, Knilans 'picked up' a flight engineer

and dedicated bomb aimer, leaving Geller to concentrate on navigating. Knilans initially flew a Manchester, 'not a very stable airplane [*sic*]', in which his confidence was not increased by a chain-smoking instructor. 'He kept his eyes roving at all times in flight to make sure we were near an airfield. He made me feel that we would have an emergency landing at any moment.' In contrast, the Lancaster was 'very comfortable to fly' and it was to pilot this aircraft that he moved to Woodhall Spa with his crew. From the outset, Knilans recognised that the pilot 'if he expected to live long . . . had to be thinking about every other member of his crew and what they were doing at any given moment'.

Knilans found that, on his raised seat, the Lancaster pilot manipulated a control column topped by a half wheel, with levers on both sides to apply the brakes. Another lever to operate the bomb bay doors was on the pilot's left, one for the flaps to his right. The pilot's right hand dealt with the four throttles, a task in which the flight engineer might assist. During flight, he must also constantly be checking 'about twenty dials and instruments'. The pilot's duties in Bomber Command's three heavy bombers were identical. But although the Stirling, Halifax and Lancaster each had the same six crew designations (bomb aimer, flight engineer, navigator, wireless operator and two gunners), the duties in the different types and variations within them were not consistent, and some squadrons further varied the standard arrangements.

Wing Commander J. H. Searby, a Pathfinder squadron commander, also enthused about the Lancasters: 'We handled them just as the fighter boys handled their Spitfires. We were that confident.' Like the Hampden, though, they could bring moments of personal embarrassment. Searby explained that, instead of the Hampden's notorious tube, a 'pee bottle' rather like a rubber hot-water bottle hung on an accessible hook for the pilot's convenience. After using it on one occasion, Searby contrived to drop the 'bottle' on the floor, with pungent results. 'They didn't talk to me for the next two days.' Other lavatorial arrangements could be troublesome, too. Searby recounted the experience of another pilot, who had left the controls to his flight engineer to answer a call of nature. As he precariously perched on the Elsan toilet, the deputy pilot frantically warned him that he could see flak ahead. 'You may jink a little but remember where I am' came the skipper's unruffled reply.

Returning from the Hamburg operation on 25 July, Knilans' crew saw no other aircraft and, over the North Sea, realised that the Lancaster was 10 degrees off course. After rapid readjustment and the wireless operator picking up homing signals, Knilans made for Woodhall Spa to look for the Flight Path Indicator lights. Yellow showed the aircraft was too high on approach, red too low; green indicated the angle to be spot on. However, cloud obscured the lights. With the instruments showing 1000ft, the bomb aimer suddenly yelled, 'there's the ground'. Knilans reacted immediately: 'Wheels up!' Almost too late. The aircraft hit a gravel pit, staggered sluggishly upwards as the pilot fought with the controls and sliced through the tops of nearby trees. Beneath the decapitated foliage, 'airmen were hurtling out of doors and windows of the barracks' built in the copse. Knilans gradually nursed his charge higher and, ignoring the altimeter, made a visual landing. When the Lancaster came to a halt, the instrument read 960ft. 'You son of a bitch,' breathed the pilot. It was 4.35 a.m. Every blade on the two port engines had been bent back. That aircraft would not be flying for some time but Knilans and his crew would. At 9 a.m. they learnt that they were going to Essen that night.

Knilans flew on the 2/3 August Hamburg raid mounted by 740 aircraft, which proved taxing in a different way. His Lancaster took off in 'a heavy gusty rainstorm'. It was, Knilans recalled, 'like flying into a bottle of ink. The unlighted, radium-coated needles were all I could see on the Sperry instrument panel before me. Our lives depended on my following the artificial horizon.' Flying down the Elbe to the target, the Lancaster was caught in a strong downdraught, and despite pulling hard on the column it continued to lose height. 'Blue streaks of static electricity, St Elmo's Fire, were flowing over the windshield and wings. Rime ice was forming on the wings and props only to break off and bang against the fuselage like flak'. Still struggling with the stick and rudder pedals, at 14,000ft Knilans ordered: 'Drop the bombs and let's get the hell out of here.' As they fell, the aircraft hit an updraught. The starboard wing was almost vertical as the bomber emerged from cloud while 'the crew sat in stunned silence'. Fortunately, Knilans managed to gain full control, but still more problems lay ahead. The aircraft was attacked by an enemy fighter and, on landing, the rear gunner discovered that one of its shells had passed through the fuselage within 2ft of him.

Field Marshal Erhard Milch, Director-General of Air Equipment, declared that 'the attacks on Hamburg have affected the morale of the people. Unless we evolve a means of defeating these terror raids [a term still used by Kammhuber thirty years later] soon, an extremely difficult situation will arise.' In fact, an embryo force capable of outflanking Window had already seen action. Major Halo Herrmann devised the use of single-engine day fighters in a tactic known as 'Wild Boar' (*Wilde Sau*). With small numbers of Focke-Wulf Fw 190s and Messerschmitt Bf 109s, it had been tried with some success on 3 July over Cologne. Without airborne radar and guided by the old system of early warning ground radar and radio beacons, these fighters effectively hunted above the altitude of the flak. At the beginning of August, though, Milch remained unhappy: 'I am beginning to think that we are sitting out on a limb. And the

British are sawing the limb off.' His temper would not have improved had he known that a Ju 88, complete with its Lichtenstein, had been captured in June. Measures were well in hand to develop the Serrate device, which homed in on the German radar signals, and install it in Bristol Beaufighters.

As July 1943 drew to a close, with the impending arrival of longer nights, targets beyond the Ruhr and western Germany became more feasible. Gordon Carter, the navigator who had returned to Pathfinder duty after escaping from France in April, took part in three of the Hamburg raids and in August also flew to other targets including Nuremberg and Berlin. But, as a fellow officer wrote, he was 'always thinking of his beloved France'.

The difficulties surrounding relationships in wartime could be seen with others, too. The Australian Bormann was devastated when a letter from 'Laurel' on 10 August called it 'all off'. He confided to his diary, 'Laurel has scrubbed me'. Frank Blackman's association with Mary Mileham did continue, though not without hiccoughs. Stationed at Eastmoor, he arranged for Mary to stay close by with Mrs Skinner. 'The problem is going to be food. I don't know how much she can do for you – but I've no doubt that will work out somehow – and I'll hope to be free on Saturday and we can buzz off into York.' In the event, that evening excursion was frustrated. 'Blast Bomber Command and all its works! Isn't it the foulest possible luck that I should have to fly this particular pair of successive nights.'

Blackman realised that Mary would reach Mrs Skinner's at about 10.30 on Friday evening and would 'no doubt be tired'. 'Nevertheless, if you care to walk along the road past the telephone box, and turn right, you will come to one edge of the 'drome and can if you want see us take off. If you do, I can't wave to you exactly – but you can be sure that that mile between us will be positively buzzing with telepathic activity.' He expected to return 'sometime before dawn' and would come to see her at about 10 a.m. on Saturday morning. Blackman added a cheerful postscript: 'I'll leave a message to be sent over – in case I have to land away or anything – so you will not be left in ignorance.' The ominous 'or anything' did not happen, but the possibility of his being lost perhaps underlay a letter later in August. 'You know, Mary, that I cannot yet ask you to marry me. Indeed, if I did, you would be afraid to say yes – being far perhaps from knowing your own mind.'

New aircrew were still entering the system. Sergeant John Allen began flying operationally at the beginning of August. After leaving school in Bognor, he had volunteered for the RAF but been made to dawdle in the Air Training Corps until he was seventeen and a quarter years old in September 1941, the age to enlist. After almost eighteen months, including service as a flight mechanic, he became a flight engineer and went to Stradishall HCU, where he was 'very lucky' to be allocated to Flight Sergeant C. S. 'Sid' Gay's crew. The New Zealander was an experienced pilot with a wicked sense of humour. During exercises, he often waited for somebody to walk aft to the Elsan toilet before going into a dive. Despite this, Allen held that 'mutual respect' soon developed between the pilot and members of his crew, so much so that they clubbed together to buy a car for social excursions into Cambridge. Like many other pilots, Gay forbade 'chitchat' on the intercom: 'If there was something to say it was said; otherwise silence.' When Allen flew with another crew on one occasion, he was 'horrified at the constant stream of trivia. Always nattering.'

During mid-1943, intelligence hardened about Germany's development of what became known as the V-weapons and in particular a production and testing site at Peenemünde on the Baltic coast. Its destruction was deemed crucial and during the night of 17/18 August, 596 aircraft were briefed to attack it in three waves. Crews were told they were to hit 'an experimental factory engaged in the production of an advanced form of RDF [radar] for the German night fighter system'. Pathfinders using H2S marked the target and a master bomber coordinated the attacks, as a small force of Mosquitoes mounted a diversionary raid on Berlin. The enemy's rocket programme was seriously interrupted by the severe damage caused, but German night fighters arrived in time to harass the third wave. They used a disturbing new technique of upward-firing cannon (known as *schräge Musik*: literally 'slanting music', but colloquially 'jazz') fitted in the twin-engine Messerschmitt Bf 110 to rake the vulnerable unprotected bellies of the Lancasters. Forty bombers were lost, almost 7 per cent of those despatched, but this was considered acceptable for such a one-off, critical target. In reality, the bombers had been saved not only by Beaufighters using the Serrate equipment to locate and attack enemy fighters, but by a lucky breakdown in communication between German ground controllers and the fighters. Fifty-five 'Wild Boar' single-seaters and 158 night fighters had been ready to intercept earlier if properly directed.

Gordon Carter went with the Pathfinders to Peenemünde. At the evening briefing, which gave the usual important details of the target, weather, bomb loads and possible opposition, as a navigator he concentrated on plotting the track to and from the target on his charts. He then rolled them up and, with all the normal 'gadgetry', tucked them into a large green canvas bag which he thereafter never let go of until it was on his folding table in the Halifax. Because he acted as bomb aimer as well, he 'also pored over the skeleton target maps, purple shaped blobs giving the target's outline and the more obviously visible features, either to the naked eye or on H2S. These had to be committed to memory for it was out of the question to play even a pinpoint of light on them during the bombing run-up, for fear of impairing one's night vision.'

Bomber Crew

After a 'one-egg' supper, Carter clambered into his flying gear: 'soft wool-lined boots . . . the foot part of which could be separated from the legging to serve as escape shoes; the long woollen underwear; a baggy, fleece-lined vest and pants; a leather helmet; a snout-like oxygen mask and intercom lead; a silk scarf and gloves, which were a nuisance to plot with, and leather gauntlets, of little use on board'. To complete the cumbersome array, Carter put on an uninflated Mae West and parachute harness, and heaved along the parachute pack with his other equipment. It was then time to clamber aboard the transport to the dispersal point, exchange words with the ground crew and pull himself through the belly hatch. As he completed his pre-operational checks, other members of the crew had their own routine to follow with the wireless operator listening to last-minute information about the weather and wind velocity, in which Carter was particularly interested.

While the aircraft was taking off, Carter 'sat on the pilot's right-hand side, belted into a foldable seat, with my feet hanging loose above the wireless operator's and navigator's well, holding the bank of four throttle levers in its fully forward position up and against the "gate" [to emergency power] until we lifted off the ground', when the pilot eased it back as the Halifax picked up speed in the air. After the wheels and flaps were up, Carter folded back his seat and 'dropped down into my cubbyhole'. He did so with a feeling of relief, fully aware that 'more than one [bomber] had ended its journey where it began, blowing up in a field a mile or so beyond the end of the runway'.

Over the North Sea the gunners tested their weapons and the aircraft crossed 'the neck of Denmark' unmolested except that 'in the far distance, off to port, the odd Swedish AA gun opened up, as a symbol of neutrality'. At the target, Carter suddenly realised that the electrical bomb-release mechanism was not working. 'The only way out was manual release, so all the crew

152

who could be spared flung themselves on their tummies above the open bomb bay and tripped the releases' when Carter gave the word. 'It worked! I saw our target indicators cascade down on to the rectangular structure and our photo plot confirmed a direct hit.'

In a sense, Peenemünde was a distraction from Bomber Command's area bombing attacks. On 12 August, Harris had written to the CAS, Portal, of his 'firm belief that we were on the verge of a final showdown in the bombing war, and the next few months will be vital'. If so, the raid on Berlin during the night of 23/24 August did not prove a happy omen. In reality, it was something of a disaster, partly because a number of crews deviated from the planned route. Seven hundred and twenty-seven bombers set out and, once more, a master bomber was detailed. Things started to go wrong when Pathfinder aircraft with H2S failed to identify the centre of the city and instead marked an area in the southern suburbs. This complication was magnified by the late arrival of the main force and some crews effectively cutting a corner by approaching from the south-west and not the briefed south-south-east direction. The bombers were therefore dispersed, with their loads widely scattered after release. Many bombs fell harmlessly in open fields; the quarter of the city in which government offices were housed remained untouched.

Furthermore, the German night fighters and flak batteries made proverbial hay. Fifty-six bombers were lost – almost 8 per cent – an unacceptable total. Undoubtedly, some were shot down because of the unauthorised route deviation. A BBC commentator flying in one of the bombers reported aerial 'chaos' as he witnessed aircraft blowing up amid a colourful display of bursting flak and shells from fighters finding their mark. Two further costly raids on Berlin, on 31 August and 3 September, accounted for sixty-nine more bombers.

The Germans were now relying on a more mobile defence, involving the single-engine 'Wild Boar' tactic and twin-engine night fighters being given more scope for initiative in a similar 'Tame Boar' (*zahme Sau*) system. Kammhuber had been replaced by General Joseph Schmid in charge of a new First Fighter Corps, with responsibility for interception passing to fighter divisions. In theory, this speeded up the entire process. Moreover, although the numbers of German night fighters rose only marginally from 554 to 611 in the last sixth months of 1943, the newer types of Bf 110, Ju 88 and Heinkel He 219 were infinitely better equipped.

Towards the end of August, the American Nick Knilans was awarded a field commission by the RCAF and duly moved into the Officers' Mess in the Petwood Hotel close to RAF Woodhall Spa in Lincolnshire. He was most impressed with the procedure of a pretty WAAF bringing him tea in bed. 'It was a nice foxhole to fight a war from that I stayed in it for fourteen more months', during which he moved to 617 Squadron. Nor was the pleasant side of his off-duty time confined to Lincolnshire. While on leave, Knilans habitually stayed at the Regents Park Hotel in London. During the afternoon, he tended to gravitate towards the daily tea dance in Covent Garden. 'It was not difficult to find a young lady looking for an evening of fun and games, too.'

Section Officer Joyce Brotherton referred to a Halifax pilot with 207 Squadron at this time, whose personality was altogether less extrovert. Twenty year old Pilot Officer John McIntosh was 'quiet and of a retiring disposition, in fact he was one of the most unassuming men I've ever met. He made no apparent effort to "run" his crew, yet there was never the slightest doubt as to who was the skipper. He had a wizard crew and they thought the world of him . . . They were prepared to take orders from him as they felt that he was the best man among them.'

154

Fierce Combat

McIntosh had flown on the Peenemünde raid and shortly afterwards to Berlin on the 23/24 August. Joyce Brotherton noted that he and his best friend, Pilot Officer Jack 'Stevie' Stephens, another pilot, 'got a shock' when they learnt of the latter target at briefing. 'They stood up to it well as they always did . . . [but] at the same time weren't keen on it.' Joyce wished them 'a good trip' as they left the Mess after their post-briefing meal: 'It seemed a long evening after they had gone.'

She later discovered that the first part of McIntosh's flight had been 'entirely uneventful' in 'reasonable' met. conditions. Skirting Hanover to the north, Lancaster M-Mother was suddenly jumped by a Ju 88 which fired as it flew towards the bomber's tail. The alert rear gunner, Sergeant Middleton, engaged the twin-engine night fighter before it passed out of range. He saw his shots ignite ammunition in the aircraft, which slowly 'turned over on its back and dived down through the cloud in an uncontrolled dive, with smoke and flames pouring from it'. Any satisfaction at this 'kill' was short-lived. The enemy fighter had severely damaged the bomber.

The starboard wing was on fire, part of the starboard tailplane, rudder and fin had been hit. There were flames inside the fuselage, which the flight engineer could not quell with the fire extinguishers. The crew fortunately did not realise that the self-sealing material on the petrol tank was alight. Why the tank failed to explode is a mystery. McIntosh turned back as soon as the extent of the damage became clear. Initially, he and the other crew members hoped that their machine might make Holland, where they could bale out with a little more chance of escaping captivity. England was a long way off. Middleton volunteered to climb on to the wing to try and douse the fire, but McIntosh refused 'the daring offer' for fear that he would be blown off.

Somehow the blazing aircraft remained aloft and, despite

155

giving the appearance of a flying torch, miraculously trudged on unmolested by night fighters. Then they were over Holland, and McIntosh decided to risk the North Sea, even though the dinghy stored in the starboard wing must have been incinerated. Slowly the damaged bomber edged its way over the dark, uninviting waters and then, to the crew's relief, the navigator announced that they had crossed the English coast. At that point, a pungent smell of burning filtered through the aircraft, and McIntosh feared a disaster when the undercarriage was lowered. He intended to land at the first possible airfield, and warned the others to be ready to bale out. Nothing did happen as the undercarriage went down and Little Snoring came into view.

As McIntosh came in to land, one of the engines cut out. He pulled up the nose and prepared to go round again, only to see that the fire had flared up dangerously. To attempt a second circuit might prove fatal, but there was no alternative. With the fire tender and ambulance visibly standing by, McIntosh calmly brought the glowing bomber down to earth. He and his crew lost no time in getting clear, as the firemen went to work. It had been a traumatic trip, and M-Mother was a write-off. But they had all survived and would complete their tour together in another Lancaster.

On 3 September, Harris was warned that 'barring an independent and complete Russian victory' Bomber Command must look to preparing for Operation Overlord, the Allied invasion of Europe planned for 1944. The 'prerequisite' had a familiar ring: 'the progressive destruction and dislocation of the German military, industrial and economic system, the disruption of vital elements of lines of communication, and the material reduction of German air combat strength'. For all practical purposes in the short term this meant continuation of the area bombing of towns and cities.

Fierce Combat

Frank Blackman illustrated a less attractive facet of human nature in a letter to Mary Mileham on 6 September: a tendency not to think of others when enjoying oneself. At the same time, he also showed the diverse interests of RAF aircrew and that Mess life was not always congenial. There was only one wireless set in the corner and Blackman complained that 'boisterous' fellows cradling beer mugs thoughtlessly spoilt his enjoyment of a music programme featuring the violinist Albert Sandler. He condemned them as 'child like' and 'bluff playmates'. Not wishing to be called 'a prig', nonetheless he had no intention of imitating them. 'Manliness,' he claimed, 'lies not in any details of carriage or behaviour but in maturity of mind, in the dream-free recognition of life and in the possession of the will to succeed.' At the time of writing, he was clearly irritated and very much out of sorts.

Shortly afterwards he was in a better mood, thanking Mary for 'a lovely weekend' and noting that he was 'in grand humour and the sun's shining and everything in the garden is lovely'. He had answered a request in Squadron Orders to design a Squadron crest and had suggested that, due to 429 Squadron's Canadian origin, it should incorporate a buffalo. The project enthused him, and it would be finished in time to be submitted for official approval the following month.

Two years after volunteering for the RAF, in September 1943, like Nick Knilans at the end of his training in Canada, Jim Parsons sailed to Britain in the *Queen Elizabeth* even less luxuriously. With forty-one other sergeants he was assigned to one compartment, where the hammocks were so closely packed that even a slight movement of the ship caused disgruntled occupants to bang against one another. An angry deputation demanded relocation. The solution offered was to shift decks every night during the crossing: from the bottom to the top in succession. The rebellious sergeants decided to stay put and endure the discomfort.

157

After a short familiarisation course on the Isle of Man to readjust to the European terrain and weather, Parsons found himself in the middle of Silverstone race track attending an OTU. Over the next fortnight, he met and 'gelled' with a pilot, Ray Harris, and they in turn gathered three more for their Wellington crew. Parsons thought the Wellington a 'nice' machine despite being slower than any in service apart from the Blenheim.

Parsons very nearly did not come through this phase of training. After takeoff, when he shared the navigator's bench, the bomb aimer would swing down into his position in the nose. During one night exercise, Parsons confidently began this manoeuvre only to see beneath him a yawning gap. The belly hatch had been left open. Frantically, he kicked out and managed to slam it, otherwise he faced a terminal plunge earthwards without a parachute. Another friend from Portsmouth was not so lucky at his OTU. As a pre-war Territorial Army member, 'Dixie' Dean had been mobilised and sent to France. On his return, 'not thinking much of that life', he transferred to the RAF and like Parsons trained in Canada. Returning from an exercise back in England, he forgot to walk straight ahead on leaving the aircraft and turned into a revolving propeller, with fatal consequences.

Meanwhile, Jack Bormann seemed to have recovered from Laurel's rejection and immersed himself in composing poetry. On 4 September, he wrote an 'ode' entitled 'Our Crew', which had no particular claim to fame but did show the importance of its members to him. It began: 'We are a jolly happy crew / With skipper named Jim Marshall / While Arnold plots us o'er the Rhine.'

The lot of another 'happy crew' was decidedly not so jolly. On the evening of 14 September, each carrying a new 12,000lb. bomb (not Wallis's later Tallboy weapon of the same weight) nine Lancasters from 617 Squadron set out to attack the Dortmund-Ems canal at low level. When a reconnaissance aircraft reported deteriorating conditions in the vicinity of the target, they were recalled. Such are the fortunes of war. As he banked to turn back, the wing of Squadron Leader David Maltby's Lancaster hit the sea near Cromer and the whole crew perished. That weekend, Maltby was set to be best man at the wedding of David Shannon to Section Officer Ann Fowler whom he had met at RAF Scampton in the run-up to the Dambusters Raid. Shannon circled for two and a half hours in the forlorn hope that survivors would be found.

Other returning crews still had to land with the large bomb, which caused bomb aimer Johnson and front gunner Sutherland in the nose of Les Knight's aircraft more than a little concern. Should they abandon their forward positions and climb up into the fuselage? Johnson reasoned there was no point. If the bomb exploded 'we'll get killed back there, or here, it doesn't matter'. Sutherland pointed to the additional strain imposed on a pilot in extraordinary circumstances like these: 'Les made a really ropey landing. I guess he'd been so long in the air because we had to get rid of the fuel and I guess he was a little nervous with this thing on board. We bounced about three times, but it stayed on, and everyone was okay, but it scared the hell out of me.'

The following night seven of those who returned from this aborted operation, plus Flight Lieutenant 'Mick' Martin's Lancaster, tried again. Most of Martin's experienced crew had flown on Hampdens and Lancasters with him. As his navigator Jack Leggo explained: 'We were together for many years . . . He [Martin] was a first class leader who had the loyalty of his crew at all times . . . a serious dedicated pilot and a friend.' Despite the persistence of the crews at the Dortmund-Ems canal, several of whom tried repeatedly to find the target in heavy mist ('right sticky to find', according to Sumpter,

Shannon's bomb aimer), success eluded them. Perhaps more importantly, five of the eight aircraft were lost. One was that of Pilot Officer Les Knight, whose crew had breached the largest dam (the Eder) during the Dambusters Raid. Knight, at twenty-two, nine years younger than two of his crew, had deservedly gained the DSO for that achievement. A devout Methodist, he neither drank nor smoked, but in the words of his flight engineer 'could fly the a*** off a Lancaster'. He was not a demonstrative captain, but could sharply quell unnecessary chatter in the aircraft when required. There was never any doubt as to who was in charge, and he was deeply respected by every member of his crew. Off-duty the crew socialised together, and as flight Sergeant Bob Kellow (the wireless operator) recalled, 'although he was teetotal, he always bought his share of the drinks'. There was a suspicion that he was inveigled into paying for more than his share and equal recognition that he knew that perfectly well. He did not seem to mind either, when members of the crew raided his parcels from home.

That night three gunners were carried, making a crew of eight. One of them, Sutherland, recorded: 'That was a hairy ride. We went in, our leader [Squadron Leader G. W. Holden] was shot down then we got in. The guy on our left was shot down in flames right near the canal. There were only two in our formation left.' At the canal, crossing and criss-crossing the area, Knight strove hard to find the target. In the navigator Hobday's understated words: 'The weather wasn't good, the moon wasn't bright enough. And we were stooging around trying to locate it.' Just as the target appeared out of the gloom, Flying Officer Edward Johnson (the bomb aimer) yelled that trees were straight ahead. Knight pulled up smartly, but still struck the top branches. As the Lancaster shook itself free, it became clear that both port engines had stopped and the tail plane was damaged. 'This happened so fast . . . I thought we'd had it,' Sutherland recalled.

Fierce Combat

Knight could not handle an aircraft which continually turned to port. The rear gunner, Sergeant Harry O'Brien, a large man, came forward 'to pull on the rudders to hold the speed', but 'we were now at a thousand feet and this was the worst feeling I ever had,' Sutherland remarked. The crew jettisoned the bomb and threw out all moveable objects, even the guns. Knight managed to get the aircraft up to almost 1500ft but he still could not stop it from persistently going to port, however hard he and the crew tried. He ordered the crew to bale out, while he struggled to keep the stricken Lancaster aloft. Reluctantly, they obeyed.

'I was first out,' wrote Johnson. By now, despite Knight's efforts, he doubted whether the aircraft was even 1000ft up. So 'I didn't follow the parachute procedure of counting and pulling the ripcord. I jumped out and pulled it.' He didn't think it would open, but to his surprise and relief it did and he 'made a fairly good landing'. O'Brien, who had been striving to help Knight, also went out of the forward escape hatch, hit the ground 'with a terrific bang', but was soon captured by an armed motorcyclist. Sutherland, who had gone aft to throw out the equipment, had to leave by the rear exit door and was terrified that he would be 'cut in two' by the tailplane as he went out. He managed to avoid this unpleasant fate. After the tailplane had 'whizzed by', 'I pulled the rigging and saw somebody's pasture below. Then I saw this barbed wire fence and I thought, Holy Jimmy, I'm going to be a guy with a high pitched voice, but I fell short.' Kellow, the wireless operator, was the last to see Knight alive: 'As I passed him on my way to reach the escape hatch in the nose of the Lancaster, I made certain he had his parachute on and we gave one another the thumbs-up.'

The seven crew members lived; Knight died, having sacrificed himself for them. His gallantry was recognised by a posthumous Mention in Despatches. In later years, whenever they met, Knight's crew toasted his memory. Flying Officer H. S.

'Hobby' Hobday (the navigator) recalled: 'We all got out in good order except poor old Les, who stuck to the controls until we had jumped. I shall never forget how he wished me all the best before I left him'. 'I owe my life to Les', he added simply. Sutherland agreed. 'He was a person that gave up his life for us . . . we've always been thankful, us seven survivors, to him for saving our lives.' Kellow wrote: 'He kept that damaged aircraft flying straight and level, so that we, his crew, would have a chance to live by parachuting to safety, but in doing so, he gave his life for us.' At the crew reunion for his ninetieth birthday, Edward Johnson movingly echoed those words.

Beyond Western Europe, by the autumn of 1943 the tide had turned in the Allies' favour. Following victory in a massive tank battle near Kursk in July, the Soviets had launched a major offensive in the south, recapturing Kharkov in the Ukraine the following month. After clearing Sicily, British and American troops had invaded the Italian mainland. In the Pacific, the Japanese were being driven back, as the American hold on New Guinea tightened.

Only British and American bombers could yet hit Germany and the strain on Bomber Command continued to mount. On the day of his crew's thirteenth operation, 3 October, the squadron commander called Knilans into his office to tell him that the rear gunner, with him since the training unit, could not fly any more. 'His position in the aircraft was the most isolated and the coldest. He had to stare out into the darkness hour after hour, knowing that enemy fighters were stalking him most of the time.' To compound matters, the gunner had received a telegram from his wife announcing the arrival of their first child, a son. Aware that refusing to fly would mean a red-ink entry in his logbook denoting LMF and loss of his sergeant's stripes, Knilans persuaded the gunner to go with him that night. They were due for nine days' leave the next day, and this would give him time to think things over. 'He flew with us and was killed by an enemy bandit,' Knilans recalled. A major drawback of the Monica backward looking radar was that it could not distinguish friend from foe. On this occasion, the wireless operator had picked up a steady signal and assumed it was another Lancaster in the stream, something which had happened before. Not this time. The mid-upper gunner was temporarily blinded in the attack by perspex splinters from his shattered turret. Knilans was too upset to accept the invitation to stay with one of his crew for the leave. He wanted to be alone.

In contrast, Frank Blackman's buoyant spirits extended into October. He expressed a 'sense of excitement' about the Soviet advances into western Ukraine: 'Now that the end is in sight things must suddenly move I think to a climax'. He then took off into a flight of fancy, which would not have disgraced interwar disciples of Smuts and the knockout theory: 'There is no doubt that a point is coming when tremendous air armadas will operate day and night with at first great losses perhaps – but with an effect that may finish the war without invasion.' Unrealistic, but an example of wishful thinking after four years of conflict.

October 1943 proved memorable for Pilot Officer Gerry South. On 1 November 1941, he had gained his pilot's wing and, to his utter despair, been immediately assigned as an instructor to a training unit. He had absolutely no operational experience, therefore, when he reached 405 Pathfinder Squadron in summer 1943. After familiarisation trips in a Halifax, including the Peenemünde raid, he acquired a 'headless' crew whose pilot had completed his tour, learnt to fly Lancasters and on 18 October 1943 found himself over Hanover. The aircraft was struck by flak and South wounded in the shoulder. But 'with the help of my wonderful crew we returned safely to base': a meagre note of a harrowing experience. Squadron records show that in the target area flak tipped the aircraft almost vertical, crucial equipment in it was damaged and, on landing, 'several small holes' were found in the fuselage. South would remain in Ely hospital for three months, during which, to his 'great surprise and delight', he was awarded the DFC for his efforts that night. 'The sisters cracked open a bottle of sherry which was shared by the ward.' On his recovery, he joined another 'headless' crew. 'Again I was lucky in having a first-class crew and though some of them finished before me, I obtained very good replacements.'

Gordon Carter completed forty Pathfinder operations on 22 October. That month, he had been reassigned to the crew of Squadron Leader Julian Sale, 'a short and robust fair-headed Canadian from Toronto' ten years older than Carter. The new navigator quickly came to appreciate the expertise of the pilot and the ability of other members of the crew. Lasting 'comradeship' soon developed, Carter explained.

It was clear now that the ambitious plans for a Combined Bomber Offensive outlined at Casablanca in January would not be fulfilled in 1943. Like Bomber Command, the US 8th AAF had suffered sustained losses. Since the heady days of Vegesack in March and the Eaker Plan in April, the Americans had experienced a torrid time. Attempts to extend the range of P-47 Thunderbolts and P-38 Lightnings by fitting drop tanks were foiled when the Germans began to attack them close to the coast, causing the fighters to jettison the tanks to obtain fighting mobility. The potentially greater range was, thus, forfeited and the bombers had to go on alone. Development of an elaborate defensive box system for the bombers had initial success, but the Luftwaffe soon devised tactics to break that up. On 13 June, twenty-two out of sixty B-17s were lost on one mission; in six operations between 24 and 30 July, eighty-eight. A twin raid on 17 August against an aircraft-manufacturing complex in

164

Fierce Combat

Regensburg and the ball-bearing factories in Schweinfurt was disrupted by bad weather, and sixty bombers were lost (six hundred men). On 14 October, 291 B-17s set out for Schweinfurt alone, and sixty more were lost, five others crashing in England. From the 260 which attacked the target, only 195 landed safely, of which sixty-two were relatively unscathed. 'Black Thursday', as it was dubbed in the American press, meant abandonment of deep penetration, daylight missions until a suitable long-range fighter escort could be found.

The long winter nights, though, now gave Bomber Command an opportunity to mount massive raids on selected targets, encouraged by a congratulatory message on 11 October from Churchill praising the Command's 'recent successes', which Harris circulated. 'The results of this campaign', the Prime Minster wrote, 'are not restricted to damage which can be seen and photographed but are reflected with equal significance in the extent to which the German Air Force has been forced from the offensive to the defensive both operationally and in new construction.' So Düsseldorf felt the weight of 577 four-engine bombers on 3/4 November. Heavy destruction in the target area was reported, with only 3 per cent aircraft losses. This raid saw another act of bravery, which resulted in the award of the VC. Shortly after crossing the Dutch coast, the windscreen of Flight Lieutenant Bill Reid's Lancaster was shattered by a Bf 110 night fighter. In the attack, the rear turret was damaged, the aircraft's control system affected, the intercom put out of action and the compasses shattered. Reid was wounded in the head, shoulders and hands, but the rest of the crew were 'unscathed' and he decided to press on to the target. However, the Lancaster was found by an Fw 190, which raked it from stem to stern, killing the navigator and 'fatally' injuring the mid-upper gunner. The main oxygen supply was destroyed, so that the flight engineer had to use the portable bottle to help Reid.

With no navigator, Reid set course for the target from memory and the aerial photograph showed an accurate bombing strike. Reid turned for home, only to face yet more serious problems. He kept fainting through loss of blood, so the flight engineer and bomb aimer were left to keep 'the Lancaster in the air despite heavy anti-aircraft fire over the Dutch coast'. Over England, Reid recovered to make an emergency landing in poor visibility at Shipdham in Norfolk even though blood from a head wound was freely running into his eyes. He contrived to control the Lancaster despite this major disadvantage and the fact that part of the undercarriage collapsed as the aircraft touched down. The citation stated that 'his tenacity and devotion to duty were beyond praise'.

The experiences of two crews on 619 Squadron underlined the danger which still faced bombers after returning from operations. One pilot hit the ground on landing, miraculously without injuring any of his crew. He was thought to be suffering from battle fatigue when he complained at debriefing that the runway had turned a corner as he put down. It emerged that he had mistaken the dimmed headlamps of a convoy, which had indeed turned a corner, for the runway. 'His voice was at a soprano pitch in the bar the next day,' wrote an unsympathetic colleague. Diverted to Scotland and number twenty in the landing circuit, another of the Squadron's pilots found himself almost out of fuel. Instead of risking a disaster, he opted to pancake on a convenient field. However, 'the flat surface turned out to be the top of a 10ft ground fog covering an apple orchard'. After the crash, the crew bolted, to find that the rear gunner was not with them. They called his name and back came the cry: 'Dinghy, dinghy.' He had fallen asleep during the long period of circling, woken suddenly when they came down and thought the aircraft had ditched in the sea. Thoroughly disorientated, he was calling the other crew members to the detached dinghy.

Fierce Combat

Towards the end of November, just after he had been commissioned, George Johnson discovered that not every peril a bomb aimer faced was initiated by the enemy. For the first time, he released a 12,000lb. High Capacity blast bomb over the target, felt a bump and looked down to see it falling: 'so that was fine'. Except that it was not. Johnson checked to find 'this dirty great bomb still hanging up in the bomb bay'. The navigator (MacLean) wanted it jettisoned, McCarthy (the pilot) violently disagreed. He was taking it back. 'Either the instrument man's a s*** or the bomb aimer's a s*** and I'm gonna find out which it is.' Fortunately next morning he discovered that the 'instrument man' had been at fault. The bombsight had been changed on the afternoon before the operation and the bomb connected to the manual-release socket, whereas Johnson as usual activated the automatic release. The bomb he saw falling had been from another aircraft and the sensation of this being dropped created either by an explosion or the prop wash of a nearby bomber. 'A series of coincidences,' Johnson remarked, but he appreciated McCarthy's determination to solve the problem and chastise the guilty party. He was mightily relieved that he was not at fault. McCarthy's determination to root out the cause of a problem was legendary, as a maintenance NCO recalled: 'Joe McCarthy frightened me. If there was anything wrong he always held the electrical NCO responsible – and would seek him out for retribution the second he landed.'

On the night of 18/19 November, Harris initiated a concentrated assault which he had long wished to unleash: the Battle of Berlin. A raid on Berlin entailed a 1150-mile round trip, a lengthy time over enemy territory and the prospect of a fearsome reception from flak and fighters in the target area. Destruction of an enemy's capital, though, was historically an ingrained tenet of political and military thought to which Harris fully subscribed. Berlin was home to 5 per cent of the German population and was the centre of government. At various times, Churchill and Portal had singled it out for attention. Moreover, several Air Ministry directives since January 1943 had pinpointed the need to attack the German capital in a bid to undermine enemy morale and, for instance, 'rub in the Russian victory' at Stalingrad, something still relevant as Soviet forces advanced relentlessly towards eastern Germany. Bomber Command argued that important industrial assets were located there: a tenth of all aero-engine and precision instrument production, a third of Germany's electrical engineering output, a quarter of its tanks. A major difficulty was the size of Berlin (883 square miles), and the fact that a third of it comprised lakes, whose surfaces did not produce the sharp H2S image acquired at ports like Hamburg. Furthermore, it was beyond Oboe range and its location such that for the final 100 miles of any approach Berlin could be the only conceivable target, no matter from which direction the bombers approached.

Nevertheless, Harris advised Churchill that if the Americans would join Bomber Command in this venture, 'we can wreck Berlin from end to end . . . It will cost between us four to five hundred aircraft. It will cost Germany the war.' The United States would not, however, play ball, and the RAF was left to pursue this dubious goal alone. Roosevelt and Churchill had their eyes firmly on a cross-Channel invasion in 1944. The Battle of Berlin would be the last opportunity to make a decisive strategic impact before that was mounted.

The 'battle' got off to a shaky start. The 444 aircraft which attacked that first night found the enemy capital covered in cloud, something not unusual in the coming months, and necessitating blind bombing. Crews rarely saw the ground. German records subsequently suggested that the bombing on 18 November was both inaccurate and only marginally effective. The plus factor was that just nine Lancasters were lost, mainly because few night fighters attempted interception. Three more times before the end of the month a total of 1571 bombers attacked Berlin. On two occasions, despite the marking efforts of Pathfinders equipped with their improved H2S sets, poor visibility hampered the bombing. During the second of these raids, elaborate measures were taken to confuse the Germans, with 'spoof' flares dropped away from the aiming point and a fake 'running commentary' to simulate the fighter controller broadcast from England. But the Lufwaffe had 'Wild Boar' single-engine fighters prowling over the city in advance of the bombers, having worked out that Berlin was the target. Five per cent of the attackers were lost, a disturbing omen for future raids.

After the Berlin operation of 22/23 November involving 764 aircraft, Stirlings were withdrawn from raids into Germany. Although they carried a smaller bomb load than either the Halifax or Lancaster, had a lower operational ceiling and more limited range, John Allen (who flew on the penultimate operation to Leverkusen) believed that they 'did a good job at the time'. The Stirling had been the first of the four-engine bombers into service, and its effectiveness was fiercely defended by those who flew in it. Critics tended to be those who trained on Stirlings before going on to another type of heavy bomber.

The fourth November raid by 450 aircraft, on the night of the 26/27th, occurred in clear weather. An elaborate deception plan, which entailed flying via Frankfurt, and approaching from the south, led to some dispersal. So aircraft flying to and from Berlin became particularly vulnerable to fighter attack. Twenty-eight Lancasters went down and another fourteen crashed in England. The Battle for Berlin, which had four more months to run was already proving expensive. So far in under a fortnight it had cost eighty-seven bombers.

The operation on 26/27 November was memorable for Nick

Knilans, now transformed from Pilot Officer RCAF to Lieutenant USAAF with a welcome increase in pay. A rear gunner who had already completed one tour replaced the one killed over Kassel in October. Before the Berlin raid, as Knilans explained, 'he did not show up to fly on a pre-flight check-up of all instruments. That night, we were attacked three times by bandits. One of the engines was damaged and feathered. The gunner said his guns were U/S and returned no fire on the bandits.' Knilans lost height, but continued to the target. 'Crossing the city amidst heavy flak bursts, this gunner twice yelled, "we're not going to make it".' Knilans 'shut him up and had the Gunnery Flight officer replace him'.

As with the Battle of the Ruhr that summer and for the same reason (not allowing respite to enemy elsewhere) Bomber Command's activity was not focused exclusively on Berlin. Operations were also mounted against other targets in Germany and the occupied countries. On the opening night, 18/19 November, 395 bombers attacked Mannheim and Ludwigshafen for the loss of twenty-three aircraft. In addition to four more attacks on Berlin in December, main force raids took place on Leipzig, Frankfurt and Mannheim. The luck of Pilot Officer Geoff Rice, who had inadvertently knocked Wallis's special weapon off his Lancaster in the Zuider Zee during the Dambusters Raid, ran out on the way to Frankfurt on 20 December. His was one of forty-one bombers lost that night, being shot down over Belgium at about 8.30 p.m. Rice woke up on the ground twelve hours later with no recollection of how he had survived, though he felt sure his flight engineer had helped him with his parachute. Unaccountably, when he came to with a broken wrist and a cut eye, his head was lying on his navigator's helmet. Sheltered in sixteen different locations by the Resistance for five months, he was eventually captured in Antwerp and consigned to Stalag Luft III on 1 June 1944.

Fierce Combat

Gordon Carter was promoted 'war temporary' squadron leader on 7 December after completing the requisite forty-five operations with the Pathfinder Force. 'Keen types' were permitted to continue for another fifteen operations to make a round sixty. Carter joined that eager band, and flew his forty-sixth operation to Frankfurt on 20 December. Perhaps he wished that he had not been so keen after all. In 8/10ths cloud over the target, the Halifax made four abortive runs at 5000ft but still could not be sure of the aiming point. The pilot therefore decided not to drop the target indicators, and the three 1000lb. HE bombs were released on what looked like a small factory. The Halifax enjoyed a trouble free home run until it began its descent for landing. 'Then all hell broke loose'. Unknown to the crew the safety cover for a target indicator fuse had become detached during the flight. As the aircraft had now come down to 1200ft, which was below the normal detonation height, the target indicator went off in the bomb bay. Then 'things happened mighty fast'. 'The plane filled with smoke and flames' and the pilot ordered the crew to bale out. Carter did so 'posthaste'. 'I remember seeing a tree upside down and instantly hitting the ground in a ploughed field' close to the perimeter track.

Meanwhile, as he was preparing to jump, the pilot Julian Sale realised that his mid-upper gunner, Flight Lieutenant Roger Lamb, was beside him frantically pointing to his parachute pack which had been burnt by the fire in the bomb bay below his turret. Unable to see his instrument panel for smoke, Sale stuck his head out of the side window and managed to get the aircraft down. As it came to a halt, he and Lamb, the only crew members not to jump, leapt out and hurtled into the distance. Very wise. Behind them, almost immediately, the Halifax blew up. Sale was awarded a bar to his DSO. The citation read: 'In circumstances of great danger Squadron Leader Sale displayed great courage and determination, setting an example of the highest order.' *The Times* headline for an account of the incident read: 'Landed Blazing Bomber To Save Comrade'. To ensure that he did not receive a bill for replacement kit, Gordon Carter was issued with a certificate confirming that his Irvin jacket, goggles, helmet, silk gloves and flying gauntlets 'were destroyed in Halifax III HX 328 J, when it caught fire and crashed on the night of December 20th 43'. The bureaucratic niceties of filing must be strictly observed, whatever the circumstances.

In the final quarter of the year, the sub-text of electronic warfare intensified. The British had developed H2S Mark III, with much improved definition. The Airborne Cigar (ABC) device was perfected to jam the night fighter VHF radios and carried in specially modified aircraft flying with the bomber stream. This required an extra man, one of whom recorded his lonely experience: 'In the Lancaster we sat in darkness, cut off from the rest of the crew. The nearest other crewman was the mid-upper gunner – his boots were at my eye level, about four feet further down the aircraft.' The Germans attempted to counter the blotting out of ground-to-air communications with Tinsel by resorting to running commentaries on different channels. The British responded by an exercise codenamed Corona, whereby German speakers broadcast spoof instructions, to the fury of the real controllers and confusion of night fighter crews. In a raid by 569 aircraft against Kassel on 22/23 October, the German ground controller had become so agitated that he began swearing. The British spoof broadcaster reacted quickly and sharply: 'The Englishman is now swearing', only for an incandescent German to bawl: 'It is not the Englishman who is swearing, it is me.' Switching to female voices to issue orders was swiftly copied by the British. On one occasion, Nick Knilans and his crew 'enjoyed a terrible row' between a German fighter pilot and a female ground controller, who was sending him incomprehensible instructions, especially when their wireless operator assured them that the offending girl was British. Eventually, instead of attempting to imitate the Germans, Corona operators set out simply to irritate them by blocking the air waves by reading lengthy passages from the writings of Goethe or the speeches of Hitler.

Joseph Goebbels complained about the humiliation of his enemy's countermeasures: 'Every month he introduces some new method which it takes weeks and sometimes months for us to catch up with.' Yet the proliferation of equipment by now being carried in British bombers paradoxically gave the Germans greater opportunity to respond. And they were not always unsuccessful in posing new problems for Bomber Command. The 'Wild Boar' and 'Tame Boar' fighters' tactics were improved and extended, so that the bomber stream could be attacked in force along much of its route. The night fighters had an improved airborne radar, SN-2, which had a range of 4 miles and was not yet susceptible to jamming. And the British handed them an unexpected bonus, by switching on their H2S sets as they left the English coast. Long-range interception equipment (codenamed Korfu), able to pick up emissions, was produced. An airborne version, Naxos-Z, came into service in November 1943 with a range of 30 miles. Initially aircraft carrying this piece of equipment were few, so they were used to shadow the bomber stream rather than attack individual aircraft, though by the close of the war many more night fighters would be equipped with it. The Germans, therefore, had by no means given up the struggle to counter the growing number of aids deployed by and in support of Bomber Command.

Nineteen forty-three had opened with high hopes of a decisive combined bomber offensive on Germany. During the year, new navigational aids like Oboe and H2S had been introduced to good effect; devastating raids been carried out on Essen and Hamburg; four hundred or more bombers were frequently being despatched to major targets. However, the Battle of the Ruhr had not annihilated the enemy war industries, partly because many of the production facilities had been redeployed. The inability of Stirlings to reach the altitude flown by Lancasters and Halifaxes made them increasingly vulnerable to enemy fighters and they had been withdrawn from operations over Germany. The outcome of the Battle of Berlin, already proving costly, remained in the balance. In truth, overall Bomber Command's loss rate was still unacceptably high and the effectiveness of its bombing far lower than expected.

Air Vice-Marshal the Hon. R. A. Cochrane, AOC 5 Group, was convinced that the Pathfinders were unable to mark small targets accurately and that their sky markers were less than effective. He argued that they spread so much in the clouds that aircraft bombing on them were liable to disperse their bombs widely. The experience of Carter over Frankfurt on 20 December, when his Halifax came back without releasing any of it markers, seemed to support the view that the Pathfinder Force had not entirely solved the problem of inaccurate bombing. More broadly, the Combined Bomber Offensive (CBO) heralded at Casablanca in January had not realised the dreams of its authors. American bombers, flying unescorted missions in daylight, on occasions had suffered truly horrific casualties: the two operations involving the ball-bearing factories at Schweinfurt had resulted in the combined loss of 120 aircraft (1200 men).

Steps were undeniably being taken, yet once more, to improve the safety and accuracy of bombers. The Americans would soon have long-range Mustang fighters in service. For RAF Bomber Command, in the last month of 1943 No. 100 (Bomber Support) Group was formed with a number of Flying

Fortress squadrons specifically equipped to jam and generally interfere with enemy electronic devices, some Mosquito squadrons carrying the new Serrate equipment and others destined for low-level intruder operations. At 617 Squadron, command of which he had assumed in October, Leonard Cheshire was poised to introduce a low-level marking technique which would transform bombing accuracy. So the future was not unpromising.

Whether it was quite so bright as Harris claimed was debatable. Broadening the strategic horizon beyond Berlin, which he would continue vigorously to attack, he assured the Air Ministry that with an average monthly bomb load of 13,500 tons, 40 per cent of the area of thirty-eight important German towns would be destroyed. By implication, that would bring the war to a premature close. On 7 December he even suggested that this could be done by 1 April 1944 if conditions were favourable. As Harris himself once said to doubters of Bomber Command's ability, 'we shall see'.

CHAPTER 6

Bitter Struggle, 1944

'Here we go round the Mulberry bush'

During 1944, excluding 100 Group, the average number of heavy bombers available to Harris was roughly double the number for 1943. With the expansion of new electronic aids carried in them, many had crews of eight, not seven, and, in the case of RAF Flying Fortresses, ten, which made manpower losses even more serious.

The year would be complicated by the need to provide support for Operation Overlord, the Allied invasion of Normandy, which, Harris bitterly complained, would have serious implications for Bomber Command. 'There could be no greater relief afforded Germany,' he wrote, 'than the cessation of any ponderable reduction of the bombing of Germany proper. The whole country would go wild with a sense of relief and reborn hope, and get down to the prosecution of a purely land war with renewed determination and every hope of success.'

Beyond this particular issue, disagreement surfaced about precisely which targets should be attacked in the enemy homeland. Harris famously dismissed those who sought to neutralise one specific area of production like ball bearings as 'panacea mongers'. He opposed picking out the synthetic oil plants once more for special attention and remained equally suspicious of calls for priority attacks on the German transportation system. Railway tracks were difficult to hit, but easy to repair, he argued. His preferred tactic remained the 'area bombing' of towns and cities, which he had inherited. Harris's views brought him into conflict with his own commander, CAS Air Chief Marshal Sir Charles Portal, and led to friction at an even higher level between the British and American authorities. Nineteen forty-four would be a rollercoaster of a year.

It opened with the continuing onslaught on Berlin. In six major raids during January, a total of 3299 heavy bombers were despatched, 202 lost (6.1 per cent – a worrying rate). As in the previous two months, operations were mounted against other targets as well: Stettin, Brunswick and Magdeburg, which brought an average loss rate of 7.1%. When a halt was finally called at the end of March, nineteen operations would have been carried out on Berlin, sixteen major attacks on twelve more towns or cities.

Such was the loss rate in these and other raids that new crews were constantly in demand. Tony Iveson had flown a Spitfire during the Battle of Britain and served as an instructor in Rhodesia before being assigned to Bomber Command. After leaving the Flying Training School at Banff, north-east Scotland, in January 1944 he went to Market Harborough OTU to fly Wellingtons and pick up five of the crew who would remain with him during his bombing tour. The procedure, as at many other training units, was for crews to sort themselves out. Firstly, Iveson acquired a fellow Yorkshireman as navigator, Flying Officer Jack Harrison. Sergeants Les Smith, who had survived a serious crash at Lossiemouth in Scotland, and Ted Wass were getting tea at the canteen waggon about four or five days after arriving when Harrison approached them to become Iveson's gunners. After being assigned to Supply and Accounts in 1939, Wass had served in the Middle East until a request for aircrew volunteers was publicised in July 1942. He lost no time in applying, the alternative being the newly formed RAF Servicing Commando to guard airfields. Wass reached Leicestershire, via the RAF Reception Centre in Regents Park whose mess was in the Zoo buildings, and various gunnery courses before securing his air gunner's brevet on 14 January 1944.

Iveson's six-man crew moved to Winthorpe HCU, Nottinghamshire, where it flew Stirlings and picked up a seventh member, flight engineer Sergeant Desmond 'Taffy' Phillips. That choice proved extremely fortunate. Phillips would effectively save their aircraft on two occasions. The crew soon learnt that Iveson, in Wass's words, was 'the boss man. You respected him, he was very strict. No chatter on the intercom.' Unlike some others, Wass never felt lonely in his detached eyrie. Always 'perfectly happy', nevertheless he welcomed Iveson's occasional quip: 'Rear gunner, you still awake at the back?'

For Gordon Carter, 'January 1944 was another of those months. On the 17th I received news that I was eligible for the RCAF operational badge, a winged "O" and Bar [for two operational tours] worn on the left-hand breast pocket.' The following day he learnt that he had been awarded a bar to his DFC for displaying 'outstanding enthusiasm for operational flying with marked ability and great devotion to duty'. Congratulations arrived from the Air Officer Commanding-in-Chief, RCAF Overseas, and Canadian Minister of National Defence for Air. The firm of which his father was treasurer, Thos Cook and Son, and the New York press celebrated Carter's achievement, too. Pride of place, though, went to a letter from his father expressing his parents' pride and adding a touching note that his mother 'carries on hopefully and keeps putting special delicacies on one side, in case you should turn up unexpectedly one day'.

During the night of 8/9 February, a promising development in target marking took place, when the Wing Commander Leonard Cheshire, OC 617 Squadron, led a dozen of his Lancasters to the Gnome & Rhône aero-engine factory in Limoges. Cheshire had insisted persuasively that only marking from low level could guarantee accurate delivery of target indicators. Protected only by a few machine guns, the site posed no major threat to the bombers, and Cheshire made three low runs over the target area to allow time for French workers to get clear. On the fourth run, he released his markers from 100ft. Ten of the eleven 12,000lb. bombs dropped by the other Lancasters hit the factory. Encouraging though this result was, it involved only a small number of bombers.

By now, Bomber Command had begun to vary its operational tactics for main force raids. The single stream was divided into two, aimed at one target or separate forces against two targets. The Germans were no longer fooled by small Mosquito diversions, as during the first part of the Peenemünde raid, so a significant number of bombers were now deployed in that role. In fact, despite only an average of fifty being available during the first quarter of 1944, the growing influence of the Mosquito should not be overlooked. Quite apart from deception ('spoof') activity or electronic countermeasure (ECM) operations with Serrate equipment, Mosquitoes flew 2034 sorties in the Battle of Berlin, often carrying a 4000lb. bomb. As that 'battle' progressed, Harris expressed concern that the enemy was 'using for his own purposes' the practice of route markers – flares dropped at predetermined points to guide the bomber stream. And to his dismay, the Air Staff had started to show an unhealthy preference for selective targets like the ball-bearing works at Schweinfurt, which Harris considered 'too small and distant a town for us to be able to find and hit'.

On 14 January 1944, Harris had received the Air Staff's response 'to your views on the question of night attack on Schweinfurt'. He was reminded of the Pointblank Directive, dated 10 June 1943, whereby 'the American strategic bombers are directed primarily to the attack of selected industries'. Air Marshal N. H. Bottomley agreed that Bomber Command's 'main aim' was 'the general disorganisation of German industry', but 'as far as practicable' that directive required Harris also to target 'industrial centres associated with those industries selected for precise attack by the American bomber forces'. This policy had been devised by the British and American Air Staffs with the backing of their respective governments. It was necessary to reduce the effectiveness of the Luftwaffe, not least with Overlord in mind. 'I am accordingly to request that you adhere to the spirit of the directive' and 'do your utmost to destroy at as early a date as possible the town of Schweinfurt and the ball-bearing factories which it contains'. In northern Bavaria, 65 miles east of Frankfurt and containing five major factories grouped round the town's railway station, Schweinfurt was believed to produce 76 per cent of Germany's ball-bearing needs. As Bufton wrote, 'every vital piece of mechanism is dependent upon ball bearings'. One of Harris's panacea targets. Eliminate Schweinfurt and the enemy war machine on the ground and in the air would theoretically grind to a halt. 'First priority must now be accorded to the destruction of Schweinfurt', Bottomley concluded. Harris had no choice.

So, on 24/25 February 1944, Lancaster F-Freddie of 467 Squadron, captained by Flying Officer James Marshall, found itself on the way to the target, which 266 B-17s had attacked the previous day. This was the RAF's first raid on Schweinfurt, for which the 734 aircraft were divided into two waves separated by two hours. F-Freddie's mid-upper gunner, Sergeant Alec Bance, recorded that, due to ice on his mask, his oxygen supply failed in the target area. The Australian wireless operator, Flight Sergeant T. G. Bashford, had the same problem, rather mysteriously noting in his logbook that 'bags of fun and games' had occurred. Bashford and Bance, in common with some other aircrew, habitually noted the number of aircraft lost on each operation (this time thirty-five), which must have made depressing reading as the weeks went by. Including mine-laying and attacks on enemy airfields, 1070 sorties were flown that night, with an official loss of thirty-six aircraft.

Flight Sergeant Jack Bormann, the bomb aimer, also referred to the oxygen difficulties, adding that the intercom failed for a time, too. He wrote a more detailed account in his diary, which was not so bland as those of his two colleagues. This was his first operation, and he admitted to having 'some mixed feelings' on takeoff with a full bomb load (11,228lb.). As the Lancaster passed through the London defensive belt, 'one hundred Jerries' were raiding London at the same time. 'Boy it shook me', believing he saw two Lancasters blown up by anti-aircraft shells. Despite light flak at the French coast, Bormann agreed that the inward flight was 'good', except for the oxygen trouble. Before Marshall got to the target area, the mid-upper gunner passed out for lack of oxygen, and the wireless operator (Bashford), going to his assistance, also fainted. The vicinity of the target was 'well lit' with 'many searchlights' and light flak forming 'a pretty red ball'. The temporary intercom malfunction happened after the bomb load had been dropped and the bomber turned for home. Unlike his fellow crew members, Bormann then noted two worrying incidents: a fighter attack, and near-collision with another Lancaster close to the English coast at dawn. It 'seemed ages' getting back from Schweinfurt to base at Waddington, near Lincoln.

An Air Ministry directive on 17 February, whilst accepting that Bomber Command's 'primary objective' would be 'the German Air Force', reminded Harris that his 'overall mission' remained 'the progressive destruction and dislocation' of Germany's 'military industrial and economic system'. The night after attacking Schweinfurt, therefore, F-Freddie went on another operation deep into Germany, to Augsburg with a slightly reduced bomb load of 10,500lb. This time 594 bombers were divided into two waves, with twenty-one aircraft lost including at least four in collisions. Bance thought it a 'good' trip with a Ju 88 fired on at one point. Bashford confirmed that both gunners did engage the night fighter, which was attacking another Lancaster. The operation had proved 'a very good prang', and Bormann agreed that it had been an 'excellent attack with the town ablaze'. He backed up Bance's account of the night fighter episode; otherwise, it had been an 'uneventful' night.

Meanwhile, Frank Blackman's luck had run out after taking off with 822 other aircraft for Leipzig on 19 February. Night fighters were lying in wait as the force approached the east German industrial centre from the north, despite attempts in the routing to suggest that Berlin was the target. Nor did a diversionary mine-laying operation in Kiel Bay work. That night, seventy-eight Lancasters and Halifaxes were lost (nearly 550 men), almost 10 per cent of the attacking force. The following day, Mary Mileham received the official telegram informing her that Frank Blackman was missing. Blackman had thoughtfully made her next of kin, although not a relative, because his elderly mother had lost her husband in the First World War. On 22 February, postmarked the 21st and clearly despatched by 429 Squadron in accordance with Blackman's instructions, his final letter arrived: 'Well Mary dear, this will tell you if something unfortunate has happened. I shall hope in due course to be writing to you again – either from Oflag something or other or, with any luck, from England on return. In the meantime, it is hard to know what to say. You have meant so much to me – and have been so very charming to me during these last few months that it is hard to say "goodbye" if only for a while. God bless you darling – and thank you again – a million times. Lots of luck and my deepest and sincerest wishes.' He would, though, never return. His aircraft had been shot down and he did not survive.

Gordon Carter's war also came to an abrupt end during the Leipzig operation. In the early part of February the crew had carried out 'plenty of training flights, practising maintaining altitude with two engines on one side feathered [props idling] or even cut out and including exercises "against" Bradford, Wolverhampton, Birmingham and Manchester'. On 15 February, they 'visited the "Big City", as Berlin was called'. Heavy cloud cover and 'much fighter activity', but fortunately 'neither the swarms of regular night fighters nor the *wilde Saue* ['Wild Boar'] daytime fighters sent up at night to sweep the sky for the telltale exhaust flames of the bombers, pounced on us'.

Shortly afterwards, the 'happily mixed bunch' of Squadron Leader 'Julian [Sale], pilot and skipper . . . Flight Lieutenant B. O. "Bod" Bodnar DFC, our Canadian H2S operator; Flight Lieutenant H. J. "Johnny" Rogers DFC, the quiet and unassuming English wireless op; Flight Lieutenant Roger "Sheep" Lamb, the mid-upper gunner; W. O. G. H. "Harry" Cross DFC, DFM, the English flight engineer; and Flight Sergeant Kenneth Knight' were given forty-eight hours' leave. They decided to go by train to London. The officers had first-class warrants, the NCOs second-class, but they all went in a first-class carriage. When challenged by the ticket collector, Sale told him 'that they were darned well staying with us, in the train as in the air'. That ended the argument.

They were together, too, when Halifax J-Johnny took off in sleet and ice for Leipzig at nine minutes to midnight on 19 February 1944. From the briefing, Carter realised that 'this would be the very opposite of a "piece of cake", namely a "shaky do"'. The aircraft had 'hardly' cleared the English coast and the gunners tested their weapons than it ran into 'unusual night fighter activity' over the North Sea. This intensified crossing the Dutch coast 'near Over Flakkee Island (how true a name!)' and 'got worse' over Germany. The enemy were waiting for them, the 'route ahead of us being brilliantly illuminated by strings of flares dropped by the Luftwaffe to light up the cloud cover far below and silhouette us starkly for the night fighters prowling about above'. Carter brooded, 'someone had obviously given the game away and we were sitting ducks'. There seemed to be 'plenty' of fighters aloft, 'nor did our own twin-engined Bristol Beaufighters, slipped into the bomber stream to pick off unsuspecting German fighters, make much difference'. The Beaufighter pilots 'had to keep their eyes peeled' for in the murk gunners in the bomber stream were apt to 'let fly' at anything with fewer than four engines.

At 23,000ft, 'higher than ever before on ops', Carter's 'fully-loaded' Halifax 'weaved gently to port and starboard, nose up and nose down, endlessly corkscrewing over enemy territory to make it more difficult for the opposition to adjust their sights', something which Carter queried 'did it really?' In their case, the answer was regretfully 'no'.

The Halifax was hit by 20mm cannon shells from a Ju 88 using the upward-firing *schräge Musik*. Carter knew that the aircraft had been hit – and badly. The fuel tank immediately exploded, engulfing the Halifax in flames. Sale, the pilot, quickly recognised that the fire extinguishers would never quell this conflagration and ordered the crew to bale out. Carter recalled that 'the average survival span of a burning aircraft was thirty

Off Cyril Barton (back, centre) with his 578 Squadron Halifax crew shortly before being posthumously awarded the VC for attacking Nuremberg in March 1944. (*IWM*)

Off F. H. Blackman, Halifax navigator on an operation to Leipzig in February 4. (*Mileham*)

Mary Mileham, in the Admiralty secretariat, girlfriend of Blackman and his next of kin. (*Mileham*)

Cologne, showing the impact of bombing. (*TRH Pictures*)

Results of raid on the V-weapon site at Pennemünde, 17/18 August 1943. (*TRH Picture*

German battleship *Tirpitz* anchored inside torpedo nets. (*BAC*)

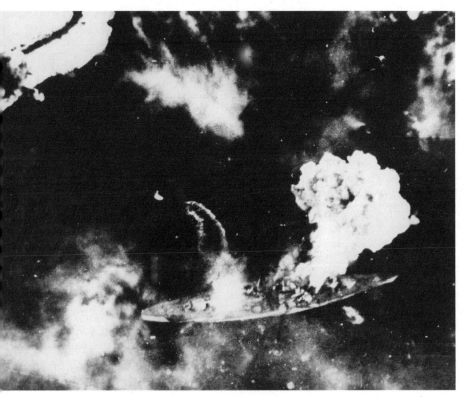

Tirpitz under attack from the air in a Norwegian fjord. (*TRH Pictures*)

Pilots with their Lanc
crews, which in 1944
attacked *Tirpitz* with
Barnes Wallis's
12,000lb 'Tallboy' bo

(Top) Fg Off J. H. Le
(centre), an American
the RAF, less the gun
extreme right. (*Coles*)

(Centre) Flt Lt R. E.
Knights, third left. (*K*

(Bottom) Flt Lt B. A.
Gumbley RNZAF, far
right. (*Grimes*)

9 Squadron crew. Sqn Ldr W. Gordon (pilot, centre) with Plt Off J. Langston on his right,
Lt P. Shirley his left. In the closing weeks of the war, Langston and Shirley would survive
an unnecessary training crash with another pilot. (*Langston*)

he perforated tail-fin of Lancaster KC-M
ursed back from Bergen by Sqn Ldr Tony
veson (second right) in January 1945. Sgt
'affy' Phillips, whose initiative twice saved
e crew, is on Iveson's right. (*Wass*)

Grand Slam. Canadian Wg Cdr J. E.
Fauquier with Barnes Wallis's ten-ton bomb
first dropped on the Bielfeld viaduct in
March 1945. (*Reed*)

George 'Johnny' Johnson, the American Joe McCarthy's bomb-aimer, who was grateful that his pilot brought him back from operations forty times 'without a scratch'. (*Owen*)

Air Cdre J. H. Searby as Gp Capt (left), who likened a bomber crew to the Three Musketeers, with Air Vice-Marshal D. C. T. Bennett, leader of the Pathfinder Force. (*IW*

F/Sgt James Watts and his fiancée Doreen Ratcliffe. Watts was killed on an operation eight days before their planned wedding. Sixty years later the people of Anzegem in Belgium dedicated a memorial to Watts' crew, and Doreen remembered 'Jimmy' as 'a lovely person'. (*Watts*)

Mary Lindsay (née Mileham) married and widowed post-war, who thirty years after his loss sought information about Frank Blackman's fate and recalled details of their time together. (*Mileham*)

(L to R) Dudley Heal (navigator), Ken Brown (pilot) and Basil Feneron (flight engineer) a memorial service for a fellow Dambuster, David Shannon. (*Author*)

25th anniversary of the Dambusters Raid. Six members of Les Knight's crew, whose l
he saved four months after the operation, behind a model of the Möhne Dam used i
the commercial film. (*Hobday*)

seconds'. He did not hesitate. 'After what seemed ages fighting the centrifugal force flattening me against the fuselage as the kite started to spin out of control, I went through the hatch.' With 'immense relief', he found himself 'on the end of a chute, albeit over Germany, because I knew that this had saved me the ignominy of having to ask to be taken off ops, with the disgrace inevitably associated with lack of moral fibre. I was simply at the end of my tether.' Reflecting years later that the 'pre-LMF' signs were a tendency to get up to 'various antics' and behave 'in an unpredictable way', Carter realised that he 'hadn't quite reached' this state. 'But I wasn't far off.'

As he floated towards earth shortly before 3 a.m. on 20 February 1944, Carter was aware that he was falling in a temperature of '50 degrees below zero or thereabouts, without oxygen, and descending through the thick of one thousand or so strong bomber stream following in the Pathfinders' wake . . . That I wasn't hit by someone's wing or my chute collapsed by the slipstreams is a wonder.'

Once more, Carter's parents received 'the long-feared' telegram informing them that their son 'is reported missing after air operations overseas'. Carter's uncles, the mother of his first pilot 'Tommy' Thomas, his squadron commander and the chaplain from Graveley, PFF headquarters at Wyton, and RCAF authorities all wrote or cabled their sympathy. At the time, they did not know Carter had survived, though he would not evade capture as he had previously done in France. A sailor shooting crows in a field disbelieved his story that he was a French factory worker. So Carter found himself in Stalag Luft III, and his parents would soon joyfully receive the news that he was alive.

F-Freddie bombed Stuttgart on 1/2 March, part of a 557-strong force which lost only four aircraft. Flying Officer Marshall's Lancaster did not have a comfortable trip, though.

The mid-upper gunner, Bance, reported being attacked by an Fw 190, at which he fired 150 rounds, hit the tailplane and with whose destruction he was credited. The Lancaster had not escaped unscathed, however. The doomed fighter had badly damaged the starboard wing, making the wireless and flaps U/S. So Marshall needed to make an emergency landing at RAF Wittering, Cambridgeshire. Bormann, the bomb aimer, elaborated this version of events, adding that the German fighter had attacked during the bombing run, the mid-upper gunner had also engaged it and a fire under the wireless operator's compartment put his equipment out of action. Until then it had been 'a good trip'. When the cannon shell struck the wing, the Lancaster had plunged from 22,000 to 16,000ft 'in a few seconds', though this appears to have been Marshall's attempt to get out of trouble. Bormann added that fire, extinguished by the navigator, had broken out when crossing the English coast at dawn; with the radio not working, their base had believed them shot down and it had been 'good to see England again; marvellous'.

Although another twenty-two bombers out of 816 were shot down attacking Frankfurt on 22/23 March, Bormann again declared it 'a good trip' for F-Freddie with no bomb hang-ups and no trouble to or from the target'. Nuremberg, for which 795 aircraft went out on 30/31 March, was altogether different. This was catastrophic. The target area was unexpectedly obscured by thick cloud and a surprise cross-wind further complicated bombing accuracy: 120 bombers actually hit Schweinfurt 50 miles north-west of Nuremberg, where, due to the faulty forecast wind, some Pathfinders dropped markers. The conditions almost exactly reversed the weather forecast, which promised cloud along the approach route and clear skies over the target. The bombers were, therefore, at the mercy of night fighters in bright moonlight along the route to and from

Nuremberg. Jamming of German equipment was useless, because in the clear air vapour trails and aircraft were easily visible. Moreover, the enemy's ability to lock on to the H2S sets meant that, by the time the bombers had reached Aachen on the German border, 246 fighters were lying in wait. Only the need for them to land and refuel prevented even heavier losses on the way home.

The result was Bomber Command's greatest loss on a single night during the war: ninety-five Lancasters and Halifaxes, almost 12 per cent of those despatched. Bormann gave the losses as ninety-six; including crashes in England, other sources suggest up to 108. Although F-Freddie had not been attacked by fighters, two rockets 'chased' it, and from the French coast onwards its crew witnessed a multitude of air to air combats. This time, the wireless equipment packed up for most of the 'very grim trip'.

The Germans had benefited from two developments in the opening weeks of 1944. On 7 January, at long last they captured an Oboe set from a crashed bomber, but that advantage was relatively short-lived. Once the loss had become known, steps were taken to overcome jamming. More worrying was arrival of greater numbers of airborne SN-2 and Naxos-Z radars the following month, increasing the killing power of the night fighters.

Amid the aerial devastation, there were many acts of individual courage. For one of them, Pilot Officer Cyril Barton gained the VC. Seventy miles short of Nuremberg, his Halifax was jumped by a Ju 88, which demolished the entire intercom system. Then a Messerschmitt Me 210 attacked, as simultaneous failure of their weapons prevented both gunners from responding. Now defenceless, Barton pressed on as the two fighters made repeated passes. In the confusion caused by lack of electronic communication within the aircraft, and understandably in view of its defensive impotence, the navigator, bomb aimer and wireless operator baled out believing that they had been ordered to do so.

Barton now faced a perilous predicament. One engine was out of action and the aircraft had no means of defending itself in the target area or on the long flight home. Nevertheless, he carried on and dropped the bombs on the target himself. As he banked away, the propeller of the dead engine disintegrated and it became obvious that fuel was leaking from two damaged tanks. Despite strong headwinds and no navigational aids, incredibly he managed not only to avoid further trouble but somehow get back to the English coast only 90 miles north of his base at Burn, North Yorkshire. Within reach of safety, the remaining fuel finally ran out and Barton warned the remaining three members of his crew to prepare for a crash-landing at Ryehope, near Sunderland. Although injured, they survived; Barton did not. The citation highlighted his 'unsurpassed courage and devotion to duty' during his nineteenth and final operation.

The Nuremberg debacle brought to a close the series of operations known as the Battle of Berlin. On 24/25 March, the last raid had taken place on the German capital, when 811 bombers attacked it. Unpredicted winds effectively broke up the stream, spreading the aircraft over a wide area including several well-defended locations. As a result, approximately fifty of the seventy aircraft lost were victims of flak.

Since its inception on 18/19 November 1943, the Battle of Berlin had mounted thirty-five major raids on thirteen towns and cities, including the German capital. Against Berlin, 9111 sorties had been launched, against the other dozen 11,113. The most disturbing statistics were that it had all cost Bomber Command 1047 bombers, with a further 1682 damaged and more than 7000 men killed or taken prisoner. As Ken Brown reflected: 'That was a battle we certainly lost.' Bomber Command had not brought Germany to its knees by 1 April, as

Harris had hoped. Six days later, in accepting that the night fighter strength had been underestimated, he wrote that 'in time' this force was likely to wreak 'unacceptable' casualties on attacking bombers. His solution was to provide Bomber Command's own night fighter escorts 'on a substantial scale'. That theory would not be put to the test in the immediate future, as operations into Germany were reduced with Bomber Command's support for the D-Day landings gaining momentum. On 4 March, Bomber Command had been directed to specific marshalling yards, airfield and ammunition dumps in northern France and warned that 'other railway targets will subsequently be detailed when the Overlord plan is finally formulated'.

Behind the front-line effort, the training process remained especially important with the high loss of bomber crews over Germany. However, for individuals the progress to operational flying was not always smooth. In March 1944, having finished his navigational course in Canada, nineteen-year-old Sergeant John Langston, who would eventually retire from the RAF as an air commodore, reached 1661 HCU at Winthorpe in somewhat unusual circumstances. Hitherto, his experience had mainly involved flights in Ansons, requiring use of maps, sextant for astro observation and loop aerial for directional bearings. He had not even seen a distant reading compass, Air Position Indicator (API), Gee equipment or H2S set, having by-passed an OTU in an accelerated scheme. He faced a steep learning curve before he could take his place in a four-engine bomber. The unit's navigational instructor, Flight Lieutenant Jim Warwick, quickly sent him up in a Stirling. The size of the cockpit area impressed him: 'Very comfortable. A huge navigation table. Shorts [the manufacturer] had been used to building flying boats.'

In between flights with different pilots, Warwick taught

Langston the rudiments of Gee and H2S, and in two months he had mastered the techniques. However, there were no crews without a navigator, so Langston soon found himself instructing others. The basis of the accelerated scheme was that too many navigators were found wanting ('washed out') at HCUs, resulting in the rest of the crew being returned to an OTU. Eventually, Langston profited from this process. Flying Officer Bill Gordon, an experienced flying instructor with more than one thousand hours in his logbook, had in the normal way gathered his crew at an OTU. His navigator, though, got the Stirling hopelessly lost on several occasions at Winthorpe and was therefore 'washed out'. Langston took his place. Gordon was 'unhappy about losing his navigator and the rest of the crew were unhappy about getting a new boy'. Langston soon proved himself, went off to a Lancaster Finishing School with Gordon and on to 630 Squadron at East Kirkby.

When he began flying operationally, Langston thought Gee 'extremely accurate', if limited in range, with enemy jamming evident as the bomber crossed the North Sea. Like other navigators, Langston found H2S particularly useful for distinguishing between water and land ('you could see black where the sea was and brilliant white where the land was'). He had to master another aid, the astro graph, a film projector on the navigator's desk which, at different stages of a flight, gave sight lines to selected stars on which shots could be taken from the astrodome. The device was totally satisfactory only in clear conditions and useful on long flights. Langston therefore had doubts about its effectiveness, especially given the time it took to operate. These were not the only aids he must manipulate. The figures on the Distant Reading Compass, positioned close to the rear entry door of a Lancaster, had to be checked on entry, the power switched on to get the gyro run up so that the readings on the four repeater compasses (for the pilot, navigator, bomb aimer and the API) were accurate. During a flight, he would constantly use the variable setting corrector (VSC) to feed in local magnetic variations and ensure that all the repeater compasses had a true north heading. As well, the navigator must make course calculations, using, for example, the API or Gee to determine the wind speed and direction.

To add to his problems, the various bits of equipment were not together. The Gee receiver over the main spar close to the mid-upper turret had to be adjusted according to the chain being used. The H2S equipment was on a rack down the port side of the fuselage over the bomb bay, the rotating dish imme-diately under the wireless operator. After a corkscrew or other violent manoeuvring, the distant reading compass and astro compass, both in the rear of the fuselage, must be reset. Until the navigator did this, the pilot relied on an emergency compass. The navigator had therefore 'to be quite energetic'. Ten thou-sand feet was the official height for the crew to go on oxygen, although to ensure night vision some crews did so before that. If the compass adjustments had to be made at 12–14,000ft, the navigator faced a difficult decision. Should he use an oxygen bottle, a cumbersome process, or gamble that he could discon-nect his main oxygen supply and finish the job before he felt breathing discomfort? Rather than 'frigging around with the oxygen bottle, I would rely on speed for short jobs,' Langston recalled. One other unofficial duty fell to him. His pilot, Gordon, had an occasional tendency to drift off course, so Langston used his long ruler to tap him on the back of his head. By the end of the first tour, Gordon's flying helmet had been indelibly scarred.

The Lancaster offered one special advantage to the navigator and the wireless operator. Not only noisy, the aircraft was often very cold, but heating from the engines came into the fuselage close to these 'two lucky guys'. This meant that Langston could dispense with his heavy gauntlets and work in the silk under-gloves, more convenient for 'fine work with pencil and dividers'. However, the navigator's desk in the Lancaster, unlike that in a Halifax, did not have convenient pigeonholes for papers and pieces of equipment. This proved a distinct disadvantage when the pilot corkscrewed to shake off a fighter or escape searchlights. The pilot would put on full rudder and dive at 'some vast speed', rapidly lose height then describe a figure of eight to regain altitude and direction. The result was 'absolute hell' for the navigator. 'The chart went one way, loose stuff all over the shop, your Dalton computer with all your calculations often fell on the floor.' Langston learnt to counter this. 'The minute I heard "corkscrew" I would lean over the table and try to gather all the stuff under my arms.' On a trip to a flying bomb site he failed to react quickly enough and everything went askew. The dividers, so critical for accurate plotting, disappeared under the table. As soon as equilibrium was restored, Langston unplugged the intercom and grovelled to locate them. At that point, the pilot tried to contact him. In exasperation, he yelled: 'Where's the navigator?' to be told by a chuckling wireless operator, 'he's under the table'. Thereafter, whenever the Lancaster neared a target, somebody was bound to inquire, 'Is John under the table yet?' It took some time to live that down.

Langston admired his pilot, 'absolutely the captain', but he added that 'in a crew, anybody could be the director at a given moment'. A gunner, for instance, issued instructions when a fighter was coming in, or the bomb aimer during the bombing run. With justification, Langston 'thought the navigator was really the right-hand man. It was bloody hard work, I tell you. You didn't stop from the moment you took off to the moment you got back. Fixing position every ten minutes, sometimes every six minutes. If you could obtain Gee or H2S fixes at these intervals, all calculations were easy.' But operational flying was rarely that simple.

John Allen's war in the air came to an abrupt end during his twenty-fifth operation. After the Stirlings had been withdrawn from conflict over Germany, Flight Lieutenant Gay's aircraft dropped mines off the enemy coast, agents and supplies to the French Resistance, a reminder that Bomber Command still had much work to do apart from area bombing. During the early hours of 11 April 1944, the Stirling was shot down at low level, Gay making a successful belly landing despite the aircraft being on fire. Everybody got out, though they would all be captured. Allen concluded that the crew owed their lives to their 'marvellous pilot'.

During March Leonard Cheshire had refined his low-level marking technique, and on 5/6 April flew a Mosquito instead of a Lancaster to mark aircraft factories at Toulouse for 144 bombers. Thirteen days later he and three more 617 Squadron Mosquitoes marked the marshalling yards at Juvisy with devastating accuracy for 202 Lancasters. 'So opened a new phase in the history of Bomber Command', 5 Group headquarters maintained, and Bomber Command declared the operation 'outstandingly successful'. Bormann, in F-Freddie, thought it a 'good trip' with the 'concentration of aiming points good' and altogether 'a good prang'.

Four days later, on 22/23 April, the technique was repeated at Brunswick for 238 Lancasters. There was a potentially dangerous complication for the attackers that night, when Les Munro acted as controller liaising between Cheshire and the main force. On the way to the target he became aware that one aircraft was transmitting continuously by R/T 'to all and sundry'. If not stopped, this would interfere with the passing of instructions to other bombers. From the nature of the exchanges, it became clear the offender was a Pathfinder aircraft. Munro therefore told his wireless operator to send a W/T message requiring all Pathfinders to check their equipment. The culprit reacted immediately.

What intrigued Munro about this episode was the incessant chatter among the crew in question. 'The only words spoken by my crew over the intercom during operational flights and even on training exercises were the giving and receiving of instructions and the identification and description of landmarks etc. I suppose in a way you could describe my plane as a flying morgue, complete silence sometimes for long periods of time, broken only by the navigator advising changes of course. I was a strong believer that the intercom should always remain clear for urgent instructions and directions in the event of fighter attack or other abnormal happenings.' He was not alone in this respect.

Although only 1.5 per cent (four aircraft) were lost, 'considerable cloud at 10,000ft' prevented many main force bombers from identifying the markers. So technically the Brunswick raid was not very successful. Two days later, they tried again – at Munich.

Pathfinder aircraft were to illuminate the area with flares; Cheshire and three other Mosquitoes would then mark the target, backed up by 617 Squadron in advance of the 244-Lancaster main force. A complicated plan required the bombers to accompany others launching a diversionary raid on Milan, which meant crossing the Alps before turning north towards Munich. Meanwhile, the Mosquitoes trailed them by two hours, after topping up at Manston flying a direct route over Germany. Warned of the intention to attack Munich a fortnight earlier, Cheshire had requested drop tanks for the Mosquitoes. 'Unfortunately, this statement was not taken seriously . . . so that the success of the attack as well as the safety of the leaders themselves was seriously jeopardised', a post-operational

194

summary concluded. As the Mosquito crews were about to climb into their aircraft at Manston, Cheshire remarked how beautiful the sunset was. David Shannon, the Australian Dambusters veteran, smartly retorted that he would rather see sunrise the following day.

En route to Munich, Cheshire's small group ran into several concentrations of flak, especially over Augsburg, but got through. It arrived over the target to find the searchlights and flak guns active. With flares already illuminating the area Cheshire dived to 700ft, identified the aiming point and marked it accurately, followed by the other Mosquitoes, as Lancasters above could be seen 'ploughing steadfastly through the thick concentration of flak'.

Although his job had officially been done, to the consternation of his navigator who was worried about the fuel situation Cheshire continued to fly over the target at 1000ft directing back-up markers. His aircraft was hit by shell splinters and, on one occasion, he almost lost control after being coned by searchlights. At length, he disengaged and turned for home, to find that for another 'full twelve minutes' he had to fly through more heavy defences. German reports would confirm that, behind him, an enormous amount of devastation had been wrought for the loss of nine aircraft (3.5 per cent). For his work over Munich that night, Leonard Cheshire was awarded the VC. 'What he did in the Munich operation was typical of the careful planning, brilliant execution and contempt for danger which has established for Wing Commander Cheshire a reputation second to none'. The raid, Bomber Command concluded, demonstrated how 'a really well-defended target could be visually dive-marked between 2000 and 4000ft under reasonable conditions'.

Two days after Munich, on 26/27 April, during the long haul to Schweinfurt in southern Germany, twenty-one bombers (over 9 per cent) were lost from the 215 Lancasters in the attacking force. A strong wind disrupted the timetable, and German night fighters took full advantage. Sergeant Norman Jackson from 106 Squadron won the VC on this raid, the first flight engineer to do so. As the Lancaster was turning for home at 20,000ft, after dropping its bombs it came under fighter attack sustaining 'many hits'. Fire broke out in the starboard wing between the fuselage and the inner engine, close to a petrol tank. Although wounded in the right leg and shoulder, Jackson secured permission to deal with the fire. Putting a fire extinguisher into the top of his life jacket, he clipped on his parachute pack and jettisoned the escape hatch above the pilot's head. He then climbed out on to the top of the fuselage and crawled backwards towards the wing. Not quite that easily. As he left the aircraft, his parachute opened, with the canopy and rigging spilling into the cockpit. The pilot, bomb aimer and navigator clung on to the rigging lines and paid them out as Jackson made his way aft. 'Eventually, he slipped and, falling from the fuselage to the starboard wing, grasped an air intake on the leading edge of the wing.' Jackson clung on but lost the fire extinguisher which was blown away. The fire had now spread and, in the formal words of a later report, 'Jackson was now involved'. In fact, his face, hands and clothing were 'severely burnt'. Unable to cling on any longer, Jackson was swept through the flames and over the trailing edge of the wing dragging his parachute behind. 'When last seen it was only partly inflated, and was burning in a number of places.' Unable to control his descent, Jackson broke his ankle on landing, his badly burnt hands were useless and his right eye closed because of burns to the surrounding skin. In this 'pitiable state', he made his way painfully to the nearest village and into captivity. Behind him, the fire had taken hold of the Lancaster and the crew baled out. Four survived; the pilot and rear gunner did not.

The VC citation acknowledged Jackson's 'incredible feat' of

attempting to quell the flames in order to save the aircraft and its crew, with little prospect of ever getting inside again even if he had doused the fire. His was a shining 'example of self-sacrifice'. Before he took off, Jackson learnt that his wife had given birth to a son and a successful operation that night would have completed two operational tours. He eventually returned to England in May 1945, and his award was promulgated on 26 October of that year.

By the close of April 1944, the focus of attention had shifted to France and need to pave the way for the Normandy landings little over a month ahead. To Harris's dismay, on 14 April control of the RAF's bombers was transferred to General Dwight D. Eisenhower, Supreme Commander of the Allied Expeditionary Force, after Eisenhower had threatened resignation if Harris's intransigence continued. Three days later, Eisenhower issued a directive: 'Our re-entry on the Continent constitutes the supreme operation for 1944; all possible support must, therefore, be afforded to the Allied armies by our Air Forces to assist them in establishing themselves in the lodgement area.' Attacks on Germany would not cease, but destruction of the enemy transportation and coastal batteries in northern France would take priority. Bitterly Harris wrote, 'thus the strategic bombing of Germany had lasted almost exactly a year'. Critics would reflect that the heavy casualties suffered during the Battle of Berlin suggested that the switch to northern France saved Bomber Command from mounting, unacceptable losses, which Harris himself had in effect admitted on 7 April.

Although drastically reduced, attacks on German targets were indeed not wholly discontinued. Hence, on 21/22 May, the mid-upper gunner Bance noted that F-Freddie flew to Duisburg in a force of 510 Lancasters and fired at a twin-engine fighter on the way back. The following night, discovering 'a new searchlight belt on the track Osnabrück–Bremen', during

197

an operation by 225 aircraft against Brunswick, he engaged an Me 210. Bormann, the flight engineer, confirmed Bance's account of the Brunswick raid, adding that 'cloud spoiled marking' and the bombing was therefore 'scattered'.

Targets in France connected with communications predominated, though. On 10 May, a 'grim' night over the marshalling yards of Lille led to twenty losses and again poor visibility interfered with accurate bombing. This was 'certainly a black day. Mac is missing; have lost the greatest pal I've ever had', another Australian whom Bance had met on the ship coming to England. 'How can I tell Esther?', Mac's English girlfriend. Dud, another lost friend, had just been awarded the DFC. 'Scotty's crew', that of Squadron Leader Smith and three others, had not returned, which 'has placed a gloom on the whole station'.

The experience of Sergeant Philip Kirby, a wireless operator with 40 Squadron, demonstrated that not all bombing of Germany took place from England nor in mid-1944 were raids carried out exclusively by four-engine aircraft or Mosquitoes. Occupation of southern Italy by the Allies opened up another axis of attack. During the night of 13/14 June, nine days after American troops entered Rome, Kirby was surprised to be flying 'in our old Wellington' from Foggia Main airfield to bomb the railway station at Munich. With extra fuel and a reduced bomb load, the twin engine aircraft struggled over the Alps well below the height of the heavy bombers higher up – an inviting target, of which flak gunners took grateful advantage. Standing in the astrodome, Kirby suddenly had 'a disturbingly good view of the ground instead of the sky'. Flak exploding under one wing had caused the aircraft to roll over, 'not a good idea in a Wellington', he thought.

As the pilot struggled to regain control of the diving Wellington, he warned the crew to be ready to bale out. Kirby helped a young gunner on his first flight to fit his parachute to the harness. Kirby was in the process of saying farewell to the pilot, when the control panel 'went up in a puff of smoke'. He wasted no more time in getting out and, with flak heavy all around, counted himself lucky to come down safely. Kirby did not evade capture, though, and spent the rest of the war in captivity.

By D-Day, in Eastern Europe the Russians had cleared the Ukraine, driven the Germans out of the Crimea and invaded Romania. In the Far East, the Japanese had been held on the borders of India at Kohima, the Americans were pressing westwards in their 'island-hopping' campaign, and having taken New Guinea were about to land in the Marianas, which would give them bases from which to bomb Tokyo with long-range B-29 Superfortresses. Meanwhile, British and American bombers continued to attack Germany.

Development of the P-51 Mustang fighter, capable of ranging deep into enemy territory and operational since December 1943, had allowed US 8th AAF bombers to resume their main offensive in 1944. Like RAF Bomber Command, they had continued intermittently to hit targets in Germany, while supporting the build-up to Overlord. Despite the diversion of one thousand bombers to the 15th AAF in Italy, by 6 June the operational strength of 8th AAF Bomber Command had reached two thousand aircraft. The horrendous losses of 1943 had not been immediately reversed, however. A concentrated effort on the German aircraft industry in February 1944, during 'big week', saw launching of almost four thousand sorties by the 8th and 15th AAFs which cost 226 bombers and twenty-eight fighters. On the other hand, from 526 B-17s and B-24s despatched to Berlin and three other urban centres by the 8th Bomber Command on 9 March, only eight were lost; on 26 April, none from 529 sent to five German cities. Tactically, the 8th and 15th

AAFs were now co-ordinated by Lieutenant General Carl A. Spaatz as Commanding General US Strategic Air Forces in Europe (USSAFE). When the CBO against Germany resumed in earnest, therefore, three bomber forces (two American, one British) were available. It helped that Harris and Spaatz, who had commanded the 8th AAF on its arrival in England, personally worked well together.

In June 1944, after the lengthy training process, Iveson and his crew reached 617 Squadron at Woodhall Spa. Surveying the new arrivals, David Shannon, who had been flying almost continuously for over two years, observed tartly: 'What are we doing getting sprogs like you, who haven't even done one bomber operation? They'll have you for breakfast.' Not exactly a warm welcome, but Iveson realised Shannon had a point. It served to sharpen his approach, but did illustrate how severely Bomber Command had been stretched. His was not the only green crew to be sent into the bitter struggle.

That month, as the Allied armies battled to expand their narrow bridgehead in northern France, Bomber Command launched continuous attacks on road and rail communications, enemy airfields, ammunition and fuel dumps, and naval targets in coastal ports. This was not the work Harris wanted for his heavy bombers. When V-1 'doodlebugs' began to fall on England, his aircraft found themselves directed against their launch sites as well. With the need for pinpoint accuracy against such precision targets, many operations would take place in daylight bringing added danger for the bomber crews.

Throughout June, only six operations occurred against targets in Germany. One, by thirty-five Mosquitoes, was on railway workshops in Göttingen, the other five on plants producing synthetic oil. Jim Parsons was now flying operationally in Pilot Officer Ray Harris's crew, and he discovered that the textbook did not always prepare him for the reality of action.

Bitter Struggle

Theoretically, the bomb aimer should not occupy his compartment in the nose until after take-off, but Parsons found it more convenient to settle in immediately. He lay on the bomb aimer's couch, on which he would sit sideways during flight as he helped the navigator by identifying pinpoints and map reading. It was easier to pick up features like rivers and roads at night than he had been led to believe. Before his first operation against a synthetic oil plant at Gelsenkirchen on 12/13 June, from 7000ft he had practised identifying target indicators dropped over Salisbury Plain at night. Now he found himself at 20,000ft over the Ruhr and the configuration was 'entirely different'. Warned by the master bomber to concentrate on the southern markers, he advised Harris accordingly. The red target indicators seemed a long way away. Suddenly, he remembered that at briefing they had been informed of a simultaneous raid to the south. Gradually it dawned on him that was where they were heading. Professional pride did not permit him to attack, so he called a dummy run and told Harris to fly back to the original location – against the main stream which was leaving the area. 'You can imagine what the rest of the crew were saying. I was not at all popular with them and swore that I would never again call a dummy run. And I never did.'

This aberration did not affect Parsons' relationship with the crew in the long run. His rapport with Harris was particularly important, because 'during the bombing run the bomb aimer is in charge of the aircraft'. It was Parsons' job to guide Harris on to the correct track: 'left, left' (repeated in case poor communication obscured the exact word), a single 'right' or elongated 'steaaaady' if properly positioned. After the bombs had been released, the bomb aimer would press a button to clear any hook-up, then physically check through a peephole. It was, Parsons recalled, a rapid learning exercise for which nothing in training could fully prepare you.

As part of the reduced effort on Germany, shortly before midnight on 16 June twenty-two-year-old Pilot Officer Geoff Packham, an experienced Whitley and Wellington pilot, took off in a Lancaster for another synthetic oil plant at Sterkrade in the Ruhr, one of 321 bombers ordered to attack despite a forecast of poor weather in the area. Flying at 18,000ft about twenty minutes from the target, flak disabled the port inner engine, put the hydraulic system out of action and, to Packham's discomfort, made 'a large hole in the nose which created a cold draught'. At reduced speed and losing height, the Lancaster arrived over Sterkrade at 'about 15,000ft' to discover itself all alone. The rest had already gone home. 'A very exciting time was had orbiting through the intense barrage of flak and being coned by searchlights while we tried to release our bombs'. Damage to the aircraft made this impossible and, at length, Packham decided to turn back with the bombs still on board.

Edging very slowly westwards, the Lancaster had sunk to 12,000ft when a Messerschmitt Bf 110 appeared to the starboard rear. Taking evasive action, Packham managed to shake it off, but the port outer engine now packed up as well. The Lancaster was therefore flying on the two starboard engines, losing height steadily and with now no hope of reaching England. Packham ordered the crew to bale out once he had steered clear of built-up areas and they all did so successfully at 5000ft. It was more difficult for Packham, the last to leave. In an effort to get some sort of stability, he shut down the remaining two engines, but the Lancaster perversely went into a spin. Eventually the pilot scrambled clear of the forward escape hatch. Realising how low the machine was, Packham immediately pulled the ripcord. The parachute duly opened, but the harness, which must have been loosened during his struggle to get out of the stricken aircraft, fell from his shoulders and left

202

him upside down held by one ankle in the straps. 'Not a happy position to be in', Packham felt. He had the wit to curl up and so landed on his rump – fortunately for his body and state of mind in 'a very soft and soggy wheat field'. As he did so, the Lancaster crashed in a colourful explosion against which a church was silhouetted. Packham made for that haven, only to spend 'a very wet and miserable night sitting on someone's final place of rest' in the churchyard. Next morning, through the vicar, he was put in contact with the Dutch Resistance. During two months on the run, he met up with his 'elderly' (thirty-five-year-old) mid-upper gunner. At length, they were betrayed and spent the rest of the war in captivity. Looking back in peacetime, Packham wrote: 'I have great admiration for the calm courage of my crew members in the action we saw, and feel there is no praise great enough for those working in the underground movement who risked their lives and families to help us.'

F-Freddie, one of 133 Lancasters, went to Gelsenkirchen on 21/22 June. This gave Bormann (now promoted warrant officer) an opportunity to take stock. 'Boy these German stooges are difficult. Flak, air to air combats, many kites going down in flames. Northern Lights show the boys up. Flak at target very heavy. Poor old Ed Dearnaly missing and Max Hill thirty-four trips – two more of my old pals. Life is getting grim again.' Squadron records agree. 'It was certainly bad luck for Pilot Officer Dearnaly and his crew as they were very close to finishing their tour.'

Three days later, on 24/25 June, F-Freddie was despatched to a 'Doodle Bug Nest' – Prouville. 'Hell of a trip. No markers so circled the defences for twenty minutes. Very grim. Searchlights, flak and fighters deadly. Many kites going down', according to Bormann. Twelve Lancasters were lost attacking this target that night; one burning fiercely passed 'a few hundred feet' underneath Bormann's. When F-Freddie bombed, it 'nearly clocked' two others. Then 'thought was my last', as the aircraft was coned by searchlights. 'We went like hell expecting tracer to come at any minute. Horrible. Very hot under the collar.' They survived, but 'Chips Cowan and Paul gone, hellish luck and wizard fellows'. His final comments betrayed the strain which so many aircrew felt but rarely admitted. 'Bugger "ops". Am getting sick of this. Berryman's crew also missing and two more from the other squadron. Feeling am losing my grip. First Mac goes, then Max and now Paul. Can't get the sight of that burning plane out of my mind – funny it should stick, have seen hundreds go down.' To relieve the tension, when not flying Bormann admitted to 'going dancing and trying to have a good time' in Bracebridge, Lincoln and Havenby.

The V-weapon sites required extreme accuracy, and for this the perfection of the new Gee-H blind-bombing device proved invaluable. Not until June 1944 did it become widely operational, although it had been in use since a raid on Düsseldorf on 3 November 1943 . Like Oboe, it was linked to ground stations, but in this case the process was reversed, with the necessary calculations being made in the aircraft, the onus for success being placed on aircrew rather than ground station operators. This system could therefore assist more aircraft than Oboe. Once Allied forces were established on the Continent in the coming months, G-H ground stations, like those for Oboe, would be moved across the Channel, thus extending the range at which this aid – and others – could operate.

In June 1944, another important acquisition for Bomber Command came into service: Barnes Wallis's 'earthquake' bomb. This 12,000lb. weapon was designed to burrow into the ground and explode beneath a target, so causing it to collapse. Its penetrative power would also allow it to go through thick concrete and armour plating. On the night of 8/9 June, 617 Squadron under Leonard Cheshire destroyed a railway tunnel near Saumur, crucial for the movement of enemy troops. And the weapon was soon used successfully against V-weapon sites and E-boat pens.

July was once more dominated by action against V-weapon sites or in direct support of Allied troops in Normandy. Towards the end of the month, four raids were launched against German cities (Stuttgart three times, Kiel once), the first of such attacks for almost two months. This sudden switch of attention back to Germany caught the defences by surprise, with the result that only 0.6 per cent of aircraft (four Lancasters) were lost against Kiel.

Jack Bormann's social life was apparently compensating for the depression shown towards the end of June. On 4 July, after a dance in Bracebridge he confided to his diary, 'am doing fairly well with Doreen', the next day taking her 'for a cruise'. Three days later he exclaimed 'boy what a life', going on to write that he had taken Doreen out in the car again. 'She's wizard and a damn nice kid. No funny business.' Between these romantic excursions, on 7/8 July F-Freddie went to a flying bomb storage dump at St-Leu-d'Esserent. Bormann's comments were brief: 'Marking good, bright moonlight deadly, many fighters. Did dummy run, silly p****s aren't we. Nearly collided with other Lancs on second run'. In fact, the fighters caused havoc. 106 Squadron lost five of its sixteen Lancasters and, overall, the casualty rate was a massive 14 per cent: twenty-nine Lancasters and two Mosquitoes from a force of 221 aircraft. On his sixty-ninth operation, Wing Commander W. I. Deas from East Kirkby went down, 'the saddest and the most grievous loss the Squadron could have. He was a popular and efficient commanding officer.'

On 18 July, F-Freddie attacked Caen. Bormann complained that it had a 'sprog second dickie [pilot]', but in another way this was a memorable trip: the thirty-first and last of the tour for him and Bance. 'The Lucky Last', according to the mid-upper gunner. 'Wizard daylight trip. Saw hundreds of a/c [*sic*] like swarms of bees when crossing the Channel.' Nine hundred and forty-two bombers were despatched against fortified positions in the area of the Normandy city, preparatory to General Sir Bernard Montgomery launching Operation Goodwood with massed tanks and infantry support on the German defences. Only six aircraft were lost. Bance was right to enthuse about the results.

During this daylight operation, covered by a heavy fighter escort bombers flew in a 'gaggle' of four or five aircraft a maximum 2500ft deep to present a wide front to hostile fighters; in effect, a vastly improved form of the Phoney War's disastrous self-defending formation. Bombers would face more opposition when they resumed the night campaign on Germany in earnest. They would benefit, however, from some important advances in the field of countermeasures. Capture of an intact Ju 88, when it landed on an Allied airfield by mistake on 13 July, yielded valuable information about the enemy's electronic capability. Two new devices were discovered. The SN-2, which homed in on bombers, could be neutralised. Its existence, incidentally, explained the falling success rate of Serrate, which had been geared to the old Lichtenstein system. The second piece of captured equipment, Flensburg, which used emissions from the Monica backward-facing warning radar, proved more difficult. So crews were advised not to employ radar sets to detect night fighters, as they could actually betray the bomber.

During the night of 24/25 July, an American pilot with 630 Squadron, Flight Officer Bill Adams USAAF, was posted 'missing without trace' on a raid to Stuttgart carried out by 614 Lancasters and Halifaxes. It later emerged that his Lancaster had been shot down by a Ju 88 near Aboncourt in France, two crew members being killed in the attack. After ordering the rest to bale out, Adams apparently then found himself hurtling downwards with no hope of making an orthodox escape. Time to improvise. Opening the side window or the upper hatch in the roof of the cockpit, according to different versions of the episode, Adams reputedly dived over the revolving propellers as the aircraft continued its near-perpendicular plunge, pulled the ripcord and survived. Picked up by the Resistance, he eventually make his way back to East Kirkby, as did three more of his crew. A fourth had been taken prisoner.

Flying with 617 Squadron to attack a V-1 storage depot at Rilly-la-Montage, on 31 July the luck of Bill Reid VC ran out. His Lancaster was destroyed by a bomb from another aircraft: five of the crew were killed, Reid and one other parachuted to safety only to be taken prisoner. Back at Woodhall Spa, he left distraught colleagues. Returning to the Petwood Hotel Officers' Mess in the early hours of the morning, he had joined in a craps game being played on the green baize of the billiard table. He won £60. On hearing that he had been shot down, his unsympathetic victims were heard to complain: 'That bugger Reid's gone off with all our money.'

For Bomber Command, the first half of August was again dominated by the need to attack V-weapon sites, their storage depots and communication targets. A single experimental oper-ation took place against Brunswick on 12/13 August by 379 bombers with no Pathfinders to mark for them. The aim was to discover how accurately an aircraft could bomb using its own H2S set. Not very well was the answer. The damage was light and scattered, towns up to 20 miles away being hit and twenty-seven bombers lost. Towards the end of the month more raids were carried out on Germany as Bomber Command came closer to renewing the onslaught. Not quite in the fashion that Harris wanted though. Success of the isolated attacks on syn-thetic oil targets in the previous weeks prompted the Air Staff to classify these as worthy of 'maximum effort'.

After qualifying as a bomb aimer and completing training, Sergeant Jim Brookbank had been posted with Flight Sergeant Bill Scott's crew to 9 Squadron at RAF Bardney in Lincolnshire. He soon recognised the contradictions of Service life in wartime. Bardney was set in peaceful rural surroundings, 'We woke to country sounds, breathed the clear country air and wondered at the miracle of nature. In this idyllic setting it was difficult to accept that we were committed to battle.' Within hours they could be coned by searchlights, attacked by fighters, hit with flak, seeing other aircraft blown up or collide. With luck, parachutes would blossom from the stricken machines; more often, not. They had, too, to fight the elements. Aircrew often quipped that 'the weather was so atrocious even the birds were walking'. Brookbank found that, in action, individual aircrew members were not fully aware of noise, which helped them to concentrate on their jobs. The bulky flying helmets, which had built-in earphone, microphone and oxygen mask attachments, meant that even the engines' throb was muffled. To Brookbank, the firing of the Lancaster's guns sounded no more than 'the sound of an office typewriter'. Flak bursts could be seen but not heard unless a direct hit came on the aircraft.

Tragedy struck during a daylight raid to Brest on 14 August 1944, when the seventeen-year-old wireless operator in Brookbank's crew was killed. Brookbank had teamed up with him at the OTU at Bruntingthorpe in Leicestershire four months earlier. 'He was young, flamboyant, extrovert, combined with a brash self-assurance which he wore as a cloak to conceal the uncertainty of his adolescence'. A flak shell killed him as he carried out his duties and his loss deeply affected Brookbank, who wrote a poem, 'Johnny Comes Marching Home', in his memory.

As need to give so much close support to the Allied armies on the Continent faded, in September the debate about where Bomber Command's effort should be concentrated intensified: transport, synthetic oil plants or the German cities. Harris remained adamant that his bombers should return in force to the cities. His major difficulty was that his superior, Portal, wanted attacks on oil targets in central and eastern Germany as well as the Ruhr basin without abandonment of area bombing. In essence, this was a question of balance and after 25 September it became purely a British matter. On that date control of the heavy bombers reverted from Eisenhower to the RAF. A directive to Harris reminded him of the long-established aim to undermine the German 'military, industrial and economic systems' but that 'the direct support of land and naval operations remains a continuing commitment'.

The naval commitment led to an extraordinary venture. The battleship *Tirpitz* had long been a potential menace to Allied shipping and, in particular, the Arctic convoys to the Soviet Union sailing off northern Scandinavia. Several unsuccessful attempts had been made to sink her in German ports in 1940–41, and since February 1942 at various locations in Norway. The RAF, Fleet Air Arm and the Royal Navy (with human 'chariot' torpedoes and midget submarines) had all tried without decisive success. Now a most ambitious plan had been devised, which put enormous strain on individual bomber crews and their navigators in particular.

Accompanied by two Liberators, carrying maintenance personnel, spare equipment and staff officers who were to direct the enterprise, and a Lancaster with an RAF film unit, thirty-eight Lancasters of 9 and 617 squadrons took off on 11 September for the USSR. A Mosquito for met. flights to the target area would follow. The aircraft made for the airfield of Yagodnik on an island in the Dvina river close to Archangel. To reach it, they would have to cross hostile Norway, neutral

Sweden and part of enemy-held Finland, which meant flying through the night and landing early on 12 September.

One bomber turned back shortly after takeoff. Of the remaining thirty-seven bombers and four support aircraft none would be lost to enemy action. Several, however, would suffer freak experiences and all face unexpected weather hazards. Approaching Lossiemouth on the Moray Firth in Scotland to top up with fuel, the two Liberators were perturbed to see a couple of Beaufighters eyeing them suspiciously. 'As our sole armament was a Verey pistol, we kept our fingers crossed,' recalled one of the pilots, but they were allowed to land unchallenged. Flying over the North Sea at 400ft below enemy radar level, the Liberators climbed over the Norwegian mountains in clear weather, which made navigation simple. Not until the weather closed in over Finland did problems arise. Ordered to maintain radio silence, the two aircraft lost contact. Flight Lieutenant G. H. Capsey's crew breathed a collective sigh of relief when a signal was picked up on the Archangel frequency. Capsey duly turned south along the Dvina river in poor visibility and, to his amazement, narrowly missed the masts of a radio station close to the Soviet city. Crossing Archangel, he was guided by a searchlight to a 'horrible little field . . . bounded on three sides by hangars and on the fourth by the riverbed'. It bore no resemblance to the briefed destination. Capsey was right to feel concern. This was Kegostrov, on another island in the Dvina. Fortunately, the Liberator did not sustain any damage and later in the morning Capsey was able to fly to Yagodnik, 12 miles upstream.

Before Capsey's unscheduled arrival, Kegostrov had already witnessed some strange happenings. Squadron Leader D. R. Wyness of 617 Squadron was about to touch down when a white horse careered across the turf in front of him. Forced to take violent evasive action, he wrote off his Lancaster whose undercarriage collapsed.

Bitter Struggle

Pilot Officer Ray Harris from 9 Squadron had difficulty in finding Yagodnik in the murky conditions and was relieved to hear his bomb aimer, Jim Parsons, call over the intercom that he could see an airfield ahead with a Lancaster (Wyness's) about to land. Harris therefore witnessed Wyness's misfortune at close quarters, and Parsons gazed down on an explosion of figures racing to escape his own bomber as it scraped over the perimeter parapet. Harris was distracted by the general confusion and managed to pitch the nose of his aircraft into a potato patch. There it lodged in a ditch with its tail incongruously pointing skywards. Trapped in his forward compartment in total darkness and with his escape hatch on the floor unusable, Parsons crawled up into the cockpit to find that the rest of the crew had already escaped. He lost no time in scrambling on to the wing to conclude 'a terrifying experience'. Undoubtedly, though, a second Lancaster had been written off at Kegostrov and two crews had therefore endured the tortuous twelve-hour journey from England for nothing.

Wing Commander J. B. 'Willy' Tait, commander of 617 Squadron, described the weather as 'appalling', and a post-operational report agreed. In 'considerable low cloud and rain' over the final 150 miles of the route 'aircraft flew just above tree tops over the most desolate country imaginable – lakes, forests and swamps. Map reading was impossible, weather conditions alone made this too difficult, and in addition it was found that the maps of the area were inaccurate – many villages and even railway lines omitted.' Tait went down to 300ft in an effort to help his navigator, as the wireless operator vainly tried to raise Yagodnik (later he found that the wrong frequency had been issued). Quite suddenly, the bomb aimer glimpsed the mouth of a river, which turned out to be the Dvina, Tait followed it and landed at Yagodnik. Only twenty-three other Lancasters did so that morning.

One was flown by Squadron Leader Gerry Fawke. His flight engineer worried about fuel ('had to sort out the engines') as his navigator, Flight Lieutenant Tom Bennett, surveyed 'a scene from a Hollywood horror movie: tips of pines sticking up through a sea of mist'. He reflected on the met. briefing: 'Cloud below 1500ft is unknown in this area at this time of year'. Bennett did find the Dvina and guide Fawke to Yagodnik, where disaster almost struck. Another Lancaster was coming in to land from the opposite direction, and Flight Sergeant A. W. Cherrington, the flight engineer, feared that in avoiding it they would finish up 'in the watchtower'. But Fawke did put down safely at Yagodnik.

Other pilots were less fortunate. Nick Knilans, the American now flying with 617 Squadron, recalled seeing 'the blazing sunset as it hung over the Orkney Islands only to sink slowly into the North Atlantic'. With wireless silence in force, the navigator had to negotiate Norway unaided in darkness. The lights of neutral Sweden eventually allowed adequate visual checks, but as dawn broke drizzle and low cloud greeted the Lancaster over Finland. Like all other aircraft that night, it flew completely alone. Knilans brushed the trees at 50ft and his wireless operator also had no success in raising the Soviets. Seeing water below, the Lancaster crew realised that they had flown too far east and Knilans turned back. He almost hit the masts of two coastal vessels with 10/10ths cloud at 150ft. After twelve and a half hours in the air, the tanks were reading empty. Seeing an open piece of land, he approached downwind through a gully, over a barbed wire fence and 'plopped down' in mud, just managing to ease round a haystack as two engines cut out. He had landed at Onega City, a primitive fighter airfield.

There he was obliged to spend the night, while his aircraft was refuelled. The crew were, however, generously fed and supplied with copious pitchers of clear water – which turned out to be vodka. Next morning, 13 September, Knilans somewhat gingerly made his way to the rain-soaked field for takeoff. His troubles were by no means over. As he lifted off, according to him, the aircraft was 'caught in downdraft'. His navigator, however, claimed that the flight engineer misheard 'flaps up' for 'wheels up'. For whatever reason, the bomber firmly hit trees, losing the pitot head, bombsight and bomb bay doors and damaging both elevators. The 12,000lb. Tallboy bomb miraculously remained secure, but Knilans was almost decapitated when a 3ft × 2½ins branch penetrated the windscreen and drove on over the main spar into the fuselage. The pilot, therefore, had to use one hand to shield his face from the wind while he coped with an overheating starboard outer engine. Not only did he land safely at Yagodnik, but the aircraft was repaired in time to take part in the attack on 15 September.

Apart from those landing at Kegostrov, more aircraft came down in unlikely places including one so remote that a parachutist had to be dropped to lead the crew to safety. Eventually, thirty-one bombers would gather at Yagodnik; six others, including those of Wyness and Harris, having been written off in crashes. The pilot of the film unit Lancaster was both complimentary and scathing: 'Navigational skill in appalling weather conditions was responsible for the greater percentage of aircraft landing at Yagodnik. There were absolutely no facilities as the beacon was U/S . . . Apart from this, maps were inaccurate and pinpoints of no value.' No. 9 Squadron maintained that only 'superb airmanship' saved the aircraft and their bomb loads, averting 'a complete disaster'.

The bombers, which set off for Kaa Fjord in northern Norway to attack the *Tirpitz* on 15 September, faced a six-hour round trip, yet more inclement weather en route and the frustration of seeing smoke canisters on board and sited on surrounding hills covering the battleship as they began their bombing run. Nevertheless, one Tallboy severely damaged the battleship's starboard bow, even though the Lancaster crews did not know it. Once at Yagodnik, they faced another twelve-hour journey back to base. The crews of the aircraft which had been written off were distributed to other aircraft as passengers. Four of Drew Wyness's crew went in the Lancaster of Flying Officer F. Levy, which found itself off course during stormy weather and crashed into a Norwegian hillside, killing all eleven men on board.

At about this time, a strange incident occurred with a 630 Squadron Lancaster. Because of the danger of collision over the home base with so many aircraft approaching, if weather conditions were poor pilots often gave the order to clip on parachute packs. On this occasion, a bomb aimer dozing in the nose woke up to hear the word 'parachute'. Believing the aircraft was about to crash and, because he was half asleep, having no idea where it was, he pulled open his escape hatch and baled out. He left behind a draughty aeroplane, with a hole where the closed hatch should have been and 'a certain amount of chaos'. Meanwhile, the bomb aimer came down safely and to his astonishment saw the outline of a stationary Lancaster close by. Making his way towards it, he was even more perplexed to discover he had landed inside the perimeter fence at East Kirkby. So he hitched a lift to the debriefing room. As he did so, the rest of his crew had patiently taken their place in the circuit. Their reaction, when they walked into the room to find the bomb aimer quietly smoking, was not recorded.

In October, Bomber Command could return to Germany with a vengeance, although something of a compromise occurred in its targeting: raids were launched on four oil plants, with the bulk of the bombing taking place on towns and cities, particularly in the Ruhr. The number of aircraft despatched daily had risen significantly: no longer was a one thousand-bomber operation extraordinary. Two separate attacks of this strength were mounted on Duisburg, another on Essen. On other nights more than a thousand bombers was sent to a combination of targets. Support to ground operations was given through attacks on Kleve, Saarbrücken and the Kembs Dam. Attempts to open up the sea approach to Antwerp by clearing the river Scheldt meant not only bombing German shore batteries, but a concerted effort to neutralise those on the island of Walcheren. Harris estimated that 42,246 tons of bombs were dropped during October on Germany's industrial centres – an impressive resumption of the offensive.

Further afield, another attempt was made to deal with the *Tirpitz*. Now anchored off Tromsø, the battleship was within direct range of Scottish airfields along the Moray Firth: Lossiemouth, Kinloss and Milltown. Fitted with extra fuel tanks and each carrying one Tallboy, in the early hours of 29 October thirty-nine Lancasters of 9 and 617 squadrons (accompanied by the film unit aircraft) took off for Norway. Squadron Leader Tony Iveson's aircraft was very nearly not one of them. As the Lancaster began to gather speed on the runway, the port outer engine failed to reach the 24lb. boost required for takeoff. The situation began to look perilous, when the flight engineer took charge. 'There wasn't any conversation, so far as I can remember,' Iveson recalled. 'Desmond Phillips recognised the problem and pulled back the other three throttles to ensure that I had even power. We just made it, but went over a hangar and 'Benny' Goodman [Flight Lieutenant F. S. Goodman, another pilot] will tell you he saw me coming and nearly dived out of his seat. We were lucky to get away with that. If he [Phillips] hadn't been on the ball and had panicked, we'd have ploughed into a line of aircraft on the peri track. There I was on the grass beyond the main runway with a fully laden Lancaster, 68,000lb., full of fuel plus the additional tank in the fuselage. It came up all

215

right, but we were very, very lucky. If he hadn't been on the ball . . .' The flight engineer's initiative had saved the lives of the crew and prevented a major disaster on the ground.

For the crews bound for Tromsø, and the navigators in particular, another hazardous journey lay ahead. Flying low over the North Sea in cloudy conditions 'with very heavy static', Gee proved useless and astro fixes 'very difficult'. A change in the wind velocity caused many aircraft to be off track crossing the Norwegian coast, but clearer weather allowed course corrections to be made on the way to the rendezvous roughly 50 miles south-east of the target. Green flares rallied the aircraft there, Wing Commander Tait waggled his wings and the aerial armada set off. This time 'horrible visibility' (low cloud) surrounded the *Tirpitz* and the battleship survived.

On 1 November, Lancasters from 44 Squadron at RAF Spilsby, Lincolnshire, formed part of 226 bombers to take part in a daylight raid on a synthetic oil plant at Homberg. After an 'uneventful' outward journey, 10/10ths cloud was found over the target and Pathfinder aircraft therefore released sky markers. The Germans, however, put up a 'very accurate' box barrage, which damaged eleven of the thirty-seven Spilsby bombers. The aircraft of Flying Officer Jack Hawarth, 'a quiet retiring Rhodesian, well liked by all who knew him', was hit by shell bursts, which shook the machine and 'very nearly deafened the crew'. According to the post-operational summary, when the situation had calmed down they saw to their horror that the pilot had been 'seriously injured and that the greater part of the instrument panel was destroyed'. Fatally wounded, Hawarth died soon after, which left the crew 'in a very critical condition'. The others did not know that the flight engineer, Sergeant M. F. Seiler, had been shot in the leg as he 'quietly' carried on his duties. The bomb aimer, Flight Sergeant G. W. Walters, took the controls to find that the Air Speed Indicator and altimeter were still functioning, although no other instrument was working. One engine was dead, and Walters had little flying training, but he offered to try to get back to England so that they could bale out over friendly territory. With his limited skills, he could not guarantee to land the aircraft. Including the rear gunner, Sergeant A. W. McAllister, who had hacked his way out of his damaged turret, the others agreed that Walters should go on. Flying above the cloud, he relied on the few instruments still left, as the wireless operator sent out: 'Captain injured. Crew baling out over England.' Walters and Seiler did eventually get the Lancaster over the coast, aided by Sergeant B. J. Saunders' 'excellent navigation', and they duly prepared to bale out. Although convinced that Hawarth, the pilot, was dead, they nevertheless sent him out on a static line, before leaving the doomed bomber themselves. Five of the crew landed safely; sadly, the wounded Seiler did not. Walters had been the last to jump and 'richly deserved' the Conspicuous Gallantry Medal he received. He had got T-Tare back to England, but it had been very much a team effort.

After the 44 Squadron Lancasters had left for the synthetic oil complex at Homberg on 1 November, a frightening sequence of events occurred at RAF Spilsby to underline the ever-present danger involved in taking off. A 207 Squadron pilot on his first operation as an aircraft captain failed to get airborne in spectacular and tragic circumstances. Australian Flying Officer A. T. Loveless was carrying fourteen 1000lb. bombs in his Lancaster. About one-third of the way down the runway, the aircraft swung violently to port – the pilot later reported that he 'felt as if something had given way, causing the aircraft to develop a will of its own and leaving him without proper control of it'. Careering off the runway, the Lancaster sped across the grass, with Loveless striving to regain control. Section Officer Joyce Brotherton, the Intelligence Officer, reported that it 'hurled itself upon one of the empty Halifaxes, at the same time flattening a small Nissen hut. By a miracle, no one was killed or even injured and the crew leapt out and ran for their lives'. All except the bomber aimer, who was trapped. Realising his predicament, Loveless rushed back to free him just before an enormous explosion occurred; almost certainly from the petrol tanks. 'A huge column of smoke rose into the air, while the flames continued to spread.' None of this was near the runway, so waiting bombers were free to take off. The Lancaster, though, was a complete write-off.

It very nearly accounted for Flying Officer J. Downing, like Loveless on his first solo operation, in one of the following Lancasters. The Intelligence Officer explained: 'When he was about halfway down the runway, an explosion which made the first one pale into insignificance rent the air. The heat had caused the main bomb load to go off. Smoke, fire and debris were hurled into the air and pieces of flaming wreckage were scattered far and wide.' Some fell in the path of Downing's aircraft, which was now going too fast to abort. 'Spectators, most of whom were lying on the ground by this time, held their breath while the aircraft passed through the flaming debris – unharmed.' However, with sharp pieces of metal strewn across the runway, the remaining six Lancasters were told not to take off.

Brotherton's report continued: 'The 44 Squadron briefing room and crew room were a pitiful sight. Not only were the windows and most of the window frames gone, but the roof was damaged, and sheets of corrugated iron were hanging down from it. The squadron offices were in the same plight and the small buildings in and around the Watch Office were in an even worse condition. How the Watch Office itself had survived was a miracle, but both the Control Room and the Met. Office beneath it were a scene of chaos and desolation.' To complete the inferno of destruction, shards of burning wreckage had been flung across the perimeter track and set another Halifax alight.

Loveless had therefore written off a second Halifax. In all, his catalogue of havoc included three bombers, a swathe of structural ruin and prevention of six bombers from taking part in that night's operation. Small wonder, perhaps, that he concluded of this dramatic performance, 'I had made an indelible impression on the unit'. He did not know that, in striving to save one of the Halifaxes, two officers had been badly injured, one of them fatally.

After so many attempts over the preceding four years, the Dortmund-Ems and Mittelland canals were at last breached in November 1944, striking a major blow to the enemy transportation system. The *Tirpitz*, too, finally met her doom, releasing for active service elsewhere the great concentration of naval vessels marooned in Scapa Flow in case she should threaten to emulate her sister ship the *Bismarck*. Flying Officer John Leavitt, an American serving in the RAF, had flown as second pilot during the October attack. This time, he captained his own bomber. Repeating the attack of 29 October, unhampered by the weather 'in a gin-clear sky', the Lancasters put paid to her on 12 November with 12,000lb. Tallboys in a devastating eighteen-minute attack. Flight Lieutenant Bob Knights, a 617 Squadron pilot, remarked on the 'black shape' of the battleship 'quite clearly contrasting with the surrounding snow-covered ground'. Unaccountably fighter aircraft stationed at Bardufoss only ten minutes' flying time away did not interfere. 'We were fortunate in not catching the enemy on one of his better days,' mused Flying Officer Fred Watts. Looking down on the upturned hull of the *Tirpitz*, Warrant Officer W. H. Pengelly in Knight's Lancaster breathed: 'Thank God for that. It's the last time we've got to come here.'

The dispute between Harris and the Air Staff over targets had again surfaced on 1 November, when Harris was directed to allocate 'the maximum effort' to 'the enemy petroleum industry and his oil supplies'. Although 'subordinate' to this 'highest priority', 'disorganisation of the enemy's transportation system should be created, especially in the Ruhr', something which Harris had always held to be of less importance. 'Here we go round the Mulberry bush', he scribbled, convinced that concentration on cities remained the best option.

Early in December 1944, Albert Speer, the German Minister for Armament and War Production, to some extent undermined this objection. 'The transportation situation in the Ruhr is the cause of our inability to send to the rest of the Reich more than a fraction of the previously despatched quantity of coal.' Availability of railway waggons had fallen from a daily total of twenty thousand to little over six thousand.

Two days before Christmas, in daylight, twenty-seven Lancasters and three Mosquitoes set out for Cologne to discover that the weather and enemy defences still posed formidable threats. The force was divided into three formations, each led by a Lancaster equipped with Oboe. Two Lancasters collided soon after crossing the French coast, a baleful omen. When it became obvious that cloud cover over the target had cleared unexpectedly, the bombers were ordered to attack alternative targets. That instruction was not received by Squadron Leader Robert Palmer in the leading Oboe Lancaster. He started the Oboe run and almost immediately ran into heavy flak, which accounted for two engines. Palmer pressed on, despite being attacked 'in force' by fighters as well having 'disdained avoiding action'. Although the aircraft was by now severely damaged, he dropped his markers in the centre of the marshalling yards before the bomber 'was last seen spiralling to earth in flames'. The rear gunner escaped by parachute, but the rest of the crew perished. Palmer was awarded a posthumous VC. In summarising his 'conspicuous bravery' over Cologne, the citation noted that Palmer had previously completed 110 operations, and 'most of them involved deep penetration of heavily-defended territory'.

remained predominantly on urban concentrations and other long-standing targets.

On the very first day of the new year, 102 Lancasters set off to breach a section of the Dortmund-Ems canal, which the Germans had repaired. One piloted by New Zealander Flying Officer R. F. H. Denton had a traumatic flight. Shortly after bombing, 'heavy shells struck in front of the mid-upper turret', fire and dense smoke filled the Lancaster. Then the nose was hit and 'an inrush of air, clearing the smoke, revealed a scene of utter devastation. Most of the perspex screen of the nose compartment had been shot away, gaping holes had been torn in the canopy above the pilot's head, the inter-communication wiring was severed and there was a large hole in the floor of the aircraft. Bedding and other equipment were badly damaged or alight, one engine was on fire.'

The Scottish wireless operator, Flight Sergeant George Thompson, realised that the mid-upper gunner was unconscious in his blazing turret, 'without hesitation' pulled him clear of the flames, beat out his burning clothing with his bare hands and edged the gunner to safety round an enormous hole in the fuselage floor. Using a fire extinguisher to tackle the flames, Thompson then saw that the rear gunner was in a similar predicament. Despite his own 'serious injuries' he made his way painfully aft to haul the gunner free and also beat out his smouldering clothing with bare hands. Having hauled him to safety, he went forward to report to the captain, who did not recognise him due to his 'pitiful' condition. Thompson then cared for the two gunners for forty minutes until Denton managed to crashland behind friendly lines near Brussels.

One of the injured gunners lived, the other died of his wounds. So too, after an agonising three weeks, did George Thompson. The wireless operator's bravery in the spite of his own horrific injuries deservedly earned him the VC. His pilot paid tribute not only to Thompson's sacrifice, but to his professional skill: 'He was the best wireless operator I have ever known – always right on top of his job.' The citation noted that Thompson 'hazarded his life in order to save the lives of others. Young in years and experience his actions were those of a veteran.'

On 13 January, John Langston, now commissioned, completed thirty-one operations and thus a bombing tour. He had become a pilot officer in a strange way. While flying with 630 Squadron, his squadron commander encouraged him to apply for a commission. So he filled in the necessary forms and was called before the base commander, 'a bluff air commodore'. After a few questions, he declared: 'You're the sort of young man we need.' A few months later, when he moved to 189 Squadron at RAF Fulbeck in Lincolnshire, the promotion came through. Now, on completion of his tour, he was looking forward to a well-earned leave and rest from operations. He and the bomb aimer, Flight Lieutenant Pat Shirley, were 'full of the joys of spring', preparing to go off on Shirley's motorbike, when their pilot, Bill Gordon, bounced up. 'Guess what? Willy Tait has just phoned and wants us to join 617 Squadron at Woodhall Spa.' Langston and Shirley chorused: 'You must be joking.' Then, according to Langston, 'insanity won and we went off as a crew. Crew loyalty, you see.'

During January 1945, inclement weather officially restricted bomber activity over Germany. Nevertheless, operational figures remain impressive. Excluding 100 Group, primarily engaged in countermeasures and mine laying, 10,370 sorties were flown to targets in Germany. These included raids by Mosquitoes against selected targets, but also main force ones on Duisburg, Hanover, Munich and Stuttgart. On four nights one thousand or more bombers were despatched, on another six more than five hundred. In that month 153 aircraft were lost, some of them two-man Mosquitoes. One aircraft was officially missing from the 598 despatched on 1/2 January, though five more crashed on home soil; on 14/15 January, 1214 sorties were flown for the loss of seventeen aircraft, excluding fourteen more crashes in England.

On 19 January, Harris received another comprehensive directive: 'The German Air Force and primarily its jet production, training and operational establishments' was to be 'a primary objective for attack'. But 'attacks on the enemy's Petroleum Industry and oil supplies are to be maintained and, if possible, intensified'. Harris was reminded that a list of 'industrial area targets' had already been issued and he must also 'meet promptly' the needs of land force operations. With regard to naval targets, 'the enemy's U-boat organisation . . . most profitable targets' should be attacked as well.

Into this latter category came Bergen in Norway. After German bases in France were lost, U-boats moved there to menace Allied shipping in the North Sea, the Arctic Circle and, potentially, the English Channel. On 12 January 1945, therefore, thirty-two Lancaster bombers from 9 and 617 squadrons, each carrying a Tallboy, took off on a daylight raid to attack U-boat pens at Bergen. The plan was to fly via Peterhead to pick up an escort of RAF Mustang fighters. At Woodhall Spa, Squadron Leader Tony Iveson found no brake power on his aircraft during pre-flight checks and switched to the reserve Lancaster. This meant getting airborne long after the others and flying directly to the target across the North Sea. No fighter escorts were seen before Iveson reached Bergen, to find it swathed in mist. He was ordered to circle by the Squadron commander, Wing Commander J. E. 'Johnny' Fauquier, in the hope that conditions would improve. On his third circuit, he was suddenly attacked by two Focke-Wulf Fw 190s, the first indication of danger being the rattle of cannon shells on the fuselage. The port inner engine had to be feathered; apart from structural damage to the fuselage, the port tail fin was perforated, the trimming wires severed and the rear turret disabled. Iveson struggled to keep the aircraft level, 'as she wanted to stand on her tail'. Before the intercom went dead, he warned the crew to prepare to bale out. Iveson explained: 'We dropped the Tallboy. Once things had calmed down and we had got out of the flak, the flight engineer found a rope to tie to the control column, which helped me keep the aircraft steady. He then went back to deal with the trimming wires. My instructions as he tried differ-ent adjustments were shouted to him by the navigator in the absence of the intercom. Gradually he managed to patch up the broken wires satisfactorily.' Once more Sergeant J. D. Phillips had saved the day. 'Without his knowledge and skill, we would not have survived', his pilot acknowledged. Returning to the cockpit, Phillips reported three caps on the floor by the rear exit, indicating that their owners had baled out.

Nevertheless, despite 'a great hole in the tailplane and one fin flapping', Iveson decided to make for home. 'Jack, where's the nearest land point?' he asked the navigator. Thus the damaged Lancaster edged its way towards Sumburgh in the Shetlands. There, unable to get the landing gear down conventionally, the aircraft circled while the emergency air system was used. Once this had been done, the undercarriage could not be raised again. Just as Iveson began his approach, 'a Spitfire turned in front of me with a dead prop'. So, with the perforated fin and under-carriage down, he had to go round again before landing. Once he had switched off and climbed out, Iveson admitted that reac-tion set in. He watched his aircraft being towed off the runway, before a Dakota could put down. It contained a concert party. After the tribulations of the day, the four remaining members of the crew attended the show that evening. Astonishingly, the con-jurer came from Iveson's home town and knew his father. Meanwhile, the three crew members who had baled out survived, only to be captured. For four months until their release, they imagined that their skipper and other three crew members had been killed.

Over Bergen, Wass had heard Iveson's preparatory warning before the intercom went dead and his turret lost power. Suddenly another Fw 190 appeared alongside the Lancaster flying parallel to it. Presumably convinced the burning bomber was finished, it did not attack. Using the wheel on the left side, Wass cranked his turret round and opened up on the enemy machine. 'All those bullets were hitting the fuselage, but they didn't have any effect. "What the hell do you have to do to shoot the thing down?" I asked myself.' At that point the fighter turned away, as Wass glimpsed a parachute leaving the rear door of the Lancaster. Rapidly he traversed the turret manually and climbed into the fuselage. He saw Les Smith hesitating in the doorway and, at his request, gave him a shove. Unlike Larry Curtis and John Langston, Wass had received rudimentary parachute training from a tower and he remembered to sit on the step and stick his head between his knees before falling forward.

Pilot Officer Jim Parsons flew with 9 Squadron on this operation, too, and confirmed the close attention of Fw 190s. After their attack on the *Tirpitz* in Norway, Harris's crew had completed its tour, but the pilot and Parsons decided to carry on for another fifteen operations and finish a second one. Hence they found themselves over Bergen with a different crew. On this occasion the Squadron's gunnery leader (Flight Lieutenant Bill Gabriel) was in the rear turret, his deputy (Flying Officer Williams) manned the mid-upper. Unknown to him, Parson's intercom had become disconnected, so he was not aware of the chaos which quickly developed behind him. He later learnt that Gabriel had exclaimed with relief, 'Oh, the Mustangs are here', only suddenly to change his mind and send Harris into a corkscrew. Parsons did not hear the warning and was taken completely by surprise as the Lancaster dived. Fortunately, as it turned out. His body went into the air, just as a cannon shell smashed through the port side and fractured a hydraulic pipe, spraying oil into the compartment. Frantically, Parsons reached for his parachute. Looking up as the aircraft straightened out, he saw Harris and the flight engineer violently gesticulating, which was when he realised that his intercom had come adrift. He now got some idea of the mayhem in progress. Dumping his parachute, he climbed into the front gun position, to find that he could not operate the weapon due to the hydraulic leak. As four Fw 190s repeatedly attacked, he could do nothing to prevent them.

Then it was all over, and it dawned on Parsons that, had he been sitting in his normal place and not taking his involuntary airborne excursion, the cannon shell would have made mincemeat of him. Some in the crew had been less lucky. The rear gunner had been wounded badly in the leg. With others committed to saving the damaged bomber, Parsons was the only one free to help him. He half carried, half lifted the 'woozy' Gabriel forward to the rest bed, where he gave him oxygen before administering morphine. The mid-upper gunner had been hit in the shin, the wireless operator in the backside.

Such was the parlous state of the aircraft that, despite using the emergency equipment, nobody could be sure whether the wheels would go down. So they took up crash positions, only for Harris to make a perfect landing with the ambulance racing alongside. Gabriel was taken to hospital where he was successfully operated on by a German PoW surgeon. The other two were treated by the squadron medical officer for relatively superficial wounds. Almost sixty years later, it emerged that since that day the wireless operator had been carrying a splinter, which had lodged near his spine but never troubled him.

Over the European mainland during February weather

conditions improved marginally, enabling Bomber Command to range more freely. Familiar targets were hit – Gelsenkirchen, Dortmund, Duisburg – and others further east like Pölitz, Dresden and Chemnitz. Harris paid tribute to the importance of H2S Mark III sets in permitting accurate raids in adverse conditions, but Oboe remained a stalwart bombing aid and, despite Cochrane's reservations and Cheshire's low-level marking demonstrations, the Pathfinders' sky markers continued to be effective. The perils of an accident had not receded, however. Squadron Leader Horsley crashed on takeoff from RAF Skellingthorpe, Lincolnshire, on 1 February, killing all but the rear gunner. As Air Commodore J. H. Searby would reflect in 1979, 'the countryside of the eastern counties today is littered with the buried wreckage of crashed bombers'.

In this phase of operations, Bomber Command's raid on Dresden on 13/14 February has attracted sharp criticism over the years. Not an obvious industrial location, the idea of attacking Dresden had originated in the Air Staff in August 1944. Operation Thunderclap was conceived as a catastrophic bombing assault on one city (Dresden being one of the suggested targets) as an overwhelming demonstration of air power designed to persuade the Germans to surrender. It was not pursued in this form, but revived in January 1945 as a joint Anglo-American venture and linked to support for the Soviet forces in their drive into eastern Germany. Portal referred to 'a severe blitz [which] will not only cause confusion in the evacuation from the East but will also hamper the movement of troops from the West'. Churchill was advised that Dresden, Chemnitz and Leipzig 'are not only the administrative centres controlling the military and civilian movements but are also the main communications centres through which the bulk of the traffic moves'. On 27 January, Harris was ordered to prepare for such an attack, and, post-war, protested that 'at the time [it was] considered a military necessity by much more important people than myself'.

Had the weather been suitable, the Americans would have bombed in daylight on 13 February. As it was the first raid was carried out by Bomber Command that night with 796 Lancasters and nine Mosquitoes, divided into two waves two hours apart. The next day, 311 Flying Fortresses supported by Mustang fighters attacked, 244 B-17s hit Dresden on 15 February and a further 406 on 2 March.

Meanwhile, the strategic bombing campaign continued against targets further west. On 20/21 February 1945, Sergeant Stan Instone flew to Dortmund as the flight engineer of a 419 Squadron Lancaster from RAF Middleton St George, County Durham, in a force of 528 aircraft. Approaching the target, he saw upward-firing cannon of a night fighter (the deadly *schräge Musik*) account for a Lancaster ahead and shortly afterwards his own aircraft suffered the same fate. The starboard middle tank burst into flames and, as the fire could not be controlled, the pilot gave the order to bale out. The navigator went forward to leave by the front escape hatch with the bomb aimer, but that jammed. The rear gunner called up to say that his turret was frozen and Instone went back to help him. As he did so, he saw that he mid-upper gunner and wireless operator had already left via the rear door.

Amid the pandemonium, the pilot held the aircraft steady. After desperate hammering the bomb aimer and navigator got their hatch open, but Instone could not free the rear gunner. Making his way forward again, he sat on the edge of the open hatch and remembered nothing more 'until I came to free falling with pieces of the aircraft dropping past me'. Instone just had time to pull the ripcord before he crashed through a copse of pine trees on to the ground; except for temporary deafness, he was unscathed. Having lost his escape kit in the swift descent,

Instone had no sense of direction and was quickly rounded up. In a prison camp he would meet up with four other members of the crew. Flames engulfing the fuselage had unfrozen the rear turret, whose occupant had escaped minus one trapped boot. Later they learnt that the navigator and pilot had not survived. Many years afterwards, Instone penned a moving tribute: 'Few words can express my feelings towards our skipper, Flying Officer L. A. Blaney RCAF. With his quiet authority and friendliness he commanded a crew with a tremendously strong bond of comradeship and, as Captain, he gave away his own chance of survival so that his crew should have theirs.'

Three days after Instone was shot down, on 23 February preceded by Pathfinder aircraft more than 350 Lancasters set off for Pforzheim. The master bomber for this operation was Captain Edwin Sales of the South African Air Force. Shortly after reaching the target area, his aircraft was attacked by an enemy fighter and one engine put out of action as the rear guns malfunctioned. Another fighter accounted for a second engine, but 'almost defenceless he [Swales] stayed over the target area issuing his instructions until he was satisfied that the attack had achieved its purpose'. With his blind flying instruments destroyed and with much reduced speed, Swales made for home 'determined to stop the aircraft and crew from falling into enemy hands'. As he struggled to keep his machine aloft, it ran into cloud and turbulence, but eventually they were over friendly territory. By now the bomber was losing height steadily and 'more and more difficult to control'. Swales therefore ordered the crew to bale out. 'Hardly had the last crew member jumped when the aircraft plunged to the earth. Captain Swales was found dead at the controls.' He was awarded the last Bomber Command VC of the war, the third to a Pathfinder. The citation read: 'Intrepid in the attack, courageous in the face of danger, he did his duty to the last, giving his life that his comrades might live.'

Bomber Crew

During the night of 3/4 March, RAF Waddington near Lincoln received a sharp reminder that the Luftwaffe remained dangerous when Ju 88 intruders paid a visit. And inexperienced bomber crews were still entering the fray to encounter stiff opposition over Germany. Mid-upper gunner Flight Sergeant Clive Watt flew his sixth operation and first night raid with 218 Squadron from RAF Chedburgh, Suffolk, on 7 March 1945, part of a 531-strong force. Taking off at twilight, the Lancaster was warned to expect heavy fighter opposition on the way to Dessau but all it met was flak, which Watt found intriguing: 'None of our crew had seen searchlights nor bursting shells at night before, so it was quite an eye opener.' Just before H-hour, a great blaze of colour appeared in front of Watt's aircraft, which seemed strangely early. The crew was about to attack when the rear gunner called that this must be a decoy location because he could see the correct markers behind him. The pilot asked for a reciprocal bearing and turned back at the same height, which Watt thought 'a stupid move' as 'many four-engined black shapes flashed by both above and below our aircraft'. By the time the Lancaster reached the target, all the other bombers had gone. They quickly dropped their bombs and made for home alone.

Twenty minutes after the target, Watt and the rear gunner picked up an ominous shadow astern, and as they feared it gradually hardened into a twin-engine fighter. Reasoning that the enemy pilot must soon see them, they agreed to unloose their six Browning machine-guns on the rear gunner's word. 'Our incendiary and armour piercing bullets bounced in all directions from the fighter's nose and engines.' After the enemy machine passed out of the rear gunner's vision, Watt continued 'to stitch it from fore to aft and wing tip to wing tip', conscious that 'the lives of six other men' depended on his accuracy, and eventually the Messerschmitt Me 410 turned lazily on its back and away. There was little time for relief, however, because the bomb aimer reported a Ju 88 to starboard. Fortunately, it did not molest them and soon disappeared from view.

Their torment was far from over, however. Unknown to himself or any of the crew, the navigator's oxygen supply had been restricted by an equipment fault. In confusion and using the wrong chart, he obtained a false Gee fix. When the aircraft should have been crossing the French coast, there was no sign of it. Further fixes did not help and the bomber floundered around for over an hour utterly lost with its petrol ebbing dangerously away. Watt could see the warning lights 'twinkling on the canopy roof' from his position. The pilot sent out a Mayday call in desperation, which was acknowledged. Then silence. The aircraft was now below oxygen height and Watt recalled: 'I cannot forget the long period sitting in my turret waiting for the inevitable conclusion.' Miraculously, two Sandra lights went up ahead and the Lancaster landed safely at Manston in Kent. The engines died as it touched down. It had been 'a close call', but the crew, according to its relieved mid-upper gunner, enjoyed the six days' leave granted to them to recover.

Pilot Officer E. T. Jetson of 44 Squadron was even less lucky that night while making for an oil refinery at Harburg in a force of 241 aircraft. On the way to the target, his Lancaster was so badly damaged by flak it became obvious that it would never reach the required bombing height and was in danger of crashing. Jetson therefore ordered the crew to bale out 'as he realised that the aircraft was getting beyond his control', according to the Squadron summary pieced together later. Warning of the low altitude, he told them to pull the ripcord of their parachutes quickly once clear of the machine. They did so, and all landed safety. Jetson had no chance himself. 'Shortly after they left the aircraft, the crew was distressed to see it dive into the ground and blow up. Jetson had given them their lives at the cost of his own.'

Flying Officer D. M. Rose (a Canadian flying in the RAF) took his crew on 14/15 March to Lutzkendorf, where 230 bombers attacked the synthetic oil refinery. Crews were warned during the morning that they would be flying that night, and at lunchtime details of the different briefings for navigators (4.30 p.m.), captains (5 p.m.) and the main briefing (5.45 p.m.) were posted. It emerged that this would be a master bomber operation, aircraft would carry a full fuel load and bomb from 8 to 10,000ft, with Rose at the lowest height. The usual gen. followed about enemy defences, met. forecasts, bomb load and the Commanding Officer's exhortation. Then off to a meal and last-minute preparations.

'We are finally ready to go out to the kite,' Rose recorded, 'all of us except the navigator', who was still working on the flight plan after the arrival of further information. As he did so, the rest of the crew went outside to wait for transport to Lancaster X-X-ray. As other crews passed and wishes for a good trip were exchanged, 'you wonder as you see them fooling about if they will be around tomorrow'. Eventually, Rose's crew (minus the navigator) reached their aircraft, exchanged words with the ground crew, climbed aboard and went through the necessary pre-operational checks. When they were satisfied, the engines were shut down and they got out for a smoke, 'hanging about waiting for something to happen. Will the trip be scrubbed?' At last, the navigator appeared, bringing the precise time of take-off. The raid was on. Ten minutes to go. Time for another smoke. All aboard once more.

One by one the four engines 'roar into life', Rose released the brake and the Lancaster taxied round the perimeter track to the head of the runway, ready to take off in the planned order. Rose mused: 'It's a nice sight seeing all the aircraft nose to tail following each other round to the takeoff position.' He did a last check over the cockpit as he waited for the green light from the control caravan to signal him away. 'I think about the load. 67,000lb. all-up weight. God! That's a lot of weight to get airborne. Still, a Lancaster will do it. I hope the engines don't fail me.' As the tail light of the aircraft in front disappeared into the distance, the signal flashed, the brakes came off and X-X-ray began to roll down the runway. Concentrating on his instruments, Rose was unaware of the crowd waving him away.

It was a clear night and, once settled on course in the air, Rose thought 'the stars are all out and you feel as if the sky belongs to you'. As the aircraft crossed the English coast, 'hoping to see it again', the bomb aimer reported 'bombs selected and fused', before silence once more. Apart from the navigator, with all navigation lights now out, crew members were searching the sky for other machines. 'Aircraft crossing just above,' reported the rear gunner, and looking up Rose identified another Lancaster. They were now deep inside France with ninety minutes to the target. The closer they got, the more tension mounted 'and the strain on our nerves seems greater'. Every ten minutes Rose called up the gunners for a report; each time he heard, 'everything O.K. back here, skip'.

A half-hour before the target, the VHF radio was switched on for orders from the master bomber. On schedule the first target indicators went down and Rose congratulated his navigator for being 'dead on track'. All at once, 'the sky is lit up with flares which are over the marking point. Everything seems bright as day. This the time to really start looking for fighters as we are silhouetted against the sky.' The Lancaster would make an 'easy target'. More markers went down; although visibility at ground level was by no means perfect 'the Pathfinders are doing OK'. Flak began to come up and suddenly 'all hell is let loose; a stream of tracer bullets is just missing by the port wing and crossing the nose'. The rear gunner 'says "corkscrew port. Go!"' Rose executed 'a hell of a dive' but 'just as I start pulling out, more tracer starts coming from the starboard side'. Two fighters were now attacking. 'I push it down further and then pull up very tightly. They come at me again. Again I push it down. During all of this my gunners are firing like mad. They can't see any results, but tell me "keep going, skip".' And then the fighters have gone; they've broken away. Rose was now 4000ft below the bombing height, and well short of the target. Although the flight engineer put on full climbing power, the Lancaster would clearly not reach the briefed height in time. With the target almost directly underneath him, Rose levelled out. The bomb aimer had just said, 'steady, skip . . . the marker is right in there', when 'a horrible blinding flash' flooded the aircraft and the rear gunner reported that another Lancaster had blown up behind them.

'All around us the flak is bursting like mad. They sure are giving us a hot time.' 'Bombs gone' from the bomb aimer interrupted Rose's thoughts. 'Steady now for the camera run.' Rose found himself 'going through the target at 6000ft and the flak is uncomfortably close'. With explosions going off on the ground and in the air, amid this mayhem 'the camera goes off' and 'I then push the nose down and go like hell out of the target area'. There was no time to relax. Away from the target, 'the still black night . . . had queer things in store for you. You never know what is lurking in the darkness waiting to pounce.' Rose checked with the crew individually and was particularly pleased to hear the flight engineer report no trouble with the engines. 'So far so good', but there was a long way still to go.

An hour after leaving the target, the rear gunner spotted an aircraft below and asked Rose to stand by 'as he thinks it is a fighter. Sure enough it is. For a solid half-hour that Ju 88 stays with us, always just a bit in front and below.' After the gunners ran out of ammunition, 'it is just a case of keeping on moving about. I do everything I can to try to shake him off.' Every now and again it looked as if Rose had succeeded, but the fighter found him again. The situation was made more 'grim' by the sight of other Lancasters 'going down one after another to the port of us. They are being shot down by the same type of kite that is on me.' Rose was determined not to give his tormentor an easy target, and succeeded. 'None of his bullets come very close to us and finally he gives up.' 'This is the worse night yet,' Rose recorded.

Over England the weather had closed in and Rose's Lancaster was diverted. With the fuel running low, their haven loomed up and they wasted no time in getting down. Incredibly, they found no damage whatsoever: 'Thank God for such a close escape from sure death.' The crew then went to debriefing, a process which evidently irritated Rose. 'They have so damn many silly questions to ask I am thankful I have landed away from base, because they don't want anything other than the important factors.' To 'quieten' their nerves each was given 'a very healthy slug of rum', of which the pilot managed to pur-loin 'three good-sized rations'. After a meal of bacon and eggs, at 9 a.m. on 31 March he rolled into a borrowed bed. 'Lord! It's good to get to bed again.' The crews of eighteen other Lancasters did not enjoy that luxury. They did not come back.

While main force bombers were active over Germany, 100 Group expanded its range of electronic countermeasures to neutralise the enemy defences. Towards the close of 1944, Dudley Heal had joined Flight Lieutenant J. G. 'Johnny' Wynne's crew and in January 1945 went with it to 214 Squadron, part of 100 Group. Such was the multitude of equip-ment being carried that Heal found himself part of the ten-man crew in an RAF Flying Fortress. After a month's familiarisation with this type of aircraft and new procedures, Wynne's crew flew its first operation on 14 February 1945. To carry out his navigation duties, Heal shared the spacious bomb aimer's position in the nose.

After less than a month, on the eighth operation, in March Heal's luck ran out. Normally, with its ability to go higher than the main force bombers, the Flying Fortress flew at an altitude above 20,000ft, but on this occasion Wynne was briefed to return at 6000ft. Heal later recalled the unpleasant result. 'After more than an hour's flying in pitch darkness from the farthest point, we were suddenly caught by searchlights and hit by shellfire. The port inner engine began to burn. Johnny ordered the flight engineer to stop the engine, which he tried to do but without success.' Heal estimated that the aircraft was about 20 miles from the Franco-German border. 'We were losing height slowly and the damaged engine, apart from the fire, was causing considerable vibration.' All attempts to feather the engine failed, and the pilot told the crew to bale out. After a struggle, Heal and the bomb aimer managed to force the forward escape hatch open, 'and I sat on the edge with my feet dangling in a black void, summoning the courage to jump. A blow in the middle of the back put an end to that and I was out. It was pitch black and absolutely silent – the contrast was unbelievable. I was turning over and over and I stretched my arms and legs to see if I could stop spinning. Whilst doing this it suddenly occurred to me that I didn't really have time for that sort of thing. I pulled the ripcord and was brought up with the expected violent jerk.' Thereafter Heal found himself 'swinging gently in the quiet and darkness' and eventually landed on the roof of a large warehouse. However, his descent had been noted. A vehicle appeared below, 'a clatter of heavy boots and loud orders shouted in what, I'm sorry to say, was certainly German.' The boots crashed upstairs inside the building, a door burst open and Heal's attempt to conceal himself failed. He was taken prisoner, as were three more of the crew. Five did not survive, and the pilot, rather like Iveson after the Bergen operation, unbelievably got the crippled aircraft home.

In a letter to Heal's parents on 24 March, he explained: 'When I attempted to leave the aircraft I became entangled in the oxygen lead and after much difficulty got free. Having relieved myself of the responsibility of the crew, I felt it my duty to try at all costs to save my machine.' He was now alone in the battered Fortress. 'I therefore decided to remain until the wing caught alight.' After about half and hour, the flames petered out, and Wynne determined to make for England. The automatic pilot was U/S so he trimmed the aircraft and climbed down into the nose to retrieve Heal's maps and log. Three times he repeated this exercise before identifying the correct maps, and 'in doing so pulled my parachute, which had to be abandoned'. Suddenly the fire ignited once more and, without his parachute, Wynne feared the worst. Miraculously for a second time the flames died out, and 'with Dudley's chart and log' he made it to RAF Bassingbourn, Cambridgeshire, something which 'I can only attribute to Providence'. Heal would later learn that it was providential that he had not at the time been in the nose, where a gaping hole had been ripped by the damaged propeller breaking off on landing.

Since hearing that he was missing, for two months the Heals had no news of their son's fate. Shortly after D-Day, they received a telegram: 'Dudley safe and well Germany awaiting transport home', sent by another PoW on reaching England. Within forty-eight hours, Heal was pushing open the garden gate. 'It had been quite an experience for me, but must have been worse for them [his parents], wondering if I was still alive . . . I was relieved to find my mother and father in reasonably good health, as were my two brothers.'

During the final weeks of the war while Heal was in captivity,

Bomber Command had continued to fly extensively across Germany, as the enemy defences faltered under the growing weight of airborne attacks and the relentless advance of ground forces. Essen and Dortmund suffered further thousand-bomber raids, Leipzig, Nuremberg and Bayreuth were attacked, as were ports like Kiel, synthetic oil plants and transportation targets, of which the Bielefeld viaduct was a high-profile location. The area around its arches was pitted by failed attempts to destroy it. That is, until 14 March 1945.

That afternoon, 617 Squadron commander Canadian Wing Commander Johnny Fauquier was set to attack the viaduct with Barnes Wallis's 22,000lb. Grand Slam. Like the American pilot Joe McCarthy before the Dambusters Raid, his Lancaster developed a fault immediately prior to takeoff. Unlike McCarthy, Fauquier could not claim another aircraft. The reserve machine standing by and already bombed up with Grand Slam was piloted by Squadron Leader C. C. Calder. Legend has it that, seeing his commander dashing towards him with arms waving and clearly bent on ousting him from the cockpit, Calder turned a Nelsonian blind eye and accelerated up the runway. If so, his bout of insubordination was worthwhile. His bomb spectacularly breached the viaduct. A postscript to this story is that Calder had allegedly been tipped off about Fauquier's intention by a loyal member of his maintenance crew, who cycled across from Fauquier's dispersal point to warn him.

The following day, a banner headline in the *Daily Express* ran: 'Our V Bomb – 10 Tons', a subheading referred to 'Ten-ton Tess' (word play on the popular comedienne 'Two-ton Tessie O'Shea') and an illustration showed how the new monster was carried. Readers learnt that eight of the ten spans of the viaduct, which carried 'one of the last two-track railways out of the Ruhr to the rest of Germany', had been destroyed in the attack. Calder explained: 'As it burst it felt as though someone had hit me severely in the back. I didn't expect the kick quite so soon. The force of the explosion caused a pain in my spine which lasted for more than a minute. We were lifted well over 500ft.' His bomb aimer, Flight Lieutenant C. B. Crafer, agreed that 'the force of the explosion was worse than the severest flak. The bomb exploded with a fantastic flash and was smothered at once by a high column of smoke.'

Revealed as the inventor of the weapon, Wallis said that he had originally conceived the bomb five years earlier, 'but it has only been recently that we have been able to use the bomb as I first designed it'. Arrival of the Lancaster with its heavy bomb-carrying capacity had reopened the project: 'Even then the bomb sighting presented difficulties, but the wonderful improvement shown by Sir Arthur Harris's crews has now made it possible.' Wallis was always at pains to pay generous tribute to the men who delivered the different types of bomb he designed. The *Evening Standard* interviewed Wallis's wife, Molly: 'We live bombs here. We have had bombs for breakfast, bombs for lunch, bombs for tea and dinner for six years now. We breathe bombs and dream about bombs.'

Up to one hundred Mosquitoes were now mounting separate bomber raids, their activities being rather quaintly described in an RAF publication: 'The enemy was being attacked by a venomous, insect-like bomber which darted here and there and dropped its bombs – sometimes 4000 pounders – in the least expected places.' The experience of one Mosquito crew during the night of 14/15 March demonstrated that even this fast aircraft could run into trouble. Flight Lieutenant Ted Dunford of 608 Squadron flew in a force of seventy-five Mosquitoes to Berlin, his thirty-fifth operation and eighteenth against the German capital. Using H2S, the Pathfinders had accurately marked the target and Dunford successfully dropped his bomb load without difficulty. The Mosquito had almost completed the level flight necessary for the camera when a warning light indicated that a radar had locked on to it. Virtually simultaneously, a flak shell burst underneath the aircraft and Dunford found he could not manoeuvre. The Mosquito insisted on moving steadily eastwards in the general direction of the Polish border. The option of baling out into the inferno below seemed distinctly uninviting.

After much experimenting, Dunford found that by applying hard rudder he could coax the Mosquito on to a westerly course. He then discovered that one petrol tank had been holed and was empty. The remaining fuel would not permit him to follow the briefed dog-leg track, so he asked his Canadian navigator, Sergeant Bob Read, to work out a direct route for home. The aircraft had scarcely settled on this when another warning light alerted Dunford that a night fighter's radar had detected them. The standard drill was to turn 180 degrees towards the incoming enemy, which Dunford managed despite his sluggish controls. Thankfully, this tactic worked and the fighter was shaken off.

Worried that the undercarriage had been damaged, he tested that successfully, followed by the flaps – not so successfully. 'Although I had been an instructor for three years,' Dunford reflected, 'spinning in the dark without aileron control had never been one of the exercises, and I lost several hundred feet before recovering.' He decided not to try the flaps again, which meant an unorthodox landing. Once over the North Sea, he requested diversion to the long, wide runway at Woodbridge, Suffolk, which meant hoping that the coastal artillery massed to deal with incoming V-1 'doodlebugs' would be alerted. He and Read held their breath, but no 'friendly fire' harassed them. Approaching the airfield, Dunford gave his navigator the chance to bale out. He firmly declined. Twice Dunford aborted the landing. On the third attempt, although travelling too fast for comfort, he put the Mosquito down 'flapless'. Read was so excited that he thumped Dunford on the shoulder, with the result that the aircraft careered off the runway and raced towards the emergency vehicles positioned at its end. Their drivers revved frantically to scatter far and wide. Dunford did manage to stop the Mosquito without further damage, though the flak had ruined it beyond repair. 'But it had got us home,' Dunford reflected.

On 24 April, more than three hundred Lancasters set out to drop high explosive visiting cards on Hitler's 'Eagle's Nest' retreat near Berchtesgaden. John Langston was on leave, so missed this trip to southern Germany. Still only twenty years old, he had already flown forty-two operations. But on 5 April 1945 he nearly lost his life in a quite unnecessary crash, which emphasised yet again that every aerial excursion, whether operational or not, was potentially dangerous. He and his friend Pat Shirley joined Bill Adams, who proved to be in a somewhat exuberant, gung-ho mood, to ferry a new Lancaster to Lossiemouth in Scotland. They were Adams' only crew members, with Langston acting as navigator-cum-flight engineer and Shirley occupying the mid-upper turret 'to keep an eye out the back'. The pilot decided to liven up proceedings by putting the flaps down and flying low over a train near Aberdeen. Heads appeared out of the windows, fists were shaken and a general impression of consternation, verging on terror, could be observed. Now thoroughly elated, Adams made off for the Moray Firth.

Approaching Lossiemouth, he saw a Wellington about to land. 'I'm not going to give way to any OUT aeroplane,' he announced. So he put the undercarriage and flaps down, side-slipped in front of the Wellington and touched down about one-third of the way down the runway 'going terribly fast'. Langston saw the runway controller 'p****** off from his

243

caravan' like a character from a Disney cartoon. Langston had no time to worry about this individual's fate as the Lancaster sped towards the end of the runway, where it was clearly not going to stop. 'Let's see how this bloody thing corners' came Adams' voice. Not very well was the answer; in fact, not at all. Langston recalled: 'We turned sharply off the end of the runway, the undercarriage disappeared, one wing came off, one engine came out and passed Pat Shirley flying backwards. The remains of the aircraft came to a halt bent in half round the mid-upper turret. I was standing up, but at the centre of rotation, so never lost my balance.' He did not remain immobile for long.

Langston and Shirley rapidly fled the confusion only to encounter an incandescent wing commander, who raced up in a truck. His face was purple and steam almost literally rose above him as he jumped out. Unfortunately, he mistook Langston, who had a mac on, for the culprit. His intemperate roar (and language) abated when Langston showed him his navigator's brevet. 'Well, where's the pilot then?' On cue, at this precise moment the offender emerged from the wreck. He was hysterical: 'I guess you gotta say I'm the pilot.' The wing commander was speechless and stomped off without another word. Adams would soon return to his native land and a career as a crop-dusting pilot.

From 16 April, Bomber Command's 'main mission' had been defined as 'direct assistance to the land campaign', support to the Soviet armies when requested, attacks on oil supplies, enemy lines of communication and naval targets. Bomber Command's final operation against the Reich took place on 2/3 May. It was feared that a strong naval fleet was being assembled in Kiel to transport units to Norway and continue fighting there. One hundred and seventy-nine Mosquitoes were despatched to attack the port and adjacent airfields, supported by eighty-nine aircraft from 100 Group detailed for countermeasure duties. One Mosquito was lost and two Halifaxes, each with eight men on board, effectively on the last day of the war. For on 4 May, forces in north-west Germany, Denmark and the Netherlands surrendered; three days later the formal capitulation of Germany on all fronts was signed to come into effect at one minute past midnight on 9 May.

With command of the air and ample protection from 8th USAAF Fighter Command, American bombers flew 88,011 day sorties in the final three months of the war for the loss of 404 aircraft (just over four thousand missing men). These figures exclude leaflet drops, some special operations and ECM flights, many of which took place at night. The last major bombing operation was by 589 B-17s and B-24s against six German targets on 24 April for the loss of six aircraft.

During the seventeen weeks from 1 January 1945, Bomber Command operating by day and night flew 62,824 sorties and dropped approximately 180,000 tons of bombs on Germany. Figures show that only 1.1 per cent of aircraft were lost. In human terms that translates into 711 aircraft, from which the majority of crews did not survive. Altogether a more awesome statistic.

There were, however, more cheerful conclusions for many families as prisoners of war returned. One involved Gordon Carter. After he escaped from France, Carter could not contact Janine, the girl he left behind. Nevertheless, he wrote numerous letters to her which he deposited with his aunt in Haslemere to be forwarded, once France had been liberated, should he be taken prisoner; a wise precaution as it turned out. In the autumn of 1944, 'having no idea whatsoever what had happened to him for one and a half years', in Carter's words, this 'tenuous link between a girl and her fly-by-night boyfriend . . . proved to her that he cared and she resolved to wait out those additional nine newsless months till he returned, despite heavy courting by the all-conquering Yanks'.

Once back in England after fourteen months' captivity, Carter lost no time in obtaining compassionate leave and making his way to Paris, where his aunt told him Janine had been working. There he discovered she had already gone back to Brittany. Carter immediately caught an overnight train to Morlaix, where he planned to take a train to Carhaix, only to find that no service ran on Sundays. He contacted the English Railway Transportation Officer (actually getting him out of bed at a distinctly unsociable hour), and that officer promptly and generously ordered his driver to take Carter to Carhaix. There the erstwhile navigator knocked on the door of a tailor's shop in the high street later that morning, 20 May 1945. An elderly lady opened it. '*Janine, c'est Gordon!*', Aunt Eugenie cried, the shop being owned by Janine's grandfather. 'Janine appeared in the doorway, rather bemused' by the 'unannounced and unexpected' turn of events.

'Having spent but a few days together a couple of years earlier we got to know one another a little better.' 'Festive meals . . . topped off . . . by a draught of *Vieille Curé* [a golden version of Benedictine liqueur]' at Janine's parents' home and long walks helped the relationship to develop. 'Those halcyon days' were enriched by the return of Janine's brother and brother-in-law from concentration camps. 'By a miracle the entire family had survived the war, including Janine's mother and grandfather who had been imprisoned for a number of months in 1943', while her brother, involved in the Resistance, was on the run.

Years later, Janine's mother admitted that, when Carter asked for her daughter's hand in marriage, 'she had undergone quite some soul-searching before giving the benefit of the doubt to the virtual stranger that I was'. Bureaucracy, though, still threatened disaster. Carter's fourteen days' leave was rapidly running out and French law required a ten-day publication of banns. Carter and Janine therefore sped off to Paris, where the senior RCAF officer extended his leave until 17 June. But there was another major obstacle. Carter required a certificate of celibacy. The old dictum of fortune favouring the brave intervened. Accidentally and fortuitously, Carter encountered a Norwegian friend, Johan Christie, with whom he had served on 35 Squadron. They contrived to concoct the required document on official Norwegian Embassy notepaper, and back to Brittany the couple went.

The statutory waiting period remained a barrier. The district attorney, though, had just returned from a concentration camp and readily agreed to help, which smoothed the way at the local town hall. On 11 June 1945, therefore, Mademoiselle Janine Jouanjean became Mrs Gordon Carter. 'A cable announcing the good news hit my unsuspecting parents like a bolt from the blue.'

The Carters would, like the traditional fairy-tale ending, 'live happily ever after', but not until several post-war administrative hurdles had been laboriously overcome.

Post-War Reflection

'All for one'

Gordon Carter was one of the fortunate members of Bomber Command to emerge from the Second World War. Either on operations, in training, flying accidents or while prisoners of war 55,463 aircrew lost their lives. A further 8403 were wounded in action or flying accidents; 9784 were taken prisoner and survived. These figures exclude non-operational staff and ground crew, of whom 8620 died through enemy action, 106 were captured and 759 wounded. Overall, the numbers should therefore read: 64,083 dead, 9162 wounded and 9890 prisoners of war.

This parade of statistics becomes more personal with respect to the experience of two bomber pilots who trained in 1943. Of the fourteen crews (ninety-eight men) which completed Tony Iveson's heavy conversion course, by the end of January 1945 only two remained operational. From those, three men had been captured and another left his squadron, so just ten aircrew were still flying. The photograph of Flying Officer James Castagnola's course is scarred with black crosses; only his crew survived. The German defences were not so depleted in the closing phase of the war as optimists had hoped.

Speaking at his old school, Winchester College, Marshal of the Royal Air Force Lord Portal neatly summarised Bomber Command's operational dilemma: 'Our original idea at the beginning of the war had been to wreck the German oil industry, but we were not then strong enough. Day bombing was not then practicable and we had not got the radar aids which we needed to enable us to hit small targets at night. We were forced to adopt area bombing as a means of generally weakening the German economy.' By 1944, Portal believed that the accuracy could be attained to go primarily for oil; Harris, on the other hand, held that area bombing remained the better option. Thus in 1945, only 25 per cent of RAF bomber attacks were against oil targets.

In his book *Bomber Offensive*, Harris recalled that, with rising bomber casualties, at the close of 1942 the 'enemy appeared to have gained a serious degree of tactical superiority . . . we were without any effective aid to navigation, and the damage we did was very far from being enough to compensate for our losses'.

The introduction of a more effective bomber stream to swamp the defences, development of an impressive array of navigational, jamming and bombing aids and, with the mass-production of heavy bombers, the ability to mount far-reaching, deep-penetration raids into the Reich significantly altered this unpromising scenario. Commencement of an American air campaign on their homeland in 1943 put added pressure on the Germans. By October 1944, Harris claimed that 'to all intents and purposes' the vast Krupps works in Essen had ceased production. Shortly afterwards, Bomber Command showed that it could breach the banks of the Dortmund-Ems canal at will, and early in 1945 destroy mighty viaducts like those at Bielefeld and Arnsberg. The accuracy which had eluded the Hampdens in 1940 was no longer beyond the capability of Halifaxes and Lancasters.

The bombing campaign was continuous from the first to the last day of the war. Harris vigorously and consistently maintained with justification that his crews did not fight intermittent battles; they did so every day and night they went out. Nor should their successes be undervalued due to controversy over specific aspects of the whole. Physically, Bomber Command did wreak havoc in Germany's industrial cities, adversely affect armament production, force the withdrawal of men and equipment from other theatres of war to combat the aerial threat and pave the way for the ground invasion of Germany. These were no mean achievements. Fundamentally, too, bomber crews were the only means of putting direct pressure on Germany between the fall of France and late 1944, over four years. What they did, and continued to do, brought hope not only to the United Kingdom, but men and women in the occupied countries of Europe. In 1971, Mr H. van Soerewyn wrote to Sir Barnes Wallis acknowledging his contribution to the bombing campaign. 'Having lived for five long years under a harsh occupation of enemy forces, we are very grateful for the work you did during these years.'

Flight Sergeant James Watts died in a Lancaster, shot down by a Messerschmitt Bf 110 near Anzegem in Belgium on 16 June 1944, eight days before his planned marriage. On the anniversary of his death in June 1945 his grieving family put a notice in the local Camberley paper: 'In proud memory of our dear son and brother.' Also listing members of the crew who perished with Watts, they concluded with the Remembrance verse, 'at the going down of the sun and in the morning we will remember them'. In 2004, his brother learnt that the community of Anzegem was planning to build a memorial to the lost crew. When Harry Watts asked those responsible why they were doing it, he received the reply: 'Well, they gave their lives so that we might be free.'

Harry Watts had already commemorated his brother in a positive way. In the army himself, on their last leave together he and James had discussed the future. If either did not survive the war, the other undertook to organise outings for youngsters who had lost their fathers. Harry kept his promise.

Doreen Ratcliffe, who had been due to marry James Watts, recalled sixty years later that he had been posted missing before and had returned with the aid of the French Resistance. 'I thought it was only a matter of time before he walked through the door. But this time he didn't come back.' An octogenarian great-grandmother, she added: 'Whenever I hear a plane go over or I see a picture of a Lancaster bomber, I always think of Jimmy. I think of him more and more now . . . He was a lovely person and was so kind to me. I remember he was also very good looking.'

In the aftermath of the end of hostilities in Europe, it was not easy for surviving aircrew to adjust to the demands of civilian life. The Canadian Ken Brown reflected that 'in varying degrees, war stains the character of all who participate. None escape, all are affected at some time.' Many were influenced in a positive manner. Nick Knilans, the American pilot who completed fifty-one bomber operations with the RAF, came to feel that the destruction of fellow human beings should be avoided at all costs and determined to do his best to help them. So he interrupted his post-war teaching career to work at a Cheshire Home for Crippled Children in India and do a two-year stint with the Peace Corps in Nigeria. At home, he laboured tirelessly on behalf of disadvantaged Hispanic families. It was perhaps appropriate that Knilans should become associated with a Cheshire Home, part of the network inspired by Leonard Cheshire, former commander of 617 Squadron in which Knilans served. Contrary to popular myth, Cheshire did not suddenly determine to devote his life to helping others as he witnessed the second atomic bomb being dropped on Nagasaki. Like Knilans, his views were formed during the bombing campaign on Germany. While not in any way condemning that action – 'what had to be done, had to be done' – as he gazed down on the destruction below like the American he thought 'surely we can manage things better than this'.

Others simply counted themselves fortunate to have survived such a costly war in human terms. Danny Walker, David Shannon's Canadian navigator on the Dambusters Raid who had received a DFC from the King and a Bar to it from the Queen, believed himself so lucky still to be alive in 1945 that he looked on every day thereafter as a bonus. Bill Edrich, a decorated Blenheim pilot and famous post-war England cricketer, made a similar remark to a Middlesex colleague, Ron Bell.

For Fred Tees, and perhaps for many others, the loss of colleagues remained difficult to bear, especially as he was the only survivor of a Lancaster crash on 17 May 1943. As a neighbour remarked, 'You had to work hard at him to get him to talk about the war'. In 1981, he travelled to Germany to see the memorial erected to his crew where their aircraft had crashed. A year later he died, leaving instructions that his ashes should be scattered over the spot.

Gordon and Janine Carter had to adjust to the peacetime environment more immediately, when they ran into galling difficulties, not least, the intricacies of practice and tradition. Having renounced her French citizenship, Janine sailed to England with her new husband. On 29 June, she encountered the quirks of royal protocol. Janine very nearly did not see her husband receive a Bar to his DFC from King George VI. Arriving at Buckingham Palace without a hat, she was delayed until ingenuity prevailed. Having spread a handkerchief over her head, she was allowed in.

Conclusion

Shortly afterwards, Gordon took Janine to Graveley to show her where he had written her name above his bunk, and more generally introduce her to people and old, familiar haunts in the area. Their days in England were numbered, however. Gordon must return to Canada to be demobilised; Janine would be unable to join him until suitable arrangements were made. With a tortuous and stubborn bureaucracy yet to be conquered, there was no indication of how long that would be. So they must part. Years later Carter wrote: 'I so clearly remember standing on the road bridge above the end of Bournemouth station platform and watching the train pull out for London with Janine on board. I almost ache as much at the memory of it as I did then.'

When Carter sailed from the Clyde on 7 July, Janine was back in Brittany having to endure 'local tongues wagging' about her rapid reappearance. Granted pre-demob leave, Carter lost no time in travelling to New York for an emotional reunion with his parents and sister at Grand Central station. 'The prodigal son had returned!' Once the news leaked out, the vivid imagination of headline writers excelled: 'Bronxville Flier Here, Awaits Bride' (*New York Times*); 'War Romance Now Unfolding – RCAF Officer Wed To Resistance Worker' (*Montreal Daily Star*); 'Gordon Carter Gives Details Of Unusual Adventures That Led To Marriage Abroad' (*Bronxville Review-Press*).

While Carter was enjoying the copious malted milk shakes of which he had dreamed in captivity, as an eligible New York resident he was peremptorily instructed to appear before a US Army draft board. Production of his wartime record quickly scotched that threat. Arranging for Janine to join him proved infinitely more difficult. 'An incredible four months' encounter with embassies and shipping lines' occurred before his wife arrived in the United States. Eventually the Carters would travel widely before settling in France in 1980 with their four children.

The second Christian name of each is that of the patron saint of Brittany past whose chapel Gordon Carter had sailed on leaving Tréboul during his escape to England in April 1943.

Memories of his wartime experiences never left Carter, as Ken Brown suggested. When he was shot down in February 1944, he had admitted strain: 'I was simply at the end of my tether.' In his letters to Mary Mileham, Frank Blackman exhibited obvious signs of stress and he apologised for his occasional bouts of ill-temper in his writing or on the phone. Post-war, Carter developed a phobia about flying, which 'almost made me physically sick with apprehension' and only eased with the advent of jet aircraft. For whatever reason, in peacetime Bill Townsend – a Dambusters pilot – never flew again except for 'a couple of hours in the draughty open cockpit of a Tiger Moth' in the 1970s. Fifty years after the events Carter experienced dreams 'of frustration and longing' about his time in captivity and 'those flak bursts are still in my ears'. In his own words, he 'developed twitches and superstitious gestures, touching this, twiddling that – sorts of ju-ju to ward off bad luck'. After what he had been through, utterly understandable.

Not all wartime relationships were so lasting as that of the Carters. The poor prospect of survival and the pressure of operations led to raucous parties and what might be termed 'high jinks'. One WAAF who served on a number of stations recalled that girls were reluctant to get 'deeply involved with aircrew members, simply because their lives were fleeting, transient. I have seen many young WAAFs distraught, suicidal even, when their boyfriends . . . failed to return from raids.' She admitted that 'it happened to me also'. Although married, with a husband overseas, she began a relationship with a New Zealander. 'I even took him home with me when our leaves coincided. I somehow convinced my parents that we were just close friends and he was so far from home.' His leave ended three days before hers, and

Conclusion

she saw him off from the station: 'We were still waving when the train vanished into the distance.' When she got back off leave, he was missing. It confirmed her belief that getting involved with aircrew, and in extreme marrying them, was a 'recipe for deep grief'. Many who did emerge from the war still happily married would disagree. But she had a point. It was risky.

Harry Humphries, adjutant of 617 Squadron at the time of the Dambusters Raid, emphasised that to aircrew riotous parties 'merely meant grasping a few hours respite before, to use their own phrase, "dicing with death" again'. But this wild scenario did not apply to all aircrew. Frank Blackman, for example, preferred classical music to drinking sessions in the Mess. Like Les Knight, who was also lost during the Dortmund-Ems operation on 15 September 1944, Flight Lieutenant Bob Hutchison, who had been Gibson's wireless operator at the Dams was a teetotaller. According to Humphries who knew him well, he 'spent most of his time writing, playing tennis or football, indulging occasionally in amateur theatricals'.

It would, therefore, be fundamentally wrong to stereotype male or female members of Bomber Command. Each had his or her own way of coping with the stress of wartime operations. Minor rituals before takeoff inspired confidence. Some crews entered their aircraft in a set order. Ivan Whittaker always watered the tail wheel and on one occasion insisted on leaving the Lancaster to perform this task having omitted to do so. Lance Howard walked round the aircraft twice; Ken Brown smoked two cigarettes. Henry Archer, who completed a tour of thirty-five ops in 1944 then lectured on this subject at an HCU, argued that everybody experienced fear and talking about it encouraged rationalisation. Excessive drinking or an acquired air of casualness, he believed, actually increased the chance of inefficiency and, therefore, danger to a crew.

The years of peace were especially difficult for friends and relatives of those who had been lost. Morfyyd Gronland, who as a nineteen-year-old had been a waitress in the Sergeants' Mess of RAF Scampton in May 1943, wrote of a 'poignant and sweet happening since the war', when sent a photograph of the grave of a close friend lost on the Dambusters Raid. Piloting a Pathfinder Lancaster early in 1944, a former Dockyard ship-wright from Portsmouth, Dennis Langford, was shot down. His body was never found, so his mother could not accept that he had been killed. She kept his room ready for his return. Jim Parsons, his Portsmouth friend, believed that she died of a broken heart when he failed to do so. Sixty years after the event, the younger sister of a gunner lost in action was distraught to dis-cover that, contrary to official records, her brother had not been in the rear turret of the Lancaster as usual that night. Six of the crew perished; the rear gunner alone survived. She still remem-bered her brother turning to wave at the end of the street, as he went back from his last leave. He had never done that before.

At the time, Mary Mileham had been devastated. She had already lost a 22-year-old brother in the Battle of Britain. Although Mary received the official telegram as Frank Blackman's next of kin, she got no further news about his fate. By then a widow, in 1977 Mary contacted the Air Ministry for information about what had happened to somebody whose memory she still treasured. The reply from the Ministry of Defence (into which the Air Ministry had been absorbed) explained that none of the crew had survived the crash in a German pine forest and that Blackman's body was buried in a Commonwealth War Graves Commission cemetery in Berlin. The writer added that Francis Henry Blackman's immediate family had long ago been given this information, presumably because the responsible authority consulted the navigator's enlistment documents. Before contacting the Air Ministry, Mary had gone to the Royal Air Force War Memorial at Runnymede,

Conclusion

which contains the names of all those with no known grave. His was not there, so she reasoned that details of his burial must be known. Having discovered where he was buried, her intention was to visit and tend his grave. Whether she was able to fulfil that wish is not known.

Another indication of the intensity of her memory was seen in a letter to the BBC. Recalling that she and Frank had attended a concert at the Royal Albert Hall, part of the 49th Promenade Season on 23 July 1943, she wondered whether a copy of the programme were available. It was, she wrote, a Beethoven–Mozart programme conducted by Sir Adrian Boult at which Joan Hammond performed. To her transparent delight, her quest was successful: 'It is indeed wonderful that the archives of the BBC are able to supply information requested' over thirty years after the event. It is interesting to note that, throughout her later married life, Mary did not destroy the wartime letters from Frank Blackman and subsequently donated them to the Imperial War Museum for safe-keeping. Among the collection were extracts from her diary, which recorded details of when they met for dinner, played bridge, visited the cinema or theatre, dates when she posted a letter to Blackman or received one from him. Her last letter was posted on 19 February 1944, the day before Blackman was lost. The entry for 21 February ran: 'Telegram Frank missing. Spent evening with Frank's mother'; for the following day: 'Frank's mother to go to Frank's brother.'

James Wright similarly had lasting memories from the war. A Londoner, seven years old at the outbreak, on 14 June 1940 with his mother and brothers he was evacuated to Llanhilleth in south Wales. His father, a painter and decorator, remained in Forest Gate until called up in 1942. James saw him only once on leave, in July 1943. Shortly afterwards, flying as a bomb aimer with 207 Squadron, Sergeant Arthur Wright was shot down.

'This became so traumatic in respect of our family to the extent that we were all ill for a long time', James recalled. He and his two brothers lost 'a complete term of schooling due to this'. After returning briefly to London 'to clear up Dad's effects . . . life went on as best we could make it'.

Movingly, James Wright wrote many years later, 'following the death of my Dad, family life was never the same . . . [it became] harder and harder for mother to cope with three grow-ing boys'. Cruelly, financial assistance was denied 'by the ladies who appeared to be one or two steps above everybody else', a criticism which did not extend to the people of Llanhilleth, whose 'love and care' he cherished. 'After my father's death _all_ [_sic_] the neighbours rallied round, as they did in all times of stress.' The pathos of a situation, which affected so many fam-ilies deprived of a breadwinner, was illustrated by a touching passage from James Wright's memoir. 'Memories of Christmas morning 1944, waking up to find that Mum had been able to purchase one blank book of rough paper, six pots of water paint, one paint brush and had been able to pop in an orange. That was my full quota that year.'

As the loss of a father or husband, son or brother seared the lives of so many, the commitment of airmen to the memory of their crews, and particularly their pilots, endured. In 1986, Gordon Carter finally found the grave of his pilot Julian Sale, reflecting that 'the calm and self-confident young man that he was lives on, graven in my mind'. Peter Brown and Dave Rodger were justified in describing a bomber crew as a small independent fighting unit. Ted Wass used a sporting analogy: a football team with the pilot as captain. Squadron Leader S. A. Booker, a Halifax navigator, went further. He likened each crew to a family.

Post-war, Jim Brookbank, former bomb aimer in 9 Squadron, published two volumes of poems 'dedicated to the families and

Conclusion

loved ones of those gallant aircrew who gave their lives'. In the second of these, *Before the Dawn*, in listing his crew during the last year of the war he not only described their lives and careers once hostilities ended but revealed that after fifty years he remained in touch with all but one of those still alive. He explained 'the strength of the bond of comradeship that exists within a Lancaster bomber crew' as being based on 'friendships built on the certain knowledge that we could all rely on each other regardless of whatever dangers should confront us'.

Perhaps the most profound example of remembrance, and one which in itself sums up the character of an RAF bomber crew during the Second World War, involved Flight Sergeant John Fraser, the bomb aimer in Flight Lieutenant's J. V. Hopgood's aircraft which crashed just north of the Möhne Dam during the early hours of Monday 17 May 1943. Hopgood strove successfully to get the fatally damaged Lancaster high enough for some of his crew to bale out. Fraser was one of the two to do so and live. In a lasting tribute to the pilot, Fraser named his son John Hopgood and his daughter Shere after the village in Surrey where the Hopgood family lived.

George Johnson, who flew with the American McCarthy on 97 and 617 squadrons, also paid tribute to his pilot: 'I shall always be eternally grateful to Joe because he took me out forty times and he brought me back forty times, without a scratch.' Commenting more broadly on McCarthy's Lancaster crew, Johnson reflected: 'We each depended on the other. We all depended on Joe for the flying, we depended on Don [MacLean] for the navigation. We depended on the gunners for keeping their eyes open.'

As the experienced Pathfinder pilot and master bomber Air Commodore J. H. Searby, echoing Alexandre Dumas' *The Three Musketeers*, put it: 'All for one.'

APPENDIX A

Sources

National Archives, Kew

To avoid a long procession of separate items, only the relevant document files are noted to give researchers a starting point.

Air 2   Citations and Awards
Air 6   Air Council memos and minutes
Air 9   Pre-war plans and Joint Planning Staff meetings
Air 10   Bomb targets in Germany
Air 14   Bomber Command papers
Air 20   Chiefs of Staff documents
Air 24   Bomber Command operations
Air 25   Operations Record Books of RAF Bomber Groups
Air 27   Operations Record Books of RAF Bomber Squadrons
Air 28   Operations Record Books of RAF Bomber Stations
AVIA 15   Ministry of Aircraft Production papers
Cab 23   War Cabinet minutes
Cab 65   Confidential annexes to War Cabinet minutes
Cab 66   War Cabinet memos

Appendix A

Cab 69   War Cabinet Defence Committee papers
Cab 79   Chiefs of Staff Committee minutes
Cab 80   Chiefs of Staff Committee memos

Imperial War Museum, Department of Documents

(*identifies a member of Bomber Command)

a. I am grateful for permission of the undermentioned copyright owners to quote from the following papers: Gp Capt K. S. Batchelor* (Mrs Rosemary Taylor), Fg Off F. H. Blackman* (Philip Mileham), F/Sgt J. Bormann* (Mark Catalano), Miss J. M. Brotherton* (David Brotherton), Sqn Ldr G. H. F. Carter* (Gordon Carter), Flt Lt I. P. B. Denton* (Mrs Celia Rambaut), Sgt R. St C. Neale* (David Hunt), Fg Off C. R. Williams* (John Oxley Library, State Library of Queensland, Australia), J. R. Wright (John Wright).

b. Every effort had been made, without success, to trace the copyright holders of these papers: L. P. Barham*, T. P. E. Barlow*, D. Bruce*, V. H. Clare*, D. M. Elliott*.

c. I have also studied the following papers held in the department: A. M. Bance*, T. G. Bashford*, G. L. Cheshire*, G. M. Brisbane* and B. J. Doran* (all Crown copyright); R. S. Allen*, F. R. W. Bagshaw*, S. C. Barratt*, J. F. Bartle*, S. A. Booker*, H. S. P. Brooke*, B. C. Bullard*, H. Burton*, F. Carr*, J. C. Claydon*, R. G. Collins*, J. C. Corby*, B. G. Dye*, A. R. Easton*, L. H. Ewels*, D. I. Fairbairn*, R. J. Fairhead*, R. Favager*, R. J. Fayers*, D. R. Field*, T. W. Fox*, L. Frith*, K. A. Goodchild*, W. K. Handley*, N. J. N. Hockaday*, D. G. Hornsey*, G. J. Hull*, H. Johnstone*, J. A. T. Jones*, A. Lens*, J. S. A. Marshall*, J. H. Mason*, G. E. Moulton-Barrett*, D. Mourton*, H. A. Nock*, C. B. Owen*, B. Oxtaby*,

R. Passmore*, E. F. Rawlings*, R. H. P. Roberts*, J. M. Southwell*, R. E. Wannop*, E. G. White*, R. H. Williams*, A. J. N. Wilson*, W. B. Wilkinson*.

d. The following accounts held in the Sound Archive were consulted: D. C. T. Bennett*, G. Byam*, L. W. Curtis*, I. Hewitt*, T. C. Iveson*, R. E. Knights*, H. J. Spiller*, Gp Capt J. B. Tait*.

e. I am grateful, too, to the following for allowing me to quote from other family correspondence and material: Mrs H. Griffith (Sgt S. Beaumont*), Mrs D. Fraser (Flt Lt J. W. Fraser*), Mrs Penny Cockerill (Flt Lt D. P. Heal*), Philip Mileham (Miss M. Mileham).

RAF Museum Hendon

The following material was looked at in the Department of Aviation Records: Barnes Wallis diaries; F. W. Winterbotham papers; H. C. Knilans, *A Yank in the RAF*, and E. M. Childs, *Kismet: A. Flight Engineer's Story* (unpublished pamphlets).

Personal Material

a. In addition to those mentioned in the Acknowledgements, I am extremely grateful to the following for giving me invaluable assistance through correspondence and interviews during the preparation of this work: N. J. Allen*, J. F. E. Brookbank*, Mrs B. Brown, P. S. Brown*, G. H. F. Carter*, E. M. Childs*, L. W. Curtis*, G. M. Dickson*, C. B. R. Fish*, Mrs D. Fraser, Mrs H. Griffith, S. Instone*, G. L. Johnson*, R. E. Knights*, H. C. Knilans*, Air Cdre J. Langston*, R. Lewis*, Mrs S. Lowe,

Appendix A

J. L. Munro*, D. Newham*, H. C. A. Parsons*, D. Radcliffe*,W. Russell, E. A. Wass*, C. Watt*, H. Watts, Mrs M. Young.

b. I have drawn, too, on material from previous correspondence or interviews with the undermentioned: A. Abels*, H. Archer*, R. V. Bell, T. Bennett*, J. Buckley*, Air Vice-Marshal S. O. Bufton*, G. A. Chalmers*, Gp Capt G. L. Cheshire*, A. W. Cherrington*, F. E. Cholerton*, J. H. Clay*, Air Chief Marshal Sir Ralph Cochrane*, C. Cole*, Mrs P. Crick, H. B. Feneron*, D. E. Freeman*, Mrs E. Gibson, R. E. Grayston*, S. V. Grimes*, Herr E. Handke (former German night fighter wireless operator), Marshal of the Royal Air Force Sir Arthur Harris*, R. J. Harris*, D. P. Heal*, Mrs E. Hobday, H. S. Hobday*, C. L. Howard*, Mrs M. Howard, W. Howarth*, F. E. Howkins*, Professor R. V. Jones, General J. Kammhuber (former commander German night fighters), E. C. Johnson*, R. G. T. Kellow*, B. F. Kent*, A. J. Lammas*, J. H. Leavitt*, G. S. MacDonald*, D. A. Maclean*, J. D. Melrose*, H. C. Munro*, S. Oancia*, H. E. O'Brien*, J. D. Phillips*, G. E. Pine*, J. C. Pinning*, J. Reed, W. Reid*, G. Rice*, H. J. Riding*, D. Rodger*, J. A. Sanders*, Air Vice-Marshal H. V. Satterly*, Mrs A. Shannon*, D. J. Shannon*, T. D. Simpson*, J. Soilleux*, Herr Albert Speer (former German Minister for Armament and War Production), L. J. Sumpter*, F. E. Sutherland*, Gp Capt J. B. Tait*, F. Tees*, F. L. Tilley*, W. C. Townsend*, Sir Barnes Wallis, D. R. Walker*, H. Watkinson*, D. E. Webb*, J. C. Weller*, Air Cdre F. M. F. West*, Gp Capt I. Whittaker*, J. Wickens*, Mrs D. Vaughan, Herr Alfred Zuba (former crew member of the German battleship *Tirpitz*).

APPENDIX B

Glossary

AA	anti-aircraft fire or guns; ack-ack
ABC	Airborne Cigar: British jamming device
a/c	aircraft
ACM	air chief marshal
Air Cdre	air commodore
AFCE	automatic flight control equipment (US device)
AFS	advanced flying school
AI	Air Intelligence, British Air Ministry, or night fighter airborne interception
AM	air marshal
amatol	explosive
AOC	air officer commanding
AOC-in-C	air officer commanding-in-chief
AP	armour piercing (bomb) or aiming point
API	air position indicator
AVM	air vice-marshal
Avro(s)	A. V. Roe & Co. Ltd
BC	Bomber Command
Bf	designation of Messerschmitt aircraft
Boozer	British airborne radar receiver

Appendix B

Capt.	captain
CAS	Chief of the Air Staff
CBE	Commander of the British Empire
CBO	Combined Bomber Offensive
CCS	British and American allied chiefs of staff committee
CGM	Conspicuous Gallantry Medal (flying)
Chastise	codename for attack on German dams, May 1943
C-in-C	commander-in-chief
CO	commanding officer
COS	British chiefs of staff committee
CSBS	course setting bomb sight
CU	conversion unit
DB Ops	Director or Directorate of Bomber Operations, Air Ministry
DDB Ops	Deputy Director of Bomber Operations, Air Ministry
D/F	direction-finding equipment
DFC	Distinguished Flying Cross
DFM	Distinguished Flying Medal
DR	dead reckoning (navigation)
DSO	Distinguished Service Order
ECH	electronic countermeasures
EFS	elementary flying school
ETA	estimated time of arrival
Fg Off	flying officer
Flak	*Flieger Abwehr Kanonen*: German ack-ack
Flensburg	German airborne radar receiver
F/Sgt	flight sergeant
Flt Lt	flight lieutenant
Freya	German early warning radar
GCI	ground-controlled interception

265

Gee	Ground Electronic Engineering, British radio navigational aid
G-H	British blind bombing aid
GP	general purpose (bomb)
Gp Capt	group captain
HCU	heavy conversion unit
He	Heinkel
HE	high-explosive
H/F	high frequency
Highball	codename for Barnes Wallis's smaller 'bouncing bomb'; two carried by a Mosquito
Himmelbett	'four-poster bed': German aerial night defensive system
HQ	headquarters
H2S	British radar navigational and bombing aid
IFF	identification friend or foe aircraft apparatus
intercom	telephone system inside aircraft
Korfu	German radar receiver for H2S emissions
LAC	leading aircraftman
LFS	Lancaster Finishing School
Lichtenstein	German night fighter radar
mag	magneto
Maj.	major
Mammut	German early warning radar
Mandrel	British airborne radar countermeasure
MAP	Ministry of Aircraft Production
Me	Messerschmitt
Met	meteorological
Monica	British airborne radar warning system
Nav	navigator
Naxos	German H2S detection radar
NCO	non-commissioned officer
Oboe	British navigational and bombing aid

Appendix B

OC	officer commanding
Op	operation
ORB	operations record book
OTU	operational training unit
Overlord	codename for allied landings in Normandy, June 1944
PFF	Pathfinder Force
Plt Off	pilot officer
Pointblank	directive or plan for the allied Combined Bomber Offensive, June 1943
PoW	prisoner-of-war
PR	photographic reconnaissance
PRU	photographic reconnaissance unit
RAAF	Royal Australian Air Force
RAE	Royal Aircraft Establishment, Farnborough
RAF	Royal Air Force
RAFVR	Royal Air Force Volunteer Reserve
RCAF	Royal Canadian Air Force
RDF	radio direction finding (radar)
RRL	Road Research Laboratory, Harmondsworth
R/T	radio-telephony
RNZAF	Royal New Zealand Air Force
SAAF	South African Air Force
SABS	Stabilised Automatic Bomb Sight
SAP	semi-armour piercing (bomb)
SASO	senior air staff officer
S/E	single engine
Serrate	British airborne radar receiver to pick up German emissions
Sgt	sergeant
SN-2	German night fighter radar
SOE	Special Operations Executive
Sqn Ldr	squadron leader

Bomber Crew

'Tame Boar'	*zahme Sau*: German tactic of using twin-engine night fighters to engage bombers to and from the target
T/E	twin-engine
TI	target indicator
Tinsel	British airborne equipment to jam German fighter control transmissions
'Upkeep'	codename for Barnes Wallis's large 'bouncing bomb' carried by a Lancaster
U/S	unserviceable
USAAF	United States Army Air Force(s)
VC	Victoria Cross
V-1	German pilotless aircraft, known as a flying bomb or doodlebug
V-2	German explosive rocket
VSG	variable setting corrector (navigator's aid) 248
WA	Western Air (Plans)
WAAF	Women's Auxiliary Air Force
Wassermann	German early warning radar
'Wild Boar'	*wilde Sau*: German tactic of using single-engine fighters over the target
Window	metal strips dropped to confuse German radar
WO	warrant officer
W/Op	wireless operator
W/T	wireless telegraphy
Würzburg	German radar used to direct searchlights, flak and night fighters

BIBLIOGRAPHY

Unless otherwise stated, all books published in London.

Adelson, R., *Mark Sykes: Portrait of an Amateur* (1975)

Aders, G., *History of the German Night-Fighter Force, 1917–1943* (English trans., 1978)

Air Ministry, *Four Lectures on the History of the Royal Air Force* (1945)

Allen, H. R., *The Legacy of Lord Trenchard* (1972)

Anderson, W., *Pathfinders* (1946)

Balfour, M., *Propaganda in War, 1939–1945* (1971)

Baring, M., *Flying Corps Headquarters, 1914–1918* (1920)

Bartlett C. P. O., *Bomber Pilot* (1974)

Baumbach, W., *Broken Swastika: The Defeat of the Luftwaffe* (English trans., 1960)

Bekker, C., *The Luftwaffe War Diaries* (English trans., 1966)

Bickers, T. B., *The First Great Air War* (1988)

Boyle, A., *No Passing Glory: The Life of Leonard Cheshire* (1957)

—— *Trenchard: Man of Vision* (1962)

Braddon, R., *Cheshire VC* (1954)

Burke, E., *Guy Gibson VC* (1961)

Carlaw, A. (ed.), *Eagles in the Sky: The RAF at Seventy-Five* (1993)

Chamier, J. A., *The Birth of the Royal Air Force: The Early History and Experiences of the Flying Services* (1943)

Charlton, L. E. O., *War From the Air* (1931)

Cheshire, L., *Bomber Pilot* (Mayflower edn, 1975)

Clouston, A. E., *The Dangerous Skies* (1956)

Collier, B., *Heavenly Adventurer: Sefton Brancker and the Dawn of British Aviation* (1959)

Cooper, B., *The Story of the Bomber 1914–1945* (1974)

Craven, W. F. and Cate, J. (eds), *The Army Air Forces in World War II*, Vols I–III (Chicago, 1949)

Bomber Crew

Crawley, A., *Escape from Germany* (1956 edn)

Dean, M., *The Royal Air Force and Two World Wars* (1979)

Douglas, S., *Years of Combat* (1963)

—— *Years of Command* (1966)

Embry, Sir B., *Mission Completed* (nd)

—— *Wingless Victory* (1973 edn)

Frankland, N., *The Bomber Offensive Against Germany: Outlines and Perspectives* (1965)

Freeman, R., *Mighty Eighth War Diaries* (1981)

Galland, A., *The First and the Last* (English trans., 1955)

Garlinski, J., *Hitler's Last Weapons* (1978)

Gibson, G., *Enemy Coast Ahead* (Pan edn, 1955)

—— *Enemy Coast Ahead* (Crecy edn, 2003)

Green, W., *Avro Lancaster* (1959)

Groves, P. R. C., *Behind the Smoke Screen* (1934)

—— *Our Future in the Air* (1935)

Hancock, W. K. (ed.), *Statistical Digest of the War* (1951)

Harris, Sir A., *Bomber Offensive* (1947)

—— *Despatches on War Operations, 1942–5* (1995)

Humphries, H. R., *Living With Heroes: The Dam Busters* (2003)

Huskinson, P., *Vision Ahead* (1949)

Hyde, H. M., *British Air Policy Between the Wars, 1918–1939* (1976)

Irving, D., *The Rise and Fall of the Luftwaffe* (1973)

Jablonski, E., *The Knighted Skies* (1964)

Jary, C., *Portrait of a Bomber Pilot* (1990)

Jones, H. A., *The War in the Air* (official history, Great War), Vols 2–6 (Oxford, 1935–7)

Jones, N., *The Origins of Strategic Bombing* (1973)

Jones, R. V., *Most Secret War: British Scientific Intelligence, 1939–1945* (1978)

Killen, J., *The Luftwaffe: A History* (1967)

Kingston-McCloughry E. J., *Winged Warfare: Air Problems in Peace and War* (1937)

Lawrence, W. J., *No. 5 Bomber Command Group RAF, 1939–1945* (1951)

Lewis, B. A., *A Few of the First* (1997)

Lewis, P., *The British Bomber since 1914* (1980 edn)

Macksey, K., *Kesselring: The Making of the Luftwaffe* (1978)

MacMillan, N., *Sir Sefton Brancker* (1935)

—— *The RAF in the World War* (1950)

Bibliography

Messenger, C., *Bomber Harris* (1984)

Middlebrook, M. and Everitt, C., *The Bomber Command War Diaries* (1996 edn)

Morpurgo, J., *Barnes Wallis: A Biography* (1972)

Morris, R., *Guy Gibson* (1994)

Munson, K., *Bombers 1914–19* (1968)

Neon, *The Great Delusion* (1927)

Norris, G., *The Royal Flying Corps: A History* (1965)

Pawle, G., *The Secret War* (Corgi edn, 1959)

Powers, B. D., *Strategy Without Slide Rule: British Air Strategy, 1914–1939* (1976)

Price, A., *Instruments of Darkness* (1967)

—— *Luftwaffe* (1969)

Probert, H., *Bomber Harris* (2001)

Procter, S., *A Quiet Little Boy Goes to War* (1997)

Raleigh, Sir W., *The War in the Air* (official history, Great War) Vol. 1 (Oxford, 1922)

Reynolds, Q., *They Fought in the Sky* (1958)

Richards, D., *Portal of Hungerford* (1977)

—— *Royal Air Force, 1939–1945*, Vol. I (1953)

—— *The Hardest Victory: RAF Bomber Command in the Second World War* (1994)

Richards D. and Saunders H. St G., *Royal Air Force, 1939–1945*, Vol. II (1954)

Robertson, B., *Lancaster – The Story of a Famous Bomber* (1964)

Rumpf, H., *The Bombing of Germany* (English trans., 1975)

Sanders, J., *Venturer Courageous: Life of Group Captain Leonard Trent* (1983)

Saundby, R., *Air Bombardment: The Story of its Development* (1961)

Saunders, H. St G., *Per Ardua: The Rise of British Air Power, 1911–1939* (1944)

—— *Royal Air Force, 1939–1945*, Vol. III (1954)

Saward, D., *Bomber Harris* (1984)

Scott, J. D., *Vickers – A History* (1962)

Smith, A. M., *Knights of the Air* (1959)

Spaight, J. M., *Beginnings of Organised Air Power: A Historical Study* (1927)

—— *Air Power in the Next War* (1938)

Speer, A., *Spandau Diaries* (English trans., 1976)

—— *Inside the Third Reich* (English trans., Sphere Books, 1977)

Bomber Crew

Tedder, Lord, *Air Power in War* (1948)

Templewood, Viscount, *Empire of the Air* (1957)

Turner J. F., *VCs of the Air* (1960)

United States Strategic Bombing Survey (Overseas Economic Effects Division), *The Effects of Strategic Bombing on the German War Economy* (1945)

Warlimont, W., *Im Hauptquartier der deutschen Wehrmacht, 1939–1945* (Frankfurt-am-Main, 1962)

Webster C. and Frankland, N., *The Strategic Air Offensive Against Germany, 1939–45* (the official history), Vols I–IV (1961)

Wells, M. K., *Courage and Air Warfare* (1995)

Periodical, Journals and Newspapers

Air Clues

Air Force List

Air Power

Army List

Camberley News

Daily Express

Daily Mail

Daily Mirror

Daily Sketch

Daily Telegraph

Dictionary of National Biography

Evening Standard

Illustrated London News

Journal of Contemporary Studies

Journal of Strategic Studies

London Gazette

New York Times

Observer

Punch

Royal Air Forces Quarterly

Sunday Express

Sunday Times

The Times

INDEX

273

Index

Index

Index

G